The Struggle for Community

ROUTE TWO PROJECT AREA

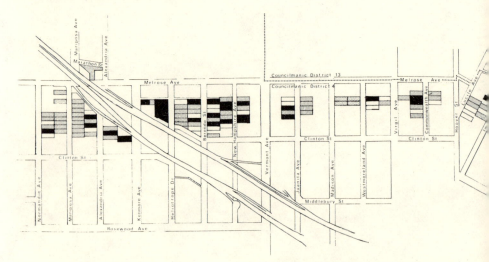

The Struggle for Community

Allan David Heskin

Westview Press
BOULDER • SAN FRANCISCO • OXFORD

Cover illustration courtesy of Mariana Payan and her children, Dawood and Muriel.

Chapter 4 is adapted from Allan Heskin and Dewey Bandy, "The Importance of Class," *Berkeley Planning Journal,* 3 (1): 47–66. Chapter 5 is adapted with permission of the NTL Institute from Allan Heskin and Robert Heffner, "Learning About Bilingual, Multicultural Organizing," *Journal of Applied Behavioral Science,* 23 (4): 525–541, copyright 1987.

Published in 1991 in the United States of America by Westview Press, Inc., 5500 Central Avenue, Boulder, Colorado 80301, and in the United Kingdom by Westview Press, 36 Lonsdale Road, Summertown, Oxford OX2 7EW

Heskin, Allan David.
  The struggle for community / by Allan David Heskin.
    p. cm.
  Includes bibliographical references and index.
  ISBN 0-8133-8338-2
  1. Community. 2. Community development, Urban—California—Los Angeles—Case studies. 3. Urban homesteading—California—Los Angeles—Case studies. 4. Relocation (Housing)—California—Los Angeles—Case studies. 5. Minorities—Housing—California—Los Angeles—Case studies. I. Title.
HM131.H399 1991
307—dc20

            91-15786
            CIP

Printed and bound in the United States of America

Contents

Acknowledgments

No book is written without a great deal of help. This one is no exception. I would like to express my appreciation to my neighbors and fellow cooperators and to the many planners and other professionals for creating through their lives the truly extraordinary story I tell in this book. I'd also like to thank the many students who helped on the project, with special thanks to Bob Heffner, Lupe Compean, Clyde Woods, and especially Dewey Bandy, who was central to much of the research. I also want to express appreciation for the advice of many colleagues, including Carl Boggs, Ed Soja, Peter Marris, and Paul Niebanck to name just a few. This book also benefitted from the aid of a marvellous editor, Rita Gentry, who made the book much more readable, and Marsha Brown, who spent hours cleaning, proofing, and laying out the manuscript.

Allan David Heskin

Prologue

In recent years a number of books have been published announcing the emergence of a new American populism.[1] The authors who employ this term refer to the actions of groups of people seeking to gain a measure of control from forces dominating their lives. These authors often couple the term populist with the term progressive. This coupling suggests a particular democratic, egalitarian form of populism well established in the U.S. tradition. As one author put it, referring to the populism of the nineteenth century, "The Populist vision, in sum, was democratic empowerment, democratic roots, and a democratic view of the commonwealth." The new populists, much in the same vein, want to give ordinary people "a voice" in matters important to their lives and create democratic institutions that "rest on the widest possible dissemination of wealth and power" (Boyte, Booth, and Max 1986, pp. 25-29).

Populism does not have to be linked with this positive image. Populism occurs across an ideological spectrum and can, in Harry Boyte's terms, simply speak to people as "victims." Right-wing populism, as he calls it, "offers scapegoats, promises great leaders, holds out vicarious victories, and invokes nostalgic images of 'the way things used to be'-- accompanied by efforts to impose rigid moral prescriptions on private behavior. . . . It breeds fear, suspicion and a sense of unbridgeable difference" (Boyte 1986, pp. 12-13).

Frank Reissman contrasts this image of populism with an ethos of progressive populism that includes "a noncompetitive, cooperative orientation; an anti-elite, antibureaucratic focus; and an emphasis on the indigenous." These new populists set as goals "doing what you can do," believe that people are "helped through helping," and share leadership. They have a "critical stance toward professionalism," are optimistic when it comes to people's "ability to change," and believe you begin with something small and build from there. Central to progressive populists' beliefs are the ideas of the cooperative community, democracy, and empowerment (Reissman 1986, pp. 53-63).

Two examples of attempts at achieving this new American progressive populism have been very much a part of my life over the past ten years. One is well known and the other not. The well-known example is the tenant revolt in the City of Santa Monica, which electorally established rent control and elected representatives to local public office.[2] The other is the Route 2 project in the Echo Park-Silverlake district of Los Angeles where some 500 tenant households successfully fought against being displaced from their rented homes and ended up purchasing some of the homes as individuals and others by organizing them into five limited-equity cooperatives.[3]

In Santa Monica I advised the early movement, studied its results,[4] and for a year worked full time for the Ocean Park Community Organization (OPCO), believed to be the most powerful community organization in the city. My assignment was to assist OPCO in the organizing of a community development corporation to attack the neighborhood's low-income housing problems.[5] Ten years ago I was recruited and served as a member and officer of the Route 2 project's new community development corporation, and some years later I moved into one of the coops and became active in coop affairs.

Both the joys and sorrows of my experiences in Santa Monica and the Route 2 project have raised many questions in my mind about new populism and taught me a great deal about its potential and the problems it faces.[6] A basic lesson has been the realization that although, as Harry Boyte has written, "Community Is Possible,"[7] it is a struggle both to attain and keep community. The battle is never finally won and the war ended. Many forces of disempowerment both outside and inside community continually work against any organization for empowerment. Community and empowerment can be attained, lost, attained again, lost again, and once again attained as long as the commitment and strength to resist the disempowering forces are present.

This dialectic of success and failure is seen from my own populist point of view with, as James Midgely observes, the "subtle influence" of anarchism (Midgely 1986, p. 16). There is no doubt in my mind that as Midgely puts it, "ordinary folk are badly done by" (p. 15); or that organization of ordinary people is "a collective means of redress" for this problem; or that decentralism and elements of anti-statist, anti-coercive views are essential to the resolution of the dialectic. I am not giving anything away by saying this. It will not take readers long to come to understand my views.

In both Santa Monica and Route 2 once the "people" came to power, they have had to face questions all democracies must face, questions central to progressive populism -- how participatory versus how representative their government will be; how public versus how private political life will be; how inclusive versus how exclusive the community will be; whether consensus will be allowed to be freely formed or will be enforced; and how issues such as differences in class, ethnicity, and gender will be confronted.

The attempt to establish new populism in a city regime as in Santa Monica is far more difficult than in neighborhood groups as the ones active in the Route 2 area. Certainly there is more political space in a neighborhood where the interests of capital are less than in a city. My interest is not, however, in the question of the amount of political space in cities or neighborhood groups. My focus is more on the internal workings of groups that have gained a modicum of "apparent" control over their lives. How having won the battle do the winners organize and reorganize themselves in the face of the continuing adversity they face? How do they attempt to establish their hegemony over their political space?[8]

Many theorists argue that the economic interest of cities in growth (the tax revenue generated by growth) and the federal structure in the United States dooms any attempt to change the nature of city politics to failure (Peterson 1981).[9] On the surface there is much in my experience in Santa Monica that seems to confirm Peterson's position.[10] However, having once established limited-equity cooperatives in Route 2, the leadership in the Route 2 project removed any similar internal logic (i.e. rising property values and equity build up) from the cooperatives. While the cooperatives must still exist in a "capitalist sea" with its structural coercive forces and ideological hegemony, there is a potentially more fertile ground for a new populist experiment.[11] What led me to this book then was my curiosity about how new populist groups attempt to establish their hegemony in the political space available to them. For this investigation the less embattled and more liberated political space of the Route 2 project has proven to be a more interesting arena to examine.

My knowledge of the Route 2 project began in 1977 when an avowedly anarchist student attending the UCLA Urban Planning Program came to me with the story of this "amazing" project. A group of low-income residents in the Echo Park/Silverlake district of the city was trying to buy two and a quarter miles of a freeway corridor. Yes, a freeway corridor! The state of California had intended to build a freeway through the neighborhood, bought a strip of property in the area, and then decided not to build the freeway. The student had attended a meeting with lots of yelling and screaming by, in his words, "reactionary" Cubans, "lefty" activists, and "hostile" Asian realtors where the resident reactionaries and lefties demanded the right to buy the state property over the realtors' objections.

I didn't know what to do with this information. It seemed too bizarre to be true, but I asked the excited student to keep me informed. He would come into my office every once in a while and continue his story. I became increasingly curious about what the heck was going on out there. As is my custom when something sounds interesting, I began to see if I could get interns from the school involved in the process. I learned that the state Department of Housing and Community Development (HCD) was assisting the project, and I contacted HCD to see if it could use help. The HCD staff members said they could and agreed to take two students. This contact began a long-term student involvement in the project.

Soon after my students began working on the project, I received a call from the head of the local HCD office. She told me that students were fine but that she wanted the professor. She told me about the formation of a community development corporation in the project and asked me to come to a meeting to meet the residents. I did not hesitate to accept the invitation. The stories the students kept telling me about this project had piqued my curiosity. Also, in a former career I had been a Legal Services attorney in Oakland, California and attended dozens of neighborhood meetings. Although I enjoyed the university and my colleagues, I dearly missed the contact with poor and working-class people that had been a substantial part of my former life.

The meeting was held at one of the residents' homes. As the students had told me, the group was very mixed by ethnicity and by gender and was very enthusiastic about its undertaking. I sat quietly at the meeting, responding only when asked about my background. I liked the meeting, and I liked the people. I returned several more times and was invited to join the board. At the time, I didn't know what an honor this was. As is discussed in the following chapters, the group did not want outsiders, particularly professionals, on its board and had rejected many other people presented by the state.

One of the reasons I may have survived, however, had nothing to do with my charms. The president of the corporation, the most vociferous advocate of community control among the leadership and a person against outsider experts sitting on the board, was out of town at that first meeting. Whatever the reason, this meeting began a very long, stimulating, sometimes painful, and usually rewarding journey.

A major fact that you must know in my telling of this story is that I later fell in love with that missing president, and having coupled, I moved into the project in 1985. In this period my objective academic distance that had already been diminished by my direct participation in the project as a member of the board was nearly overcome. I have tried to protect the reader from my excesses by involving various of my students in the research. Dewey Bandy, whose dissertation is on the formation of limited-equity cooperatives in California including Route 2, helped on many parts of the book, particularly on the subject of class.[12] Robert Heffner contributed heavily on the issue of ethnicity.[13] Lupe Compean interviewed many of the Latino residents in Spanish. Clyde Woods helped on the issue of race. I have discussed my observations with them and encouraged them to question and probe my experience in the project.

I feel very much, in my own way, like Leroy Ellis who wrote the book *White Ethics and Black Power* (1969). He questions the ability of participant observers to grasp the true story of a community project. He claims a role for the "partisan observer" in the analysis of such undertakings. There are facts and feelings you simply cannot know unless you were there on the inside of an event. Moreover, people will not tell you about certain facts and feelings unless they have known you for a long time. These facts and feelings are what my involvement has gained.

My case is different from Ellis' however. As a black man entering a black neighborhood, he had to overcome the distance a university education had created. My problem is much greater. My background is more petite bourgeois than working class. Further, I am Anglo and an Americano in Route 2 terminology and speak only English. Americanos are in the minority in the Route 2 project where many of the people are monolingual, Spanish-speaking immigrants, i.e. Latinos.[14]

Because of the language barrier, I have had to rely on informants and interpreters more than I would have wished. This has only added to the inevitable barrier between the researcher and the studied. As Elliot Liebow, a white man studying a black neighborhood, notes in *Talley's Corner*, there was always a "wall between us [that] remained" (Liebow 1967, pp. 250-251). As Robert Emerson notes, in the best of situations, a researcher cannot go fully native and become a regular member of the group (Emerson 1983, p. 183). The persistence of distance is one of the lessons I have learned. Across this distance, however, fieldwork is in the first order "relational." The work by its nature changes both the studied and the studier. "Researchers' attempts to form close ties with some people will inevitably antagonize others." There are no "'magic moments' where prior evasions, distancing, and suspicion finally drop away." The studier and the studied merely achieve "a different sort of relation than one had before" (Emerson 1983, p. 181).

There are many ways to tell the story of the Route 2 project. John Van Maanen in his book, *Tales of the Field*, sets forth three methods of reporting ethnographic research: realistic, confessional, and impressionistic (1988). He places the anthropological objective approach to reporting on research in his realistic category. He is very critical of this approach. He puts many newer ethnographies which openly report the story through the eyes of the researcher in the confessional category. In the impressionistic category he puts all the "good stories" researchers tell each other at conferences or at social events but rarely publish. He calls on researchers to combine the confessional and impressionistic approaches in writing up their work.

With Van Maanen's words in my ears I set about to write. I know that others could have seen a different reality than I experienced and likely would have drawn different conclusions from what I saw.[15]   As Van Maanen describes impressionistic tales, most of what follows is the product of stories that have been told and retold inside the project in conversations with residents and outside in conversations with colleagues and friends.   They have been "reinterpreted in light of new understandings and continuing dialogue with the studied" (Van Maanen, p. 118). Many of them represent the "exceptional" events rather than the "common and routine occurrences" (p. 108).

Beyond Van Maanen's affirmation of my approach, you should know that in my academic life I am, among other things, an experiential educator who attempts to teach praxis, i.e. the integration of practice and theory.[16] My students work for government, non-profit groups, or the private sector and are asked to observe their experience critically. In class and in written assignments they demonstrate their understanding of the integration of practice and theory in their work. This book can be seen as my effort in this direction, my paper on part of my praxis of the past ten years. I have observed, I've talked to others involved and interested in populist efforts, I've read what seemed to be relevant theory and accounts of other's experiences, and I've written about my experiences.

The end result is a book that places a story against a backdrop of theory. I report on how theory can come to life and how nuances of theory can work themselves out in the particular, concrete situation. Many times I have heard one author or another's words come from the mouths of the people I was observing. At times I've heard penetrating criticism of one or another theory. There have been times when I've asked what people think of a particular theory. On occasion I've given one of the project leaders the article or book I thought was relevant and asked for comments.[17]

Antonio Gramsci[18] would refer to many of the leaders of the Route 2 project as organic intellectuals.[19]   These are people who have the capacity to image an alternative future, to generate a counter-hegemony in the interests of the group with which they align themselves, and understand how to take steps toward that future in the real world of praxis.[20] I've been fascinated at just how theoretical many of the people in Route 2 are; how they have theories of how society and its parts work; how they act on these theories; and how these theoretical people, much as in Gramsci's theory of the organic intellectual, can influence the progress of a group.[21] This fascination permeates the book, and in many ways what follows is a book about organic intellectuals and how they attempt to establish their vision of hegemony in a group.[22]

When I read Gramsci's work, I get the impression that an organic intellectual, particularly one aligned with the working class, is an intellectual that is correct in his or her revolutionary thought, i.e. intellectuality is viewed unproblematically. This is not the reality of the situation. The working class may pick as intellectual and cultural leaders individuals who can be brilliantly effective at relating theory and practice or choose intellectuals to follow who, at the level of tactics, either disconnect theory and practice or engage in theory-based practice that is very inappropriate, and even destructive, in a given situation.[23] This is clearly a factor in why movements fail. In one light moment I thought of calling the latter group organic pseudo-intellectuals. This seemed too convenient an out to keep the theory pure, and I passed on the idea.

The Route 2 project has been through many phases. It successfully passed through a period of mobilization and activism when the people gained the right to buy the property and a development phase in which the cooperatives were formed. A length of time has also passed when the cooperatives have experimented with the problems of managing themselves. One approach has not dominated as happened in Santa Monica. Instead many competing ideologies have swept the project. Various forms of populism have expressed themselves. The dominant mode has varied from a very pure form of new progressive populism, through a form akin to interest group pluralism, to a form of clientelism. Traditional left ideology and individualism have also expressed themselves, but to a lesser degree. For writing purposes I have simplified the ideological categories' titles to "populist," "pluralists," "clientelist," "traditional left," and "individualists."

As the leaders of each of these groups asserted themselves, the process and the very form of the project organization changed. When the participants in the Route 2 project were uncertain about which way to turn, the organic intellectuals defined the dimensions of the hegemony that governed the outcome.[24] The result of the shifts in direction has meant the process in the Route 2 project has been open, public, and cooperative as well as conflictual, consensual, and private. There have been moments of exemplary public talk and periods when private talk dominated. There have been moments of community and extraordinary empowerment, and there have been moments when community was threatened and disempowerment reestablished.

Although I focus on particular individuals in the project, I have chosen to omit the names of the actors in the story with the exception of the politicians. The omissions are intended to give what level of privacy and confidentiality is possible in telling such an intimate story (in modern parlance to give them "deniability"). I have also omitted the names because I did not want to tell a story of personalities although there are some wonderful characters that took part in the Route 2 project. When I discussed issues that arose in the project with the residents, they would often want to talk about whether so and so was a "jerk," a "saint," or perhaps another more colorful characterization. It is the individuals' ideas in which I am interested and not whether they were jerks, saints, or whatever. I see their ideas as driving the objectional or laudatory behavior, and it is the interaction of individuals with different views, particularly of people with the ability to create a modicum of hegemony, that I investigated.

Chapter 1 presents an overview of the Route 2 story. Many of the external disempowering forces are introduced in this chapter. The following chapters are organized around the different views of the competing ideologies in the project on the meaning of community, empowerment, and disempowerment and the role played in the project by class, ethnicity, and gender. The chart that follows summarizes the differences between the three dominant groups.

The populists were Athenian in their approach to community and did not see power as an important concept in settling their internal affairs. They stressed the need for the members of the community to express their will to participate through self-reliance. The populists emphasized their working-class commonality, were suspicious of professionals, celebrated their ethnic homogeneity, and saw the sexes as equals fully capable of leadership and participation in the public talk of the community.

The pluralists saw the cooperatives as they did the world, as a place of conflict where community was at best a product of compromise. Their governing principle was power. The path to power was through a realization of rights and the development of competence. In their struggle, ethnicity in its U.S. racial sense rather than class was the dividing line between groups, and they sought allies across class lines to garner more power for their group. In the pluralists' tradition gender would also be seen as a generator of dividing lines, but as with class, in the Route 2 project the pluralists did not stress this category.

The clientelist concept of community was social as opposed to the political concepts of the populists and pluralists and was akin to family. They accepted class domination as inevitable but insisted on a benevolent leader (patron). They saw homogeneity as a requirement for community and saw exclusion of hostile elements as the path to homogeneity. Ethnicity was also a central category, but in the clientelists' case ethnicity was more based on immigrant status than in the racial terms of the pluralists. Gender differences were acknowledged. While women could be leaders, they were to do so in networks behind the scenes, in private talk away from the public world of men.

As you can see in the following table the differences are often quite extreme. It has meant at times that the project has travelled on quite a rocky road. These conflicts on top of the demographic diversity in the project are, however, what makes it so interesting and worthy of study.

Summary of Ideologies

	POPULIST	PLURALIST	CLIENTELIST
COMMUNITY	POLITICAL (Athenian) (cooperation) (us)	POLITICAL (arms length compromise) (us & them)	SOCIAL (familial) (consensus) (us)
EMPOWERMENT	ABSENCE OF POWER (self-reliance) (will)	GETTING POWER (having rights) (competence)	DOMINANCE (good patron)
CLASS	ANTI-PROFESSIONAL (class important)	PRO-PROFESSIONAL (ally in power) (interest group more important)	PRO-PROFESSIONAL (patron)
ETHNICITY	HETERO-GENIETY (no sub-organization)	BASIS OF INTEREST (race) (sub-organization)	HOMO-GENIETY (immigrant) (exclusive)
GENDER	EQUALITY (women can be open leaders in inclusive public talk)	(not a category)	DIFFERENCE (network of women in private talk)

The book ends with an Afterword. In the Afterword I place the story in the context of community planning practice and theory rather than let the story be the driver of practice and theory text. For those of you more comfortable with the more traditional approach of a theoretical chapter preceding the story rather than the integration of practice and theory in a text of thick description, you might want to read the Afterword first. To me it is an Afterword.

My experience in the Route 2 project has taught me about the complex character of the issues of community and empowerment. New populism has a difficult road ahead that it must negotiate to both achieve its end and maintain its goal; hence the title of this book: *The Struggle for Community*.

Notes

1. Boggs (1986); Boyte (1986, 1984, 1980); Boyte and Riessman (1986); Boyte, Booth, & Max (1986); Delgado (1986); Evans and Boyte (1986); Bouchier (1987); Viguerie (1983).

2. Many people have written about Santa Monica including Kann (1986); Boggs (1986); Clavel (1986); and Shearer (1982).

3. For a definition of limited-equity cooperatives see Chapter 1, pp. 8-9.

4. See Heskin (1983).

5. I helped create Community Corporation of Santa Monica which has proven to be a productive organization in the city. At this writing it is approaching having built or rehabilitated 300 units of housing in the city and has won several national and international awards for its activity.

6. Carl Boggs (1986) and Mark Kann (1986) state my position on the Santa Monica movement. After the tenant political organization, Santa Monicans for Renters Rights (SMRR), won city elections in 1981, there was an outburst of mass participation in the populist style in Santa Monica. Committees and working groups of citizens were formed to study any number of issues. This approach didn't last long. "Progressive" consultants were brought to the city from throughout the country to tell the city what it should do. Expertise and management replaced populist visions of community and democracy as the dominant themes. Important decisions were increasingly made in closed sessions attended by small groups of people who relied on the city staff's or its consultants' analysis. Political correctness haunted the effort much as it did in Britain with the Labor Party's local strategy (Gylford 1985). After three years of this professionalization of the movement, the tenant political organization lost its majority of the council seats and political control of the city. The loss of a majority on the council brought on calls for democratization of the tenant movement. The reform adopted was the replacing of private nominating meetings with the selection of candidates at public conventions. Power brokering, traditional in conventions of political parties, was tried by the old leadership at

these conventions and failed. A new leadership once again espousing a new populist line of community, democracy, and empowerment emerged. During the winter 1988 elections SMRR made a comeback in the politics of Santa Monica and regained a majority of the city council seats. The establishment in the city is wondering what this reemergence of SMRR will mean. I share this curiosity.

7. Boyte (1984).

8. My emphasis is more on the enemy within than the pressure from without. As Antonio Gramsci put it with victories "the enemy to combat and overcome will no longer be outside the proletariat, will no longer be an external power that is limited and can be controlled. . . . The new man, in his every act, has to fight the 'bourgeois' lying in ambush" (Boggs 1964, p. 103).

9. Others, while acknowledging the constraints, see sufficient political space for such regimes to at least partially succeed. Stone (1987); Elkin (1987); Swanstrom (1988, 1985).

10. The initial movement in Santa Monica was a slow growth movement. This slow growth effort was partially abandoned at the same time as the participatory governmental form because of the "necessity" for commercial growth to raise the revenue to support an undefined progressive social agenda. This effort, however, has led to a second slow growth reaction that is now playing itself out in the city. This debate is not the subject of this book. If it was, I would argue with Peterson's position. Much of the truth in Peterson's position is based on a liberal, redistributive, welfare state image of equity. Populism does not share this image.

11. The issue of property values and the effect of decisions on property values is removed in a limited equity cooperative. Had they chosen a condominium or some other unrestricted market form of ownership, Peterson's observations might have been equally applicable in the neighborhood case as well. As is discussed later in this prologue, the notion of "ideological hegemony" was derived by Antonio Gramsci who observed insurgent movements "strive to create their own consensual legitimacy or counter-hegemony presence in both civil society and the state" (Boggs 1984, p.159).

12. Heskin and Bandy (1986a, 1986b, 1985).

13. Heskin and Heffner (1987).

14. I am Americano as distinguished from a Latino. This refers to U.S. citizen as opposed to immigrant from a Latin American country. It gets a little more complicated because it involves identity as well as actual status. One might have forsaken his or her immigrant background by assimilating or on the other hand be so identified with the cause of immigrant Latinos as to be an honorary Latino.

15. As an aside I should say that I do not feel a great deal more unsure of my findings than those of my own and my colleagues' quantitative work. The questions one chooses to ask and the form of the questions often determine the results of a more quantitative study, and as I know from many debates with friends and foes over the meaning of data, interpretation of the numbers is, in a complex field such as mine, much a matter of personal and ideological choice.

16. Heskin (1978).

17. Sometimes working-class people can say very direct and humorous things about a book with which they agree.

18. The concept of hegemony employed in this book is that of Antonio Gramsci, an Italian Marxist politically active in Italy in the 1910s and 1920s. He was jailed in 1926 by Mussolini's fascist government. He remained in prison for virtually the rest of his life. He died in 1937. He wrote voluminously as a journalist before being imprisoned. While in prison, he wrote his major work which was later published as *Selections from the Prison Notebooks* (1971). Gramsci saw the dominance of the liberal capitalist state as being based in more than just its potential coercive power. He saw the state gaining the freely given consent of the populace to its domination through the formation of ideological hegemony with the assistance of bourgeois intellectuals who work to ensure that the hegemony penetrates every possible element of civil society. A major component of his response to this perceived condition was the necessity of the formation of a revolutionary, working-class counter-hegemony with the assistance of intellectuals aligned with the working class. While the situations examined in this book are far short of the Gramscian aim, the idea that it is necessary to hegemonize a population with an alternative vision, i.e., to gain its consent to a different undertaking, when one seeks social change, even at the level of new populism, is central to this work. There are numerous important books on Gramsci's life and intellectual work. Among the authors who have influenced my interpretation of Gramsci are Boggs (1984 and 1976) and Adamson (1980). The work of Laclau and Mouffe (1985) and Bocock (1986) has also been helpful.

19. In Gramsci's conception organic intellectuals are individuals who "would be simultaneously 'leading' and 'representative,'" of the working class (Carl Boggs 1984, p. 223). Organic intellectuals could be "intellectual defectors from the bourgeoisie," but in the long run they would "have to be a 'new type of intellectual' generated through the class struggle itself" (p. 224). In Gramsci's scheme intellectualism was not "a specialized type of mental work associated with conventional scholastic or literary traditions, but was an integral part of everyday life-culture, social relations, work, politics" (p.220). "All human beings are in the final analysis 'philosophers.'" The difference between the masses and the organic intellectual is one of "quantity and not quality" (p. 143). Organic intellectuals would be active in "practical life, as constructor, organizer, 'permanent persuader,' and not just a simple orator." They would not only discover and create new ideas but also "disseminate" them and in the process furnish "cohesion" to class formation (p. 220).

20. As Laclau and Mouffe (1985) put it, engage in "articulated practices." These authors take the ideas of Gramsci beyond direct organizing of the working class itself to the organization of "oppressed" groups that could be stitched together into a larger movement. This is implied in Boggs' interpretation of Gramsci's rejection of economism, focus on civil society, and concept of "bloc" (1984, pp. 228-230).

21. Carl Boggs (1984) in discussing Gramsci's theory of organic intellectuals states Gramsci's view of the intellectualism of the people that matches my own: "Gramsci looked upon all human interaction as in some measure 'intellectual' to the extent that everyone 'contributes to sustain a conception of the world or to

modify it, that is, to bring into being new modes of thought.' Or, put differently, 'the majority of mankind are philosophers insofar as they engage in practical activity and in their practical activity (or in their guidelines of conduct) there is implicitly contained a conception of the world, or philosophy'" (p. 220). The organic intellectual is a philosopher who both learns from and forms the bases of the philosophy of the people.

22. My feeling is very much captured in a Gramsci quote Boggs (1984) includes in his work: "If you're not able to understand real individuals, you can't understand what is universal and general" (p. 206).

23. Schon (1983) articulates the problem of divergence of theory and practice.

24. This establishment of dimensions was more in the nature of moral/philosophical instruction than rule making. As stated by Bocock (1986), "The concept of hegemony which Gramsci developed meant, in part, that people of all non-exploiting classes should give their consent . . . as a result of education and understanding, not through processes of manipulation and imposition by a party elite" (p. 22). Boggs (1984) quotes Gramsci elaborating the point: "Ideas and opinions are not simultaneously 'born' in each individual brain: they have had a center of formation, of irradiation, of dissemination, of persuasion—a group of men, or a single individual even, which has developed them and presented them in the current form of political reality" (p. 209).

1

A Struggle for Community

When a family's home is threatened, the family will fight to save that home. When a group of families' homes are threatened, they will often organize and fight to save their homes together. If the families are composed of poor and working-class people, they usually lose their fight, particularly if the attack is coming from the state. Sometimes their troubles are assuaged by help to move, but they usually move. The incidents in which they win, where they stay, are heroic tales that need to be told and retold. Only a few such tales exist in the modern literature. This book adds another to the short stack.[1]

In 1975 a group of tenant families met to fight for their homes in the Echo Park-Silverlake district of Los Angeles. The tenants occupied housing owned by the state of California in a proposed freeway corridor (Route 2) that was to be sold off after the freeway project was abandoned. When the fight was over in the early 1980s, the tenants ended up the owners of this housing either on an individual basis or in collective ownership in five scattered-site cooperatives. To win they had to sustain a five-year fight most people said could not be won. Since winning, the tenants who ended up as cooperators have had to struggle with the task of collectively owning and operating their housing.

In this chapter the main events of the Route 2 corridor story are presented. The material is organized into the three distinct stages of the project. The first stage consists of the tenants' mobilization and social action to win the right to buy the property. The second stage involves the period when the housing was purchased and rehabilitated and the cooperatives were organized. The third stage focuses on the operation of the cooperatives. You will find many up and many down periods in the story. The Route 2 story mixes moments of gaining community and losing community; of empowerment and disempowerment. The struggle against external displacing and disempowering forces is never finally over. Moreover, once a moment of victory is attained, a new set of internal disempowering and potentially displacing forces emerge.

The tenant population of the Route 2 corridor is primarily made up of working-class families representing skilled and unskilled labor with very low to middle range incomes. This unifying characteristic is unique in a population that is both ethnically and ideologically diverse. The population is over two-thirds Latino, including immigrants from at least 14 Latin American nations and Chicanos, about a quarter Anglo, with many ethnicities represented, and the remainder is approximately equally Black and Asian.[2] Very few of the residents are multi-cultural or multi-lingual. At least five distinct ideologies have at one time or another been manifested in the leadership of this population. Initially individualist, new populist, and traditional left approaches were represented in the leadership. Beneath the surface lay a clientelist ideology held by much of the resident population. Later, interest-group pluralism was introduced into the project. Each ideological group contributed in its way to the overall project.

The ideological differences have meant that the population has had to work through differences in the meaning of community and empowerment and the significance of class, ethnicity, and gender throughout its collective story. All the groups believed in collective struggle against the state, but there the commonality ends. Each group used different methods and sought different ends. The individualists struggle for individual gain, the new populists seek collective self-empowerment through self-help, and the left seeks to confront the state to hold it accountable for care of its citizens. The pluralists' focus is on expressing collective self-interest through mobilizing power. The clientelists are more accepting of state power but demand reciprocity and seek security in family.

In the first stage of the project a coalition of individualists and new populists dominated. The left activists were isolated not long after the organizing began in earnest. The new populists took over in the second stage when the cooperatives developed. Individualist and clientelist elements were also active in this period. As the development period was ending, an interest-group pluralist approach became dominant. Then as the cooperatives stabilized, the ideology of the project leaders became more mixed. An amalgam of what had preceded can now be found, but it is in this period that clientelism has been given its day.

As will be discussed in detail in a later chapter, women played a major role in the history of the project and continue to be over-represented in the leadership. There are more adult women than men living in the project either as single heads of household or alone. There are, however, a significant number of men present either as part of family units or alone.[3] Well over two-thirds of the units are occupied by families, many of them large families. Nearly 60 percent of the units in the project have more than one bedroom and a quarter have more than two bedrooms. There are three five-bedroom apartments and one six-bedroom apartment in the cooperatives. Typically each bedroom in these large apartments is occupied by two children.

The Route 2 story actually has its beginning in the late 1940s when the Division of Highways, the most isolated, insulated, and powerful arm of government in the state of California began its 25-year spree of highway building. The Division of Highways controlled one of the largest collections of gas tax revenues in the nation that, augmented by federal money, approached one billion dollars per year. This budget and an autonomous structure allowing it to operate virtually free of legislative control led former governor Edmund G. Brown to say that if the Division of Highways wanted to build a road through the state capitol, no one would know how to stop it (Haas & Heskin 1980).

In the mid-1970s the completion of the transcontinental highway system, increasing environmental concern, and community protest led to a reappraisal of state priorities and put an end to the highway boom. In this period the Division of Highways was replaced by a smaller and less autonomous California Department of Transportation, called Caltrans. When Edmund Brown's son Jerry Brown, a decidedly anti-freeway governor, was elected, freeway plans were postponed, and many were later cancelled.

The reversal in policy, however, left Caltrans in the middle of a number of projects. Many of these projects were to be constructed through populated areas. It is Caltrans' practice to rent dwellings they purchase in scheduled freeway corridors until they are demolished to make way for the construction of the freeway. The highway "bust" left Caltrans as one of the biggest landlords in the state. In 1978 it owned some 5,000 units of housing in California, with 3,000 located in Los Angeles.

Among the Caltrans units was property purchased between 1960 and 1975 to extend the Route 2 freeway through the Echo Park-Silverlake district of Los Angeles as the beginning of the Beverly Hills freeway planned to parallel the Santa Monica freeway that runs from downtown Los Angeles to the coast at Santa Monica. Caltrans' Route 2 property consisted of a collection of some 544 units of housing in single-family homes, duplexes, triplexes and apartment buildings on more than 200 parcels of property stretched over a two and a quarter mile long and a block wide strip about two miles west of downtown Los Angeles.

The Beverly Hills freeway, after passing through Los Angeles, would have disrupted parts of the wealthy town of Beverly Hills. This meant significant, powerful opposition to its construction. With the shift in popular attitudes against freeway construction as an aid, this opposition was able to obtain cancellation of the first leg of the building plan many miles away from Beverly Hills in the more working-class Echo Park-Silverlake district of Los Angeles. No organized opposition to the freeway is remembered by long-term residents of the Echo Park-Silverlake area. They do recall, however, that the threat of the impending freeway and the purchase of property by Caltrans had a destabilizing, deleterious impact on the neighborhood.

During Caltrans' ownership of the Route 2 housing, it was occupied by approximately 1,500 tenants. Caltrans used the excuse of the scheduled demolition of the structures to forego adequate maintenance of the property, half of which was over fifty years old. When the freeway plan was cancelled in 1975, housing conditions in the corridor had deteriorated to the point that Caltrans had become known as one of the largest slumlords in the region.

Stage One: Mobilization and Social Action

Organizing in the Route 2 area began immediately after the freeway project was officially cancelled. A group of first-wave, anti-Castro Cuban residents who lived in single family-homes in the corridor circulated a petition among the residents of the corridor (103 signed) and presented it to Governor Jerry Brown. They requested that they be permitted to purchase the homes they occupied before they were offered to the general public, what they called a right of first refusal. The petition found its way to both Caltrans and the California Department of Housing and Community Development (HCD), to the office of state Senator David Roberti, and the offices of the local council members Peggie Stevenson and John Ferraro (the corridor crosses two council districts). All the recipients of the petition began in one form or another to work on the Route 2 problem.

Caltrans balked at the idea of giving the residents a right of first refusal. As one HCD staff person put it, Caltrans' position was "those people don't have a right to anything; it's not their property." Besides such a practice was against established procedures, and, Caltrans argued, illegal. HCD, a quite liberal organization under the Brown administration, and the politicians, including state Senator Roberti, a liberal who represented the area and who later became Speaker Pro Tem of the state senate, were more supportive. Caltrans had kept the rents low on the housing in the corridor and many low-income families lived in the units. There was a fear that sale on the open market would result in the displacement of many of the lower-income residents.

In 1976 the senator, to overcome Caltrans' objection to the legality of the tenants' request, obtained a state attorney general's opinion stating that the tenants could be given the right of first refusal to the property.[4] The opinion shifted the issue from the question of whether the tenants may buy the property to the question of how they could buy it. Caltrans and HCD were part of the same super agency, the Business and Transportation Agency, and an internal struggle ensued within the agency over who would handle this question. The struggle repeated other such turf fights Caltrans and HCD had in the past in other parts of the state. In the end HCD was assigned the lead in coming up with a solution for the Route 2 problem.[5] The resolution of this question was not easy. As one HCD staff person put it, Caltrans "died hard."

Having won the internal fight to take the lead in the Route 2 project, HCD set about to do what was to be the first in a series of feasibility studies on various approaches to Caltrans selling the property without causing displacement. In October, 1976 HCD enlisted the help of the City of Los Angeles Community Development Department (CDD) to work on the problem. CDD working with HCD hired a consultant with experience developing properties such as those in the Route 2 corridor to formulate alternative solutions to the problem.[6] Caltrans, for its part, set about the process of establishing the market value of the homes. Whatever happened, Caltrans wanted to make sure it realized a maximum return on its investment in the Route 2 corridor.

Caltrans' position and the issue of price became increasingly important during the feasibility investigation. Between 1975 and 1977, between the tenants' original request and serious consideration of how the request might be met, an inflationary real estate spiral had increased the value of the Route 2 corridor homes by some 50 percent.[7] Even the price of homes once affordable to the more moderate-income residents of the corridor began to move out of their reach. This problem was exacerbated by the deteriorating condition of the homes. The homes would have to be repaired to obtain financing.[8] If the residents had to pay for these repairs, the homes would become even less affordable.

Real estate prices continued to rise as Caltrans took its time determining the market value of the homes. The residents could see the problem building and became angry. They believed they should not be punished for the delay by having to pay more for their homes, and they demanded that they be allowed to buy their homes at 1975 prices, the year they submitted their petition. Caltrans staff was seriously troubled by this new demand and again maintained that it would be illegal to comply with the residents' request. To sell the homes at below the current 'fair market value' would be a 'gift of public funds' in violation of the state constitution.

With the growing roadblock of increasing prices and deteriorating conditions in their path, it was clear to the original activists that they would have to take action beyond their petition if they were to buy their homes. They decided to mobilize the people who lived in the corridor. In March 1977 the first corridor-wide meeting was held in a neighborhood school with the ostensible purpose of introducing the city's feasibility consultant. All the residents were invited to attend. The senator's office cooperated by sending out the invitations.

Some of the traditional left residents who were active in the alternative print and electronic media learned who the consultant would be in advance of the meeting and used their sources to research the consultant's background. Their discovery that the consultant was a developer who dealt with buying, rehabilitating and selling homes like those in the Route 2 corridor led them to worry that the consultant might have entrepreneurial interests in the property. The media group came to the meeting to present the information to the other residents.

The school auditorium was packed for the meeting by more than 300 people. The left activists passed out copies of the information on the consultant as the people entered the hall. When the consultant was introduced, he was asked to confirm the truth of what had been learned. A heated exchange followed. The assembled group with the support of the council members decided to insist that the consultant work under an advisory committee of Route 2 residents. They won the argument, and a second meeting was scheduled to be held at the council field office a week later to elect a steering committee for what became the Route 2 Tenants Association (R2TA). About 100 people filled the council office to overflowing at this follow up meeting.

Weekly meetings of the elected committee began from that point on. The early discussions about what should happen in the corridor produced a "no displacement," one-for-all-and-all-for-one position. Whatever plan produced by HCD and the CDD consultant had to provide housing within the corridor for all the residents, high and low income, those in single-family homes and those in multifamily buildings. With this position established, the committee, dominated by the single-family residents, moved to expand itself with more multifamily residents at another mass meeting.

While the residents were organizing, Caltrans' position against any sale to the residents hardened. The Caltrans position remained, "We are not in the housing, welfare, or other type of business. We are in the transportation business and are using taxpayers money" (*Northwest Leader*, March 24, 1977). In mid-1977 Caltrans cut off communication with the tenants. The tenants responded with the one mass public action in the entire struggle. One hundred tenants helped form a one-day picket line at Caltrans' Los Angeles headquarters (*Northwest Leader*, September 21, 1977). With some of the media-connected residents' help, full media coverage was obtained (*L.A. Times*, September 8, 1977).

Soon after the demonstration Caltrans reversed itself and rejoined the process. The residents believed that their action had significant impact on Caltrans. Caltrans seemed to be very uncomfortable with such negative publicity. It is, of course, hard to tell what brought Caltrans back. The tenants demonstration was accompanied by pressure from the senator's office and support by HCD staff.

The belief that Caltrans was publicity shy led some of the traditional left residents among the leadership of the corridor to urge the group to take a public confrontative style in approaching the resolution of their problem. This position set off a debate fairly typical of this period. The populists in the group wanted to exploit Caltrans' discomfort with the threat of further demonstrations but did not want to carry out the threat unless there was no other option. This group felt the residents would have more maneuvering room for what it saw as their very radical demands without the intense public scrutiny the media can bring. It caused some shouting and hard feelings in the committee. In the end, the populists with the support of the individualists won out.

In the period that followed, the legality of the tenants desire to buy the property at a reduced price was established by two major legal acts. First, the state attorney general was again asked for his opinion. This time the question concerned the legality of a below market sale. In a public press conference during the attorney general's unsuccessful 1978 campaign for governor, he declared that the state could sell the property to the tenants at a discounted price to prevent the negative environmental impact of displacement (*Northwest Leader*, April 27, 1978).

Second, in 1979 state legislation passed setting forth a procedure for the sale of the property to the tenants at an affordable price down to the original purchase price of the property (S.B. 86).[9] The bill had been drafted through the collective efforts of the HCD staff, the tenant leadership, and the senator's staff member, Michael Woo, who later replaced Peggie Stevenson as councilperson for one of the districts covered by the Route 2 project. The residents' position on the contents of the legislation was a product of intense debate between R2TA and HCD and within R2TA. HCD favored keeping the housing as rental housing because it would likely ensure the long-term affordability of the units and would be *relatively* easy to accomplish. Most of the tenant leadership wanted to escape tenancy and become owners.

The traditional left activists were the only residents voicing opposition to the ownership idea. They complained that buying the property would transfer the state's responsibility for neglected property to the residents. If the tenants failed, they would not be at fault. Failure would be because the property was in such bad shape. The left activists wanted to confront the state with its failure to meet its responsibility and demand it meet its obligation to provide housing for its population. It is an argument that has taken place in other places with varying results, but, in this instance, it didn't catch hold of the group.[10]

The populist activists hit upon the idea of forming cooperatives as the logical next best choice to renting the units. Cooperatives permit the total wealth of their members to be used to accomplish what their individual wealth might not and fit the all-for-one approach of the leadership. Cooperatives also have an advantage over other forms of ownership in that cooperatives are eligible under federal law for what is normally considered rent subsidies. Many of the residents needed this assistance if they were to stay. The mix of ideology and pragmatism in the choice of cooperatives could be seen as a theme for the populists' approach to the issues that followed.

The individualists, primarily the activists living in single-family homes on separate parcels, did not want to be included in the cooperatives. They supported a coop plan for the residents of multifamily parcels and those who lived in single-family homes who could not buy their homes by themselves, but they wanted the opportunity for individual ownership of the single-family parcels. The argument was more heated than might otherwise have occurred because much of the single-family leadership was Cuban. The Cubans argued that they had not escaped the collectivity of the Cuban revolution for collectivity in the United States. They were adamant and, with HCD support, they eventually won the day. The HCD staff, having lost on the rental idea, felt the single-family program was politically more palatable and feasible. The coop idea was more speculative.

The result of the discussions was that the legislation was divided in two parts. One related to single-family dwellings and the other to multifamily dwellings. The single-family portion called for the state to repair the property and sell it to individual residents at an affordable price down to original purchase price. Caltrans would rehabilitate the single-family homes, and modest controls would be placed on resales to ensure against early speculation in these low-priced, high-valued houses. Over time the new owners would escape any restriction. The multifamily property was to be sold to a developer to create "limited-equity" cooperatives for the residents of the property. The developer would be responsible for bringing the condition of the property up to the standards necessary to obtain financing. The state's failure to accept responsibility for repair of the multifamily property and the very low income of many of the residents made the question of feasibility of the cooperative idea a real one.[11]

Cooperatives are not common in California, and the limited-equity cooperative was a new idea in the affordable housing field. A housing cooperative is a corporation in which each of the residents own a share of stock and has the right to occupy a housing unit owned by the corporation. A shareholder in a limited-equity cooperative, as defined by state law passed in the same year as the Route 2 legislation, may not receive more than 10 percent per annum simple interest (not compound interest) on the purchase price of the share when it is sold. The law also limits, forever, the possibility of residents obtaining further access to the building equity in the property. For example, if the cooperative is dissolved, all proceeds must be given to the government or a charitable organization.

Caltrans now reluctantly went along with the process and next prepared a negative declaration (in lieu of an environmental impact report) stating that sale of the property to the tenants was necessary to prevent displacement of the tenants and that the sale would not result in any negative environmental impacts.[12] In a stormy public hearing in May, 1979 (the one my students told me about), opposition to the sale was expressed by local real estate and business interests (*Northwest Leader* May 23, 1979). These objections were noted, and the project moved on to approval before the California Transportation Commission, the state commission that supervises Caltrans' activity.

In August of 1979 some of the individuals who testified against the project in April filed a law suit attacking the below market sale of the property, as Caltrans had, as an unconstitutional gift of public funds. The plaintiffs were represented by the Pacific Legal Foundation, a conservative public-interest law firm that had several exCaltrans employees on its staff, one of whom 10 years later became Director of Caltrans. With Legal Services help, the tenants drove back the attack a year later. Although the legal fight was won, the law suit clouded the situation and delayed the progress of the sale of the property.

The years 1978 and 1979 were like a roller coaster ride for the leadership. It won a number of victories and celebrated after each victory, but each victory seemed to be followed by yet another battle. The residents still did not own the property and many problems lay ahead. Internally, the division of the property into two programs had the effect of dividing the residents and the leadership. Many of the multifamily residents felt the residents of the approximately 120 single-family parcels got the better end of the deal with the state. About half of the leaders lived in these properties and, more importantly, most of the Latino leaders were in this group. Over time as they bought their homes, these individuals left the organization leaving a racially and ethnically diverse group but one without a real immigrant Latino presence. It would take years to overcome this problem.

Stage Two: Developing the Cooperatives and the Federation

In 1979 it was decided that HCD should handle the sale of the single-family housing and following the residents wishes and the legislation, that a housing development corporation be formed to handle the disposal of the multifamily property. The group incorporated with the name the Route 2 Community Housing Corporation (R2CHC).[13] The initial board was made up primarily of the populist multifamily residents on the R2TA executive committee. It received initial technical assistance from the HCD staff and consultants hired with a small state grant, the Los Angeles Community Design Center, a non-profit organization that provided architectural and planning services to low-income people, and a Los Angeles Bar Association group named Lawyers for Housing.

The Design Center studied the condition of the property, finding it in need of substantial repair, and surveyed the residents disclosing that the residents saw the two and quarter miles of the corridor as crossing through three very distinct areas rather than one neighborhood. The Design Center study led the R2CHC board to decide that multiple coops should be developed rather than one to maximize the chances of social cohesion within the cooperatives. Three cooperatives, one for each area, were considered, but one of the areas was so large that it was decided that it should be subdivided into three cooperatives where major streets crossed the corridor. Lawyers for Housing worked on creating the legal forms necessary to carry out the plan. The presence of the consultants and the HCD staff often made R2CHC meetings in this period more like professional conferences than community meetings.

State funds were soon obtained to hire yet another staff person, an organizer for the project with the title "Community Education Specialist." The organizer was supposed to help in the latest iteration of the feasibility study by collecting information from the residents and educating them about cooperatives. Circumstances, however, led the organizer in another direction. Not long after the organizer was hired Caltrans announced that all rents in the corridor would be raised by 10 percent. The leadership was immediately concerned that an increase would cause the displacement of the poorest residents. In addition, since Caltrans had neglected the properties, many residents felt a rent increase was unjustified.

Everyone had discussed the deterioration of the property, but with two and a quarter miles of property not everyone was fully aware of the dimensions of the problem. Since the organizer visited all the residents, she was one of the few people who was familiar with the actual conditions of all the property. She had been shocked by what she had found. One family, for example, had lived in a unit with no roof over their kitchen for four months. Pictures were taken of the worst cases, and in the midst of the rent increase crisis the organizer brought them to the leadership. The leadership decided to call a mass meeting of the residents to discuss how they should respond to the rent increase and the condition of the property.

The pictures of the deteriorated housing circulated during the meeting. They shocked the membership as they had shocked the leadership. The residents did not want Caltrans to displace the tenants directly through a market sale, indirectly through allowing the property to deteriorate to the point it could not be repaired, or though a rent increase the residents could not afford. The discussion led to a decision to strike, to refuse to pay the increase. They would not pay the increase until the property was repaired and an ability to pay test was made part of Caltrans rental procedures for any rent increases. The one-for-all spirit prevailed.

The strike put the whole project at risk. Mass evictions were possible and as is discussed in Chapter 4, HCD did not support the residents' decision. The department felt a strike would make the negotiations for purchase of the property more difficult. There was also the possibility that the membership would not support the strike and undercut the legitimacy of the leadership. The moderate-income single-family-residents were particularly pressured. It was hard for them to take a chance on losing what they had worked so hard for, but many of them did participate in the strike. When the next rent came due, some 80 percent of the residents did not pay the increase.[14]

The resident leadership decided to go back to a more public strategy for this crisis. They invited state officials to tour the property and see the conditions for themselves. Caltrans and representatives of the various political offices involved went on the tour. The media also came along and afterwards labelled Caltrans the largest slumlord in Los Angeles. Even some of the Caltrans officials expressed shock at what they found. After seeing an entire wall of mildew in a unit, one of the heads of Caltrans gave his card to the resident with instructions to call if it wasn't repaired immediately. In a few months both of the tenants demands were met, at least on paper. A means test was established for any rent increases.[15] No increase could result in the rents becoming more than

25 percent of a tenant's income, and a commitment was made to repair the property.

With some effort, the proposed rent increases had been withdrawn, but the fight to have the property properly maintained, to have Caltrans live up to its commitment, was a long one. It brought another political actor to the fore in the project. Michael Roos, the local state assemblyman, who was to become the majority leader of the state assembly, led the political fight to have the property repaired. He went so far as to have the Caltrans budget modified to include the specific requirement that the Route 2 property had to be repaired before senior staff people in Caltrans could be paid.

The assemblyman not only did what he could to force the repairs, he also blunted another Caltrans initiative that could have endangered the project. One of the responses of Caltrans to the call for repair was to begin to declare buildings beyond repair and to order the relocation of the tenants to other supposedly more habitable units. From the tenants point of view emptying buildings would be likely to remove these properties from the project. Vacant buildings in the neighborhood are subject to vandalism that, in turn, can lead to destruction of the building. Destruction would have not only saved repair dollars, but also would free the property from the discounted sale price provisions of the law. Vacant land was to be sold at market value.

Most of the tenants were scared out of one twenty-unit building before the tenants' association learned of Caltrans' actions. Two tenants hung on and at the tenants' associations' urging, refused to move. The assemblyman investigated and with the threat of litigation by R2TA backing him up, convinced Caltrans to abandon this plan.

The political support that the Route 2 tenants received is unusual. At one point the speaker pro tem of the state senate, the majority leader of the assembly, and the president of the city council represented the area and actively supported the project. Their support arose partly from the seriousness of the potential displacement of the residents of the neighborhood, partly because Caltrans had many enemies from its aggressive past, and partly because of the attractiveness of the multiethnic, low-income group of people carrying on such a long struggle. One of the political aides used to take great pleasure in referring to the group as the "mouse that roared."

Although Caltrans eventually repaired some of the buildings, they could not or would not act to solve another major problem. There was a substantial amount of overcrowding in the corridor. Caltrans had not paid attention to how many tenants lived in a unit. More than ten people lived in some one-bedroom apartments. Allowing overcrowding was not only a questionable policy, it could prevent the cooperatives from obtaining federal rent subsidies and financing. Two-thirds of the residents needed federal Section 8 assistance to be able to afford the monthly carrying charges that covered the mortgage payment, insurance and maintenance, and other miscellaneous expenses of operating the coops.[16] Overcrowding is not permitted in Section 8 assisted units.

Caltrans did, under pressure, agree to stop renting units and keep them empty for the coops to use to relieve overcrowding. Agreements like this resulted from long negotiations at meeting after meeting with various Caltrans personnel. Caltrans' main office in Sacramento sent one after another bureaucrat to deal with these "obstreperous" tenants, but one after another they were repelled.[17] While the tenants' political support helped, they also were good negotiators. They were particularly good at controlling the agenda of the negotiations, the secret of success in many negotiations. For example, they used the existence of R2TA and R2CHC to advantage. They would often cut off Caltrans' efforts to divert attention from the tenants' agenda by saying what Caltrans was interested in was a matter for the other organization and would have to be considered at a separate meeting with that group. Although the members of the two organizations were nearly identical, this tactic seemed to confuse Caltrans bureaucrats and kept them off balance.

The overcrowding problem also generated leadership and staff interest in the empty lots that Caltrans had accumulated by purchase or demolition of buildings that had fallen into disrepair. In 1979 R2CHC obtained options on some dozen such lots throughout the corridor at 1979 values. It planned to develop additional housing on these lots to relieve the overcrowding in the existing housing. Before R2CHC could hire its own staff, the HCD staff came to the board of R2CHC with a proposal to hire a consultant to develop more than a hundred Section 8 housing units on the lots.

In spite of its nervousness at its inexperience in the development of housing, the board went along. The consultant contacted several developers to help put a development package together. As the meetings with the developers approached, the board became increasingly nervous about the idea. It seemed too much too fast. It was not clear that so many units were needed to relieve the overcrowding, and the board felt development on the proposed scale might turn the neighborhoods surrounding the corridor against the entire project. The leadership had gone to the surrounding homeowners groups to get support for their effort to buy their homes. Most of the groups have given their support, but they had expressed reservation about the development of more housing.[18]

Instead, the board proposed a phased solution with the development of sixteen units on the largest lot first. The HCD staff was upset. They accused the leadership of various anti-affordable housing sins and indicated the Section 8 new construction program was ending, but the board's position held. A new consultant and the board put together a proposal for a sixteen-unit project that was to be a sixth coop, Imogen Cooperative. It was funded by the Federal Department of Housing and Urban Development (HUD). The Section 8 program did end and only one other lot was later purchased and developed with other funds.[19]

The HUD commitment to the Imogen project was almost lost some months later. A board member learned that the project funding was in danger due to HUD funding cutbacks. The board contacted its political support for assistance. One of the supporters called a former intern working in the White House. A call from the White House was made to the local HUD office inquiring about the funding of the sixteen-unit project. The project was not dropped from the commitment list. It was discovered, however, that due to a technical error in the paper work by the consultant, the project was set up as a rental project rather than as a cooperative. This error was unfortunate. The paper work was changed so the project could later be converted to a coop, but the conversion has never taken place. The story of Imogen is told in Chapter 5.

In 1980 R2CHC received funds from the City of Los Angeles in the form of a Community Development Block Grant (CDBG) to begin the development corporation. The city Community Development Department that administers CDBG funds was skeptical of the project. They had never heard of limited-equity cooperatives and inquired about the legality of such a thing. Under political pressure, they granted seed money for R2CHC, but they never believed anything would come of it.[20] With the help of the HCD staff, additional funds were obtained from the state through Caltrans and HCD. The residents participated in grant writing that resulted in additional funds from various private foundations. A director was hired, and work began in earnest. When the project became a reality rather than an idea, the staff grew from the director and organizer to office workers, rehabilitation inspectors, an assistant director, and additional organizers. At its peak R2CHC had nine full-time employees.

Once the project started to develop, the board of R2CHC was transformed. The R2CHC board, consistent with the populist beliefs of the leadership, decided to amend the corporation's bylaws formally to change itself from a self-appointed body to a federation of coop representatives with the number of representatives dependent on the size of the coop. Boards for each cooperative were formed and elected representatives were sent to serve on the R2CHC board. Some of the original leadership, who did not become coop board members, were retained as members at large. At its peak the board had seventeen members. The story of this transformation is told in Chapter 4.

The R2CHC office was a storefront with the aura of a people's office. It was furnished primarily by the residents with items donated from their homes or purchased at garage sales. The aura, although not intentional, was soon to pay dividends. The hardest problem the staff faced initially was obtaining financing for the purchase of the property. Cooperatives are not common in California, particularly low-income, scattered-site cooperatives. Many lenders literally laughed at the idea. Even the National Consumer Cooperative Bank established by the federal government to finance cooperatives refused to make a loan to the project. A consultant the bank hired wrote a sympathetic report after a visit which in short said, "nice people; too bad." Things couldn't have looked worse. The whole project would fail if financing was not obtained.

The last best chance for financing was a group name SAMCO, the Savings and Loan Mortgage Company. SAMCO is a coalition of savings and loans institutions that make high risk, socially responsible loans. The R2CHC board had decided to try to develop the Dayton Heights cooperative first. It was the smallest and needed the least rehabilitation. The board and staff felt the lenders would be most comfortable with that cooperative, and R2CHC would have the chance to learn its job on the easiest of the cooperative groupings. The director and assistant director waited nervously all morning for the SAMCO representative to come for a tour of the Dayton Heights cooperative. They cleaned up as much as they could to make the office presentable and waited nervously. When the representative didn't come, they finally went off to lunch. The only person left in the office was the administrator busy at work on the books of the organization when the SAMCO representative came in. She barely looked up when he asked for a map of the corridor. With a map provided, he went off.

When the director and assistant director returned from lunch, they rushed out to find the SAMCO representative but were unsuccessful. The next day they got a call with the news that the loan would be made. The SAMCO representative had been very impressed by the no frills style of the office and attitude of the administrator. He saw Route 2 as the real thing, a no-frills, people's project, just what SAMCO was set up to support.[21]

With financing in hand, a commitment for some 200 moderate rehabilitation Section 8 certificates were obtained with some difficulty from the City of Los Angeles Housing Authority to help subsidize the rents of the low-income residents. The Housing Authority had the responsibility of issuing and administering the HUD Section 8 certificates. The Housing Authority was in substantial disarray and quite capable of not using the certificates and returning them to HUD. The problems within the Housing Authority had become so great that in the mid-1980s its director was to be fired under an investigatory cloud and its board dissolved. The Housing Authority was not supportive of the Route 2 project and getting it to commit the certificates was no easy matter.

R2CHC was regarded as a maverick developer. The residents had pushed their way into the housing development field with the help of their political supporters and not gone through normal professional channels. The residents did not show the bureaucracy the deference it expected from those courting assistance, and some of the bureaucrats resented having the project foisted upon them. Even without this history, a group like R2CHC would likely have had problems. In the 1970s and early 1980s Los Angeles city agencies rarely supported non-profit housing developers, much less non-profit developers of cooperative housing. Most of the subsidized housing in the city has been built by for-profit developers. With few exceptions, non-profit organizations such as churches had acted more as sponsors of a particular government-initiated project rather than as developers.[22]

When the Housing Authority refused to cooperate, the residents once again turned to their political support. This strategy, however, was not sufficient this time. A Housing Authority consultant, like others, had issued an opinion that the Route 2 project was unfeasible and would never obtain financing. This analysis legitimized the Housing Authority's refusal to make a commitment of the Section 8 subsidies to the project. The problem was that the logic was circuitous. Given the low income of the residents, without a commitment of the Section 8 certificates financing was impossible. Finally, under political pressure and in the belief that financing would not be obtained, the Housing Authority wrote a letter stating that it would contribute the certificates if financing were obtained by a certain date. With this conditional commitment of Section 8 certificates, R2CHC obtained the SAMCO loan within the time constraint and the project moved on.

In 1981 the options to the property for the first two cooperatives, Dayton Heights and Silverlake, were obtained by R2CHC and assigned to the cooperatives in question, and the property was immediately purchased.[23] The purchase of the first cluster of property was an occasion for joy, but the joy was short lived. In the Silverlake coop a group of tenants protested the purchase of their homes. They wanted to purchase the property where they lived as the single-family residents had, even if purchase made them the landlords of their neighbors who could not afford to buy the property. As has happened elsewhere at such moments in the life of other projects, this group launched a drive against the formation of the cooperatives.[24] The revolt was soon ended at yet another mass meeting, but it sapped energy from the project. The event is discussed in detail in later chapters.

The project proceeded with the development corporation carrying out the rehabilitation of the property under contract with each of the cooperatives. Some rehabilitation was necessary to correct problems Caltrans failed to solve; other work was necessary to combine units to make large apartments to house overcrowded families. The repairs necessitated by Caltrans' neglect and the necessary large-scale consolidations were very expensive.[25] There was not enough money provided by the moderate rehabilitation Section 8 program and the city to accomplish these tasks adequately, but R2CHC kept going.[26]

If the necessary work was major, the tenants had to be temporarily or permanently relocated. Each coop formed a relocation committee to handle the problem. A corridor-wide relocation committee was formed that was modeled after the federation of the coops in the development corporation to deal with inter-coop moves. The corridor-wide relocation committee later became the corridor-wide membership committee to deal with membership policy. It was later to play an unintended but significant role in a reorganization of coop activity.

Once SAMCO agreed to fund the first cooperatives other lenders agreed to participate. In 1982 and 1983 the remaining options were obtained and assigned, and the property was purchased for the Four Streets, Marathon, and Alexandria cooperatives.[27] During this period the development corporation rehabilitated 200 units spread over nearly the length of the corridor. Problem after problem began to emerge. The contractor selected for two of the cooperatives was in so much trouble that he had to be let go in the middle of the job. This created more problems, but with many people losing sleep over the problems, the property was rehabilitated, at least to the satisfaction of the inspectors from the lenders, the Housing Authority, and the city's Building and Safety Department. Unfortunately in the chaos of this period many physical deficiencies in the property went uncorrected. They were to come back to haunt the project later.

The chaos associated with the rehabilitation inhibited community building in the cooperatives. Many people were moving, were often inconvenienced by construction delays, and, in some cases unhappy with the results. The leadership wanted to use self-help in the rehabilitation process, but no developed self-help program exists in Los Angeles. Both government and the financial institutions vetoed this approach. In other U.S. and Canadian coop projects, self-help has been a major community-building activity.[28] The work provided by the residents helps bond them to the coop. Given this potential benefit and the trouble the project had with contractors, it is too bad the residents could not give it a try.

As the coops emerged from the development phase in the mid-1980s and stability returned, community building became increasingly important. Of particular concern was the absence of the immigrant Latinos in the leadership of the project. A reorganization of the R2CHC staff emphasized the organizing of the Latino population and resulted in the eventual firing of one of the organizers who was not having significant success in this effort. This decision, in turn, led to a heightening of the involvement issue and yet another mass meeting.

The meeting held to discuss the firing and its aftermath are the subject of a later chapter. The meeting was very uncomfortable, but it led to increased Latino participation. Unfortunately, the time lost in solving the problem left the most heavily Latino coops in trouble. Among them was Imogen, which was planned as a sixth coop. To this day it remains a rental project owned by the development corporation.

Stage Three: Operating the Cooperatives

With the completion of the rehabilitation, the federation of the cooperatives turned its attention to managing the cooperatives. The forces that had blocked the use of self-help during the rehabilitation of the property had also insisted on private, professional management. Just as the rehabilitation had not worked out as hoped, there were problems in management. The federation decided to organize a company and take responsibility for management just as R2CHC had for development. Grants and loans were obtained and staff hired for the project's newest organization, the Nuestra Management Company.

At the same time, the cooperatives began to admit new members in vacant units left over after the completion of the relocation process. Among those admitted was a group of bilingual, bicultural Latinos with activist, organizing backgrounds. Most of these people, almost instantly, began to play a leadership role in the cooperatives, coop federation, Nuestra, and the corridor-wide membership committee.

Several of the original populist leadership stepped aside in this period, making more room for new leadership in the cooperatives. Some of the early leadership had liked learning about development and were interested in working on further development projects. They stayed on the board of R2CHC. With the federation's blessing, they reorganized the R2CHC board back to its original form of a self-appointed board that now included elements of the original leadership and many of the outside supporters of the project. The board of Nuestra was then structured like the former board of the R2CHC with representatives of the cooperatives and became the home of the federation. This reorganization had the unintended effect of removing from the leadership of the cooperatives most of the people who had developed the political sophistication and political contacts that had served the project at critical points in its history.

The change in leadership was dramatic. The new leadership of the cooperatives had not experienced the period of struggle in the formation of the cooperatives and had not shared in the organizational populist culture developed in that period. They came out of 1960s and 1970s ethnic movements and had a confrontational, interest-group approach. One of their first acts in the coops was to form a "Latino caucus" to look after the interests of Latinos.

As happens so often in social change movements, the new leaders tended to take what had happened before for granted. They had their own heartfelt agendas for the project. They saw the cooperatives as having potential other than housing cooperatives and began to talk of moving into other socially supportive ventures in food, youth activities, child care, and health. Towards the end of the development phase of the project a grant had been obtained for youth organizing. Some of the coops had gang members among their residents, and the leaders wanted to confront the problems this presence created. Two youth organizers were hired with the grant, which was then taken as a model of what should follow. The two youth organizers became, de facto, staff to the people interested in socially supportive work.

The new leadership with the support of its youth staff and the staff of Nuestra expressed their interest-group approach a few months later by restructuring the projects' organizations. They did not like the ambiguity of the federation model of cooperative management and reformulated the board of Nuestra into a self-appointed board to distance it from the cooperatives. In actuality Nuestra's board was made up primarily of the old leadership that had not withdrawn. With this move the federation was said to have been removed from Nuestra. The formation of a new organization, the Route 2 Foundation for Human Concerns (R2FHC), was announced that was to act upon the social agenda of the new leadership. The committee working on creating the new organization was made up primarily of the new leadership. They claimed that the federation now resided in their new organization, but it was not clear what they meant.

Great confusion and disarray accompanied these changes and factions began to form. For example, the corridor-wide membership committee became a faction when they declared themselves independent from Nuestra, if not the coops. They put their energy into the formation of R2FHC, but did not merge into that organization. They were, in effect, a faction in a faction. Some members of the new factions also turned on R2CHC when the president of R2CHC, still a channel for funding the new project in the transition, refused to sign a check for a youth trip. She would not sign the check because there was no insurance to cover the outing and no budget for expenditure of the youth money. In anger elements of the new leadership claimed R2CHC had been stolen by the old leadership from the masses. In this same period, after years of working together in both R2TA and R2CHC, one of the coops under the new leadership objected to having its affairs discussed openly at Nuestra meetings. The problem they didn't want discussed was their inability to pay its Nuestra management fees.

The growing internal problems could not have come at a worse time. Shortly after hiring a new director, the Housing Authority was judged "troubled" and fined over $1,000,000 by HUD for failing to properly inspect the property under its jurisdiction. Under pressure to comply with HUD regulations, the Housing Authority inspectors descended on the coops (and other subsidized units throughout the city) inspecting all 200 units nearly simultaneously and demanding repairs within five days in units they had passed a year or two earlier. If a unit failed the reinspection in five days, it would be placed on "abatement" which meant that the Section 8 payment stopped until the unit passed a later inspection. This was not the HUD rule, but the reality.

No further reinspection was scheduled until requested by the owner. The Housing Authority, however, lacked the administrative capacity to handle the reinspection requests. With all the subsidized landlords in the city in the same boat, the phone lines were constantly jammed. If a landlord personally came to the Housing Authority office to ask for a reinspection, he or she faced a long and not always successful period in the waiting room of the Housing Authority. The mail didn't seem to be an effective channel of communication either. The system simply broke down.

Although many lengthy meetings were held, the Foundation for Human Concerns never got off the ground. Less than a year after its inception the organization dissolved amidst quarrels among various factions including a split between the two organizers. The political skills of the interest-group pluralists that might have been directed at the Housing Authority's impasse never found that target. Instead they were absorbed by the infighting. The effort of organizing the foundation sapped the limited energy in the coops. The conflict also contributed to the exhaustion of those running Nuestra.

The distancing of Nuestra from the cooperatives left each of the cooperatives free to express their individual self-interest rather than to search for collective solutions. With many units going on abatement and the income of the coops dropping, two coops began to threaten to withdraw their business from Nuestra. Concern was growing. The pressure from the leadership conflicts and Housing Authority actions resulted in a complete turnover in the Nuestra staff. With many of the potential leaders distracted and quarrelling, the board of Nuestra tried to regroup.

The problem of the Housing Authority withholding large sums of money from the coops for failure to repair units within the required time was exacerbated when the Housing Authority failed to do its Section 8 paper work with HUD properly. HUD refused to pay the Housing Authority under its overall Section 8 contract. The money stopped whether the units were repaired or not. At this point, some of the original leadership returned. They encouraged the group to go back to the political allies of the project for help. A call to the council offices resulted in a meeting between the council offices, the coop leadership, and the new director of the Housing Authority. The director brought checks of multiple thousands of dollars for the cooperatives to the meeting. The log jam was broken, and the money again began to flow. Nuestra, however, was mortally damaged. One of the coops left for an outside management company. The Nuestra board considered another reorganization or dissolution. They chose the latter, and all the coops joined the first at the new management company.

This period also saw the departure of much of what I have called the interest-group leadership from the Route 2 cooperatives. After the discovery that the board members in the troubled coop that had espoused the right of secrecy had allowed each other great leeway in not paying rent, the membership of that coop forced an election, replaced the board and evicted the people who had exploited the situation. In another coop, once strong and now troubled, as is discussed in later chapters, members started disrupting meetings demanding the departure from the board of the new leadership, and later evicted several of this group, again, for non-payment of rent.

With the subsidy money returning to the cooperatives, their economic situation began to improve. New leadership filled the voids left by the evictions of the interest-group leadership and stabilized their cooperatives. Three of the cooperatives that had been distracted by all the confusion finalized the process of cooperative formation by selling shares.[29] In several of the cooperatives immigrant Latino leadership began to emerge. The Latino leadership brought with it yet a third style of leadership to the project. They were neither new populists like the original leadership nor interest-group pluralists like the leadership that followed. Their approach was clientelist. They in turn have generated yet a new set of issues for the cooperatives to resolve.

The story is not one with an ending. It is likely that future events will be as interesting as past, but the phases of the project examined in this book will end here.

Conclusion

The Route 2 corridor residents won their initial fights against displacement with the help of unusual political support and excellent technical assistance. Caltrans was a formidable foe and local real estate interests complicated the problem. Even with political support it took skill for the residents to survive the threat to their homes. It also took a great deal of luck, a fact that is hard to study and little written about.

Once they gained control of the property, the residents faced a whole series of obstacles to develop the cooperatives. The bureaucracy was not supportive; the private sector thought the residents' ideas laughable. Clarity, persistence, and support helped overcome these obstacles. Then obstacles in the form of the technical difficulties of carrying out the project's goals replaced the old obstacles. Without a history of other such projects in Los Angeles as a guide, every step involved experimentation with both positive and negative results.

Once technical obstacles were surmounted, internal ideological divisions and a loss of clarity created a new set of problems. The Housing Authority's difficulties exacerbated these problems. Instead of receiving external assistance at a crucial time, the project faced new potentially displacing forces. The attempt at self-management did not succeed, in part for technical-political reasons and in part because of the internal processes. Still the residents struggle continued the process of trying to stabilize their collective lives. In the following chapters this process will be examined in more detail.

Notes

1. See discussion of displacement fights in Hartman, Keating and LeGates (1982) for a review of the literature on displacement. For individual books on cooperatives see Helman (1986), the story of a project in Montreal, Canada similar to the Route 2 project; and McDonald (1986), a similar story with the exception that the displacees joined together to build their cooperative from Liverpool, England. For New York stories see Leavitt and Saegert (1990) and Kolodny (1973). For an equally heroic tale that involves saving neighborhoods although not against a direct act of replacement see St. Anthony (1987) and Fraser (1972). Also Dewey Bandy who is currently on the staff at the Cooperative Center at U.C.

Davis is working on a book with additional California stories of resistance to displacement being transformed into housing cooperatives including three farmworker cooperatives in the central valley of California.

2.   The Latino immigrant population consists of people from Mexico, Cuba, Guatemala, El Salvador, Puerto Rico, Ecuador, Nicaragua, Peru, Costa Rica, Columbia, the Dominican Republic, Chile, Panama, and Argentina. I have used the term Black rather than African American because that is the term used in the Route 2 project. For a discussion of race vs. ethnicity as a category see pp. 96-97.

3.   Some of the men are not permanent members of the household and, therefore, are not likely to be involved in the cooperative. Single women and married women who no longer have a husband, usually through divorce, often have male friends that slowly become part of the household and sometimes participate.

4.   This was an unpublished letter in response to the Senator's question. The letter was dated April 26, 1978.

5.   This was a period of freeway versus housing fights in the state. The Route 2 issue was very similar to an inner agency question that was resolved in HCD's favor in Oakland that also resulted in a limited-equity cooperative, Oak Center Homes. In that case Legal Services stopped the building of the Grove-Shafter freeway until replacement housing was provided. The agreement to develop the cooperative was part of the settlement of the litigation. In the Route 2 case the HCD staff having won this first turf fight was able to threaten a rerun of Oakland.

6.   The consultant was paid $5,000.

7.   The vast majority of the appraisals exceeded $25,000 which was a price higher than a majority of the tenants could afford to pay.

8.   The consultant's report shows that the units will each require more than $5,000 in rehabilitation work (*Northwest Leader* July 21, 1977).

9.   S.B. 86 adds Article 8.5 (commencing with Section 54235) to Chapter 5 of Part 1 of Division 2 of Title 5 of the Government Code, and amends Section 118 of the Streets and Highway Code, relating to surplus property.

10.   This date was prevalent among activists in New York during the late 1970s. The position of the traditional left activists in the Route 2 project was expressed in a pamphlet entitled *Housing Abandonment in New York City* put out in 1977 by an activist group in New York entitled Homefront. The more radical populist response was articulated by Steven Barton in a piece published in the *Review of Radical Political Economy* (1977). The debate was also articulated by Tony Schuman, stating the Homefront position in a letter to the *Planners Network* that appeared in issue #16 (October, 1978, p. 3), and a response by Barton in #17 (January, 1979, p. 7), and a reply by Schuman in #18 (March, 1979, p.4).

11.   The legislation offered alternatives if the cooperatives were not feasible. The property was to be maintained as affordable rental housing for the residents. If this was not feasible, the property was to be sold on the open market as affordable housing. Finally, if no other course proved feasible, it was simply to be sold.

12. The California Environmental Quality Act (Pub. Res. C. Sections 21000 et. seq.) requires that environmental impact reports be prepared on projects with significant environmental impact. If the project will not result in a significant impact, a negative declaration may be prepared instead. For a discussion of negative declarations see 50 Cal.Jur.3d 354-355.

13. The articles were filed in June, 1979.

14. This is what the organizer reported.

15. As a result of the tenants' action in the Route 2 corridor, Caltrans adopted this policy for all their property statewide.

16. The residents of the Route 2 Project received assistance under the moderate rehabilitation portion of the Section 8 program. This program is normally thought of as a rent supplement program. It is also available to support the carrying charges in a cooperative. Under the moderate income Section 8 program the federal government (HUD) pays the difference between 30 percent of the residents' adjusted gross income and the fair market rent as determined by HUD to the cooperative to help support the rehabilitation of the project and its operating costs. For a discussion of the history of this program see Hays (1985, pp.146-153).

17. The characterization of obstreperous was a favorite term of one of the Caltrans managers sent to deal with the problem. I had the good fortune of earning this title at one meeting in which I challenged the administrator's interpretation of California law.

18. Portions of the Route 2 corridor are in an area which contains slow-growth activists who are part of a group known as the Hillside Federation, a federation of homeowner groups. For a discussion of this group's actions in the Route 2 area see Heskin and Garrett (1987).

19. When the Route 2 project was completed, R2CHC owned a lot that it had intended to convert into a community center in the largest cooperative. Funds could not be identified to develop the center, and R2CHC entered into a joint venture with other non-profits to develop 18 units of affordable housing on the lot supported with redevelopment funds.

20. The funding for R2CHC was never made a part of the normal funding cycle of Community Development Block Grant recipients in the city. Each year the Community Development Department would find unspent funds from previous years to provide minimal support for the R2CHC staff and overhead. Once the rehabilitation started the expansion of the R2CHC was funded out of the rehabilitation loans that now rest on the cooperative's property.

21. The loan from SAMCO for Dayton Heights (31 units) was for $553,000 at 10.9 percent interest. R2CHC also obtained an interim construction loan from Security Pacific Bank in the same amount and CDD provided a $57,000 no interest loan to assist in the rehabilitation.

22. The most notable exception to this general rule is the Watts Labor Community Action Committee (WLCAC). WLCAC has been a very active non-profit housing developer in the South-Central part of Los Angeles since the late 1960s.

23. The Silverlake cooperative (43 units) received both its interim and permanent loan from Security Pacific Bank in the amount of $779,000 at 14.5 percent interest. CDD added $43,000 in the form of a no interest construction loan.

24. See Helman (1986, p. 126).

25. In the end there were fewer housing units but many more bedrooms in the project.

26. In the Route 2 project less than $10,000 per unit was spent on rehabilitation. In contrast, in the beautiful Milton-Park cooperative project in Canada which is roughly the Canadian equivalent of the Route 2 project $50,000 per unit was spent on rehabilitation (Helman 1969, p. 172).

27. Four Streets (97 units) received an interim loan from Crocker Bank and its permanent loan from SAMCO in the amount of $2,240,000 at 13 percent interest. It also received a $519,000 no interest loan from CDD. Marathon (66 units) received an interim loan from Crocker Bank and its permanent financing from Aetna Life and Casualty in the amount of $1,635,535 at 13 percent interest. CDD added a $266,000 no interest construction loan. The same actors also financed the Alexandria (38 units) cooperative in the amount of $939,500 at 13 percent interest with CDD adding $207,000.

28. I visited the Milton-Park project in Montreal (Helman 1986) and discussed the self-help component of the project. The organizers told me that the self-help rehabilitation portion of their program was the basis of the cooperative organizing. It was hard for them to imagine forming a cooperative without it. In their opinion it bound the residents to the property and converted them from tenants to owners. Self-help has also been the common practice in the New York cooperatives. See Urban Homesteading Assistance Board (1986) and Kolodny (1973) for reports of the New York experience.

29. There was no rush in the cooperative to sell the shares. One had sold its shares earlier. One has yet to sell its shares. Approximately 80 percent of the residents bought shares when they were offered. Over time the cooperatives are approaching 100 percent shareholders. As renters move out they are replaced with shareholders.

2

Community

There is no doubt that community is an important word to the people who live in the Route 2 project. It is also clear that the residents do not agree about what the word means. The new populists see community as expressed in the specific social relations among residents of the project. The pluralists and clientelists see community as an expression of interests and identity not necessarily bounded by the project. The populists and pluralists have a partial, functional vision of community while the clientelists have a more totalized view. The meaning of community that has controlled the discourse in the project has changed with the changes in the ideological position of the project's leadership. This chapter discusses the various ideological views of the leadership on the subject and then traces the debate over the meaning of community through the story of the collective experiences of the residents of the Route 2 corridor.

The new populists did not see the Route 2 project as central to their lives. It was something they wanted and to which they gave many hours, but it was not to be the center of their lives in other than a temporal sense. The battle to establish the cooperatives took more time and energy than they likely would have given had they known what they were getting into, but having begun the fight, they were not about to lose, particularly to Caltrans which continually angered them with what they saw as one insult after another.

The populists certainly were not looking to create cooperatives that would recreate or recapture the small town atmosphere against which liberals and new communitarians have rebelled (Yack 1988).[1] What they hoped for was the formation of functional communities. Their image was not, however, your usual image of a functional community. The populists are working-class men and women of many ethnicities, and they have experienced oppression on multiple levels. If they were going to do this project, they wanted to create coops that would be an oasis from this oppression. They wanted the cooperatives to be places of political contemplation and psychological safety where justice would be the common concern.[2] As described by authors such as Benjamin Barber and Scott Peck, they wanted to create communities not in ties of friendship but in the spirit of inclusive neighborliness where community members would be able to relax their preconceptions, ideologies, prejudices, and values sufficiently to hear, understand, and accept others whose outlook and values are different from their own (Barber 1985 & Peck 1986).

Within this community of neighbors, the progressive populist vision of democracy is to be practiced. Community-based democracy requires open debate along with a high level of cooperation and activity among the community members. The citizenry of the community is bound together more by common participatory activity toward a common goal than any underlying contract or formal membership (Barber 1985, p.219). Voluntary civility of empathy and respect among participating members ideally replace the citizenry's concerns for the accountability of its elected representatives.

Homogeneity is not required, or even desired, in the populist community. Rather heterogeneity is very close to an essential element of this community formation and renewal. It is only through difference, through an acknowledgement of the distance between people as in Buber's concept of I and thou, that the joining of community is possible (1970). It is, of course, only through the repression of conflict and the insistence on conformity that homogeneity can be approached. Heterogeneity on one or another dimension of humanity is common in groups if it is permitted.

The question of the role of heterogeneity versus homogeneity in community has been very important throughout the Route 2 project's history. The Route 2 corridor has had a very heterogenous population from its early beginnings. Together in the space called Route 2 lived a population ranging politically from anti-Castro, anti-communist Cubans to members of the radical New American Movement and ethnically from immigrants from fourteen Latin American countries to U.S. born Blacks, Asians, Chicanos, and ethnic Anglos.

The early populist leadership helped organize this heterogeneous group of residents into a self-interested collectivity to fight Caltrans, but they did not see themselves as working toward a community based solely on self-interest. They were not interested in establishing the kind of community envisioned by people who talk of the financial or business communities. Cooperatives, particularly the limited-equity cooperative with a blanket mortgage, create a common interest, but as the name indicates, limit the element of self-interest.[3] The new populists were very aware of the pressure this contractual form puts on its members to come together and the constraint on self-interest the form presents. They saw the contract and the common interests as bringing people together. Living in a common area, having a shared history, and establishing interdependent contractual relationships can start the conversation, but these by themselves, could not make the community they sought. Direct participatory democracy is the additional needed essential element.

The pluralists who excitedly moved into the cooperatives after they were developed also saw the cooperatives in political terms. To the pluralists, who were primarily Latinos but also included blacks, the cooperatives were part of a larger cause and a wonderful base from which to work. They were not an end in themselves. Housing was only one need of poor and oppressed people in this society and the members of the cooperative were only a segment of those with these needs. The population in the cooperatives had to be subsumed under this larger community of need.

Their political community was less the dialogic community of the populists than a place in which equal rights are practiced (Mansbridge 1983, pp.233-251). The pluralists wanted direct democracy, but in their case participation was more a requirement than an encouraged product of an open process. The interaction they sought was more formal. They saw even this small project as made up of factions and saw their faction as composed of those that were with them.[4] The overall community within the cooperative in the pluralists' view is a negotiated compromise of interests. As is discussed in the next chapter, the basis of the negotiations is power, relative power of the factions, and not the common concerns of the larger group (Dahl 1961 & Polsby 1963).[5]

Clientelists were present throughout the history of the project but not very vocal until after the development period ended. The clientelists were to a large extent but not entirely Latino immigrants. They sought a more traditional totalized community of family where blood ties, culture, or ideology is the prime element that holds people together and serves as a cause to exclude the outsider.[6] Their vision of community is more focused on survival than the other groups because the clientelist immigrant status puts them in a different strata of the working class than the other groups. The populists and pluralist mainly have skilled and unionized jobs in the primary work force. The clientelists tended to be in the secondary labor market.[7]

The clientelist community is one that insists on consensus formed through private talk and not on synthesis generated through public debate. It employs a unitary form of democracy that seeks homogeneity very much as Barber describes in his book, *Strong Democracy* (Barber 1984, p.219). The clientelists' community like that of the pluralists also have external links, but these links are to the obligations of immigration, to family in the economic immigrants' case and to political struggle in the political refugees' case.

Neither the pluralists' nor clientelists' communities are necessarily safe places. In the pluralist community the non-participants are either ignored or confronted as another faction. If they are in a weaker faction they may be run over. In the clientelist community a dissident may face exclusion. To the individual or family dependent on fellow immigrants, this poses a very serious threat.

Two other ideological groups that participated in the development of the project were not full partners in the community debate. The individualists, just as the name suggests, were not interested in the cooperatives and the community that might exist in them. They were not interested in joining with the other residents of the project beyond what was necessary to obtain individual ownership of their home. The traditional left activists had an exclusive style related to the pluralists and clientelists. They were interested in organizing a correct cadre of activists to confront the state. What kind of community would have followed had the residents taken this path is not clear. They like the pluralists and the political refugees in the project were fighting a bigger fight.

In the beginning of the Route 2 project the extraordinary diversity in the Route 2 corridor's population ensured debate on nearly every issue except the desire to avoid displacement. These debates have always been intense. In the formative years of the project static division was hardly possible except, perhaps, in the debate over the issue of single-family versus collective ownership. In this there were populist individuals among the initial organizing group who had the capacity to define the initial process and kept the debate open.

These individuals and the pluralist and clientelist leaders that followed them acted very much in the mode of working-class organic intellectuals as defined in the work of Antonio Gramsci. Organic intellectuals conceptualize and philosophically elaborate ideas (Adamson 1980, p. 145). They are masters at praxis, the bringing together of practice and theory, and they can, therefore, be leaders with a particular capacity to imagine alternative futures (Boggs 1984, p. 223). Organic intellectuals need not be members of the working-class *per se*, but they must align themselves with the working-class. When the intellectuals are not from the working-class it is said they contribute the knowledge and the working-class passion (p. 225). In this case the intellectuals were working-class and combined the two elements.

Organizing for Democracy

The first corridor-wide meeting of Route 2 residents in 1977 led to the formation of the first formal organization in the corridor, the Route 2 Tenants' Association (R2TA). The structure of the organization was hotly debated. The traditional left activists wanted a dues-paying membership organization to separate "who is with us from who is not" in the struggle with the state. The populists wanted an organization of all the residents of the corridor that was continually open to any residents who at a particular moment in a debate of an issue wanted to participate. As the populists pointed out, their approach had a pragmatic advantage over the left's idea. Aside from its vision of an open community, it also allowed R2TA to claim the entire population as members in negotiations with Caltrans rather than to limit those the organization represented to dues-paying members. With this in mind the individualists sided with the populists.

With the individualists' support the populists won the argument, and R2TA was born as a very open organization with a shifting active self-selected membership from the entire population dependent on who participated rather than who joined. If the shifting membership didn't adequately represent the whole population or some group within it, it would be up to that segment to become active in R2TA and express itself. The controlling group's responsibility was to be open to such a challenge even if it meant changing who controlled the organization. Many of the individualists, particularly the Cubans thought this was a crazy idea, but they came to appreciate the approach. One of the Cubans told me it was the most important lesson he learned during his participation in R2TA.

The option of becoming active was from time to time taken up by one or another dissident group. The incidents reveal what took place in the project and make up much of this book. The requirement of self-initiative, however, posed increasing structural problems as the project moved along. When the active group shifted from the politics of R2TA to the technical development phase of R2CHC, the group's dialogue became increasingly sophisticated. Newcomers had a hard time understanding what those who had been active all along were talking about, and it was hard for them to catch up. This problem was particularly severe for the monolingual Spanish-speaking population. The language problem is discussed in Chapter 5.

The organization initially functioned at two levels of decision making: the mass meeting and the executive committee meeting. The executive committee was elected at various mass meetings and expanded from time to time as the need arose. For example, the original members of the executive committee primarily lived in single-family residences. More multi-family residents were added to the committee when the issue of how to handle the multi-family property was going to be addressed. Whenever an issue seemed major enough to require mass involvement, the executive committee called a mass meeting. For example, a mass meeting was called to discuss the issue of whether the cooperative form should be used to buy the property. Mass meeting or not, all the meetings were open, and everyone who attended could participate. Participation usually included having a vote whether the participant was elected or not.

Initially the R2CHC board was made up of the people elected to the R2TA executive committee who wanted to be on the corporation's board. Later people joined the board as they came to meetings and expressed interest in serving on the R2CHC board rather than by election at mass meetings. During the period of negotiations with Caltrans, the executive committee of R2TA and the board of R2CHC both functioned. The populist resident leadership insisted upon full involvement in all negotiations. As matters progressed, even twice-a-week meetings were inadequate to ensure full participation.

Together the executive committee and the board added a third level of organization called the "war counsel" to fill the gaps in resident control. The war counsel was a mixture of residents, staff members of political supporters, and R2CHC and HCD staff who discussed the strategy for negotiations. It met on a few hours notice during the day to plan responses to unexpected eventualities. Everyone who volunteered to be on the war council was called for such emergency meetings. Those who attended reported on the counsel's actions at their next board or committee meeting.

After each coop was formed, individual coop boards were elected by everyone who resided in the coop who wanted to vote. When an issue was particularly significant, in the R2TA style, a mass meeting of the coop's residents was called. Once the coop boards were elected, the R2CHC bylaws were amended to make its board a federation of the elected coop boards. In addition, committees were formed in each coop and on a corridor-wide basis.

Each of these meetings was open. To ensure as much access as possible meetings occurred regularly at the R2CHC office rather than in people's homes. At the height of the organizing effort approximately seventy meetings per quarter were held in the Route 2 project office. Copies of the schedule were posted in the office for any resident who wanted to attend the next meeting. Interestingly, although cooperative membership legally depended on ownership of a share in the cooperative corporation, there was no rush to sell shares in the cooperative, to close membership. It was not until several years after the purchase of the property that the shares were, in fact, sold.

The populist chair of R2CHC personified the style of the organizations. Her approach was inclusive and open. She refused to differentiate between the development corporation, the cooperatives, and the residents. There was only "us." If someone angered about some part of the process of coop formation approached the board of R2CHC with a complaint, he or she would invariably start off with the statement "You . . ." At this point the chair would look over her shoulder and ask "Who are you talking to? I only see us here. We are all in this together." She would never let a statement of division go by.

A Test of the Open Democracy

The openness of the process and the insistence of democracy by the populists received a major test when the second cooperative was purchased. Some of the tenants in this coop had been talking with the Caltrans staff about the possibility of direct sale to them rather than the coop. They knew that the single-family residents could purchase their homes. These individualists wanted the same opportunity even though other residents in their parcels could not afford to participate, and they would in the process become their neighbors' landlord.[8] They had not initially organized against the coop's purchase of the property because they thought it would never happen. Unfortunately for them, they were wrong.

The leadership of the dissident individualists responded to the notice of the coop's purchase of the property by passing around a petition questioning the motives of the R2TA and R2CHC leadership. They alleged double dealings on the part of the leadership and demanded to see all the paper work involved in the project. In addition they alleged that the leadership was guilty of various racist practices. The boards appeared vulnerable to this charge at this time because there was little Latino participation in leadership positions after the departure of the Latino activists who lived in single-family residences. The petition called for a stop to all activity pending an investigation. Many people were concerned and confused and signed the petition. The leadership responded as in everything else by calling a mass meeting. Nearly a hundred people from the just purchased cooperative crowded into the R2CHC office for this extraordinary event.

In response to the allegations the leadership had multiple copies made of all the central papers of the project and brought them to the meeting for the residents. When people entered the room, it was edged with stacks of copies of documents. The leadership of the coop conducted the meeting. They began by calling on members of the R2CHC board and staff to present a description of the coop development process. They used graphics prepared for the meeting to illustrate each step in the process and held up the appropriate papers for each step so people would know what they were talking about. The presentation was followed by a raucous round of questions and answers. The information seemed to satisfy the people who attended, and the revolting group was isolated.

Consistent with the populists' pragmatic approach, the groups' openness to internal conflictual resolution of their differences was not matched by an interest in aiding opponents in expressing their opposition outside the project. The external world does not necessarily offer support for a populist community. As discussed in Chapter 4, it is a place of class struggle where working-class people must fight for what they get. Different rules apply in that arena.

The ground breaking for Imogen, the new construction project, took place shortly after the mass meeting to hear the dissidents' claims. Many public officials who supported the project attended. The energy in the revolt had already dissipated, but one of the leaders of the dissidents showed up at the ground breaking. Significantly, he was by himself.

He approached the president of R2CHC, who was master of ceremonies for the event, and demanded access to the microphone to read a statement of protest. The president told him that he would be placed at the end of the agenda for the event. He fumed and waited. Residents of the project talked to him, kept him busy, and screened him from the public officials. Aides to the public officials in attendance were informed of the problem and helped keep their bosses and the dissident separated. The planned program took a long time. By the time it was almost over most of the dignitaries had left. When it was finally over, the leadership walked away. Residents supporting the project pulled the plug on the microphone. The dissident found the microphone dead and left in disgust.

Good luck played a big role in the revolt's early failure. Even though the mass of people dismissed the revolt leadership they fought on for a while after the meeting by trying to attract media attention. They were only moderately successful. Just by chance a major media contact person who could have energized the group with media stardom was the roommate of a former HCD staff person who had worked on the Route 2 project. When the revolt leader called the contact, he was not in his office, and the leader was referred to his home phone. The former Route 2 staff person answered the phone when the call came in and that was the end of that.

Further, the usual sources of assistance for oppressed tenants all knew about the Route 2 project and were turned off by the "I want mine" attitude of the revolters. When the few remaining participants in the revolt began a rent strike, eviction actions were brought. One of the strikers found his way to a conservative activist lawyer who became interested in the tenant's story.[9] When the revolting tenant, however, refused to pay his rent into escrow with the attorney, a matter of conservative principle, the conservative activist attorney lost interest in the case, and the revolting tenant leader was evicted.

Limits to Inclusiveness

There was a limit to the populist belief in inclusiveness just as there was a limit to their promotion of open debate. The experience of another coop that faced a serious crisis soon after its formation reveals the limits to inclusiveness. In this case the board members of the coop discovered their president had embezzled some of the coop's reserve funds. In the formative period of the coop he had carried almost the entire load of running the coop's affairs and had served on the R2CHC board. He had befriended and helped many of the people in the coop and recruited many of the board members into active participation in the coops' affairs. They in turn felt considerable affection for him.

Like many of the working-class coop residents of the corridor, the coop president always lived on the edge of financial disaster. He held all sorts of jobs including cab driving and delivering flowers and had been trying for some time to get a college degree. He drank a lot and was often late and sometimes inebriated at the meetings he was to conduct, but he was exceptionally sharp when sober. People were not happy with his erratic behavior, but most looked the other way because of all the "good" time he put in. He would sometimes say that his Route 2 project work was like therapy for him. It gave him something constructive to do that kept him out of trouble.

Unfortunately, in the last few months of his presidency, he became drug dependent and his dependency got the best of him. Exploiting a bank error, he took cooperative funds to support his habit. When the problem was discovered, the other board members met, immediately removed him as president, and secured the remaining funds. The coop was insured for this eventuality, so the problem did not result in a substantial financial loss to the coop.

When the former president was confronted with the loss, he immediately confessed and stated his intention to make good the loss. The remaining board members did not believe that the he would be able to keep such a promise, but out of deference to their former leader they agreed to give him a chance. They told him he would have to act quickly because they would have to notify their insurance company to protect the coop, and they told him that they were considering prosecuting and/or evicting him. Interestingly, he said he would rather be prosecuted than be evicted and lose his home of many years.

What to do beyond removing the president then became the issue. Should they prosecute him and should he be evicted? After long deliberations the coop board members decided that they would move to evict him and not prosecute unless they had to for insurance purposes. The discussion in the board meetings included questions of what would be best for the coop and what would be best for their friend. They felt that a clear statement had to be made that this behavior would not be tolerated and that only the sharpest of actions might bring him around given his addiction. Coop members who had either first-hand experience as former substance abusers or as people who had substance abusers in their families believed that remaining in the coop as a guilty past president might promote the self-degrading image that can accompany addiction. This argument seemed important to at least one member of the board who was having a hard time voting for eviction. It at least blurred the lines between whether evicting the past president was hurting or helping a close friend.

The former president did not accept the decision of the board and demanded a hearing before the whole coop. Because of the seriousness of the situation, the board granted his request. A meeting was called both to elect his replacement on the board and hear his plea.

The meeting called to discuss the eviction was an extraordinary one, reminiscent of a mainland Chinese commune gathering in the revolutionary period described in the book *Fanschen*.[10] After the election, the past president addressed the assembled membership confessing his crime, stating that he had been sick, and asking for enough forgiveness for his mistake that he might be allowed to remain in the coop and make recompense any way he could. The coop members recognized his past service (some felt he had almost earned the amount of money he took with the time he had put in) and thought he had "guts" to get up in front of everyone and confess as he did. The discussion was going back and forth between forgiveness and eviction with the forgiveness position appearing to be winning, when one populist member, who was not on the board of the coop but was a leader in the federation, took the floor and made an impassioned plea for eviction. In the speech she demonstrated how an organic intellectual generates the hegemony for her position at moments of crisis where a community group is uncertain.

The member began by describing the coop venture they had all set upon and reminding the audience that they all knew it would not be easy to work together. Her position was that the only chance of making it was if they could truly trust each other. She said that she was poor and had access to the development corporation's checking account in the past. She had often looked over at the corporation's checkbook when she didn't know where the next dollar was going to come from to feed her children, but she knew if she stumbled and "borrowed" some money that the whole effort could fail. She said it was not the money the past president took that bothered her, it was the breach of trust. Her argument swung those assembled toward eviction, and the decision was made and carried out by the board.

No one felt good about participating in this decision. It was not comfortable to wield the heavy hand of justice, but the consensus was that it had to be done. Stuart Henry writing about decision-making in cooperatives in England discusses the difficulty of taking disciplinary action with the "network of intimacy" formed in cooperatives (Henry 1983, pp. 181-197). He quotes one coop member as saying disagreement seldom occurs "because we know, trust and respect one another's perhaps differing feeling about situation, we take each other into consideration, and make as much effort as possible to accommodate one another in most situations" (p. 183). Those in positions of responsibility in the Route 2 project experienced similar considerations. The past president had gone too far. He broke the chain binding the people together, and they decided to expel him from the group.

This case demonstrates the political process required in the direct democracy of community. The decision-making process involved a public discourse raising legal concerns, personal compassion, community values, and collective history. Participation admitted all these differing concerns into the decision-making process and then sifted them out through public dialogue.

Decision making among the Route 2 cooperatives in this period was characterized by what Barber calls "public talk." Public talk is much more than the shrill advocacy of private interests. Public talk "entails listening no less than speaking." It is "affective as well as cognitive," and "its intentionalism draws it out of the domain of pure reflection into the world of action" (Barber 1985, p. 174). It is a form of conversation that permits a community to discover its mutuality, clarify its values, develop affinity, and take action. Public talk provides the vehicle through which individual interests, concerns, and conflicts can be located and acted upon within a public context.

Public talk both derives its vitality from community and also contributes to building it. As the embezzlement case indicates, public talk is not conversation among strangers. It occurs between members of a community who personally know one another, who have worked and struggled together. Common experience allows the admission of the affective, common experience, history, and personal character into the dialogue. It is precisely at moments of intense communal tension and crisis that public talk can be the means through which community can be reaffirmed.

Finally, this incident reveals the necessity of safety required in the formation of community. The residents used the term trust, but it is very much the same idea as having a safe, open environment where leadership can be challenged as it was by the troubled past president. It is ironic, however, that here exclusion was required to maintain inclusiveness. Peck discusses how difficult it is to maintain community (1987). He gives a somewhat similar example of exclusion in his book. A failing of the collective in his example leaves a hole in the totality and creates the type of sadness felt at the eviction of the past president.

The Breadth of Inclusiveness

Although openness to member participation suggests an organization's inclusive democracy, its presence is not sufficient to judge the organization. The organization's membership selection must also be examined. The Route 2 neighborhoods are among the few heterogeneous neighborhoods in the heavily segregated city of Los Angeles (Research Group on the Los Angeles Economy 1989). The cooperatives fit right into the heterogeneity of the area. Part of this arises from residents' choice of a place to live and part from the *laissez faire* rental policies of Caltrans.[11]

The heterogeneity of the Route 2 corridor population inhibited discrimination in the coops in any way that the term is normally employed. In addition, the leadership of R2TA and R2CHC was assertively anti-discriminative. The early leadership repeatedly made statements about the non-discriminatory nature of the project, and the residents who took on leadership of the coops in the formative years repeated these statements almost like a pledge of allegiance. Inclusiveness in a housing cooperative is, of course, a limited concept. There are only so many housing units available at any one time. Choices have to be made between applicants when a unit becomes available.

Each coop's membership committee usually interviews between three and five applicants from a long waiting list for a vacancy.[12] Membership on the committee is open to any member in the cooperative who wants to serve. Typically the neighbors living next to the units are invited to participate in interviews. Great deference is often given to the preferences of the neighbors that choose to attend.

Questions of financial eligibility are settled before these interviews.[13] The primary criteria used by membership committees is the applicant's skill level, how the applicant might contribute to the operation of the cooperative, and the applicant's level of need. Over time various committees members have valued one of these criteria more than others.

The cooperatives' ethnic mix is usually represented on the membership committees as it was in the example that follows. This committee was made up of an apolitical Anglo, who is married to a Chicana, an apolitical Chicano who is married to a Filipino, a Latina who is the daughter of a Mexican and Cuban marriage, and two Central Americans, one an economic immigrant and the other a political refugee.[14] The committee interviewed three applicants at its meeting for a three-bedroom Section 8 unit in one of the rougher parts of this particular coop. Two applicants were very shy Mexican immigrant families. The third family was from Nicaragua. The husband of this family claimed to have been a former officer in Somoza's army.

The couple from Central America stood out in the interviews. They were aggressive in inquiring about the coop and the obligations of the residents. They had been sharing a single-room apartment with two other families since coming north and were anxious to find a place of their own. If the coop accepted them, they intended to take their obligations seriously and contribute their skills to the group. The two shy Mexican families did not actively engage the committee.

When the interviews were over, the committee began to discuss the families interviewed. The Anglo and Chicano were attracted by the Central American applicants' aggressiveness and the family's potential for contributing to the coop. The more political Central American on the committee responded with horror at the thought of what she saw as Somozistas moving into the coop. In Spanish she tried to express her anguish with the other Central American, who is almost fully bilingual, translating.

The two favoring members responded with two arguments. First, they could not hold what people did before they came to this country against them or they would have lots of trouble with a great many of the present residents of the Route 2 project. With Latinos from so many countries living in the Route 2 cooperatives all sides of the political disputes in Latin America were represented in the corridor. Second, following a liberal, civil libertarian line, they argued that one cannot hold a family's politics against it in such matters. The dissenting member responded that this was not a matter of politics. This man and woman were part of a murderous army; it was not simply a matter of a Republican as opposed to a Democrat.

The discussion raged on for quite a while, but the dissenting member never said anything directly against the particular applicants before the committee. Her attack centered rather on who they represented and the background from which they came. She said, for example, that people from Somoza's army would never participate in or support the coop no matter what they said in the interview. The apolitical Americanos were troubled by her systemic approach and her failure to consider the personal qualifications of the applicants. They knew what the dissenting member was referring to when she said that the applicants would not support the coop. One of the other coops had problems with a Central American resident who claimed to be the brother of a recently assassinated general in his country, and another with a *Cuban who organized against the whole Route 2 project stating that limited-equity cooperatives were communistic. They felt, however, that the applicants before them were very different. They saw that the former captain was aggressive and tough, but they felt the particular area he was moving into needed aggressive, tough people to deal with its problems.

The two remaining members of the committee were less involved in the discussion. The Latina liked the family and didn't comment on the political questions. The other Central American sided with the dissenting member but only mildly. When the vote came, the two Central Americans each voted for one of the Mexican applicants. The other three members of the committee voted to admit the Central American family. The dissenting member was very upset, but the other Central American who was also a member of the board of directors of the coop said she would support the committee's position when the matter came before the board.

The dissenting member of the committee was not satisfied, and a few days later she indicated that she wanted further discussion of the matter. The president of the coop felt the first process was fair but agreed to hear the member out at the next board meeting. She did not, however, show up at the appointed time, and the board went on to approve the admission of the family.

The now very unhappy member stayed away from the meetings for a week or two but returned to serve on the membership committee which the newly admitted members subsequently joined. Later, the women in the two families were both elected to the board of the coop by the membership where they served together amicably. The political member explained that their amicability was based on her discovery that the new member was apolitical and not consciously part of Somozas' policies.

A Threat to Inclusiveness

Interestingly, the threat to inclusiveness in the cooperatives has not come from discrimination of any sort as it's normally conceived.[15] It has emerged rather from the pluralists' sense of struggle for power between factions and the clientelists' more unitary concept of community. During the pluralist days in the project control over the admissions process became an important issue in a larger dispute between factions in the cooperative. The issue in the context of pluralism is presented in what follows. In the unitary form of democracy admission to and continued participation in the community is based on blood or brotherhood.[16] The discussion of the clientelist challenge to the open democracy of the project follows the pluralist discussion and continues in later chapters.

As described in Chapter 1, after the development of the coops was completed, a group of interest-group pluralists moved into the coops and soon took positions of leadership. They were people who saw the world as a place of conflict, a conflict which they and like-minded people had not won.[17] They were people of moderate means who had many scars from fighting an oppressive and racist society.

The first institutionalization of the pluralist conception in the project was the formation of the "Latino caucus." Organized by some of the new residents of the cooperative, it included the new leadership and like-minded people in the pre-existing immigrant Latino resident population. There was particular concern over the low level of Latino participation in the leadership and over the recent failure of Imogen to convert to a cooperative. The caucus set about investigating past grievances (in the process attracting some of the dissidents that had revolted after the purchase of the first cooperative) and ensuring Latinos' rights were protected in the project in the future.

The nature of this group's approach was demonstrated by their response to an immigrant Latino member of one of the coops who appealed for help with a "problem" she faced. She wanted to be on the board of her coop to represent as she put it, "her people" in a cooperative whose membership was two-thirds Latino. She was convinced that she would be discriminated against in the election because she was Latino. In fact, she was not very popular with her neighbors, some of whom were Americano leaders of the coop who thought of her as standoffish.[18] The Latino caucus, convinced of the need to fear a power play by the hostile Americano leadership, decided to try a power play of their own to ensure the caucus member's election.

Everyone in the coop received written notice of the mass meeting several weeks before the election was to take place. Then with the help of a sympathetic organizer who was also a member of the caucus, caucus members visited Latino members of the coop thought to be supportive and asked them to come to the election meeting to prevent the exclusion of the Latina from membership on the board. They did not visit the other members of the coop or give any further reminder of the meeting.

The election meeting was unusually tense. The Latinos recruited to the meeting were ready for a fight. Attendance at the meeting was light, and the battlers made up the vast majority of those present. A spat broke out when a Chicana member, not in the fighting group, seated in front of the translator complained about having the translator talk too loudly into her ear. Charges of racism were yelled out. The translator moved and the meeting continued.

When the election started, the Americanos did try and raise a technical objection to the candidacy of the Latina in question, but this was quickly dismissed before it became an issue. The candidate's husband worked for R2CHC, and R2CHC had a rule that no one who was paid by R2CHC could be on its board. One of the R2CHC board members in attendance quickly dismissed the objection because the election was a coop election, not an R2CHC election. The question of whether she could sit on the R2CHC board as representative of the cooperative would have to be settled later. Besides the candidate was not the employee; her husband was the employee. The election was then held, and the Latina fearing discrimination was elected. The Americanos were certainly unhappy when they figured out what had happened, and they successfully encouraged the Latino organizer who participated in the visits to take an early retirement from employment in the project.

As is discussed in Chapter 5, there were many structural problems in involving the Spanish-speaking population in the leadership of the project, but to the extent I could tell there was no intention of exclusion. Taking an active role in the coops meant taking on a great deal of responsibility without any significant remuneration. The rule that an individual couldn't get paid and be on the board sometimes meant giving up a chance at remuneration. Responsibility was something active residents were anxious to share. The conversations I overheard among the Americanos expressed more anger at having to carry the work load than a desire to exclude anyone interested in serving.

In the period of this power play there was a substantial turnover in the leadership of the project. Many of the Americano leaders stepped aside. They had been holding on through the development period, and now that their "job" was done, they decided to refocus their lives on other activity. They were replaced primarily with the new activists that had moved into the project. The long-time Latino membership still, however, was not significantly represented in the leadership. The new leadership moved quickly through the individual coops' membership committees to the corridor-wide membership committee and through the coop boards to the board of Nuestra.

The federation model of the corridor-wide committees and Nuestra seemed to particularly bother the new leadership. The corridor-wide membership committee asserted its independence from the Nuestra board and stated it would only report to the individual coops. The Nuestra board was, however, made up of the elected leadership of each coop. The new people on the Nuestra board took the position that the cooperative federation model created two basic "conflicts of interest." One, found in all cooperatives, involved, the conflict between acting as the service provider and the client. The other involved the conflict in being in the federation with other cooperatives that may have different needs and interests.

The problem was put in pluralist self-interested terms, the opposite of the "us" approach of the original leadership. The spokesperson for the new leadership told me that he could not represent the interests of the federation, Nuestra, and the individual cooperatives. Where the leaders of R2TA and R2CHC worked to discourage any distinctions between us and them, the new leadership insisted upon it. To them the distinctions were a reality that could not be denied. The project had succeeded thus far without acknowledging this "reality," but it would go no further.

A Revolt for Respect

Jane Mansbridge in her book *Beyond Adversary Democracy* (Mansbridge 1980, pp. 233-251) sets out two competing concepts of equality in democracy, one focuses on equal respect and the other on equal rights. The populists relied more on equal respect to conduct their business while the pluralists were more concerned with equal rights. Meetings which had been conducted with an informal tone of inquiry and debate became much more formal. For the first time attention began to be seriously paid to such things as Robert's Rules of Order. Points of order began to fill the meetings. Mansbridge's findings are that the equal rights approach is often selected when a sense of equal respect is lacking. It is a response to conflict. In this case the equal rights approach was imported into the project by people who had experienced years of disrespect. From my perspective its introduction into the project was a response to conditions in the society, not within the cooperatives. Conflict followed its introduction rather than the other way around.

The nature of the conflict engendered is illustrated by a power struggle that took place in one of the cooperatives between the "new" residents of the cooperatives and the "old" residents who had been

Caltrans tenants. In one cooperative the transformation in leadership from populist to pluralist happened particularly quickly when an illness caused the established populist president of the cooperative to retire in mid-term. At a board meeting rather than a mass meeting the board members selected one of the new pluralists to take the ill leader's place. This individual who was a fully bilingual and bicultural Latino had been an organizer of low-income Latinos and was seen as more knowledgeable about the ways of the U.S. than many of the immigrant Latinos. He functioned as the primary organic intellectual representing the pluralist point of view.

The populist leader was an Americano woman who had worked through long-time Latino women neighbors to maintain contact with the Latino members of the cooperative. As a general proposition the immigrant population went along with the activities leading to the formation of the cooperative but were not formally active in the cooperative leadership, certainly not in proportion to their numbers. It is hard to say in retrospect whether this nonparticipation arose from trust resulting from a unity of purpose and equal respect as Mansbridge describes or from alienation and passivity (1980).

The new pluralist leader assumed that the lack of Latino participation was the result of a lack of proper organizing by the old leadership and set out to correct what he saw as under-representation of Latinos in the active membership. In addition to utilizing the available organizing staff, he personally tried to activate the Latino membership. He spent hours talking with and encouraging participation by his neighbors. His primary measure of activism was attendance at board meetings.

The populist leaders argued with some of the project organizers about the importance they placed on attendance in earlier years and stressed that people were different, had different talents, and that there were many ways for people to participate. Some residents liked meetings, others did not. The populists felt that residents had to be allowed to participate in their own way and urged the organizers to find many ways for each person to contribute.[19] Even if meeting attendance and vocal participation in the public talk that took place at meetings was an ultimate goal, organizers, they argued, could not always expect participation to begin with attendance at meetings.[20]

The pluralist leader held a different view. He wanted as many people as possible to come to meetings, to be involved, to participate in the formal process of the coop. He made it a practice to go around the cooperative before a meeting and personally invite the people he met to the next meeting. On repeated occasions the residents would promise to attend, sometimes within hours of the meeting, but they would not show up.

After many months of unsuccessful efforts to encourage the immigrant population to attend meetings, the new leader became discouraged, even angry, and shifted gears. He had seen the resident Latino population as the mass to be organized. Now he saw them as a group to work around. Moreover, if the old membership was not with "us" (his group that was running the coop), then they must be against us.[21] He began to treat the old membership as adversaries. He gathered his allies around him and focused on filling periodic vacancies in the coops with supporters in his effort. He voided the waiting list and created his own list of potential participants in the cooperative.

The behavior of the pluralist leader was consistent with the theory of David O'Brien (1975) who criticizes the populist approach to cooperative organizing and community building. O'Brien believes populists lack an understanding of the central role of individuals' self-interests in neighborhood organizations. He sees the populist model as having a misplaced faith in altruism and calls for the application of what he calls the "exclusionary principle" in such efforts (p. 178). His exclusionary principle posits a universal need to exclude people from the group and its benefits if they do not participate. The threat of exclusion then forces participation. From time to time active residents sought to apply the exclusionary principle in the Route 2 project. The no displacement pledge of the original leadership and the presence of the Section 8 subsidies with their own set of protective rules, however, made exclusion virtually impossible. Carrying charges on Section 8 units are set by the Housing Authority; the units must be maintained and pass annual maintenance inspections conducted by the Housing Authority, and residents of Section 8 units can only be evicted for cause. The populists consciously, as O'Brien would predict, were not interested in using exclusion. The pluralist leader's treatment of the long-time residents as adversaries went as far as anyone's in trying to actualize the exclusionary principle.

The pattern of nonparticipation by the Latino immigrants and the "new" residents running the coop continued for about a year. Rumors of financial trouble began to spread across the cooperative as the period of trouble with the Housing Authority and Nuestra ensued. The cooperative's financial troubles were exacerbated by the new board's decision to loan a large sum of money to another cooperative that could not repay the loan as promised.

The coop sought to avoid further trouble by trying to save money in its operations through a partial separation from Nuestra. The separation increased the trouble of both entities. Nuestra's billing for its services (purely a matter of accounting) encouraged the cooperatives to pick and choose among its services and obtain others elsewhere. The coop stated it only wanted to buy the inexpensive services. An unusual period of bargaining between the coop and Nuestra followed. It was the arm's length bargaining of pluralism rather than the collective problem-solving of the populists. The problem from Nuestra's point of view was that Nuestra's only customers were the cooperatives and if all the services were not purchased, it simply could not function. The coop briefly experimented with alternatives, but soon returned to the Nuestra fold. It was an unfortunate adventure when such an adventure could not be afforded.

The old members began to meet and discuss events. The coop's financial trouble was not their only complaint. Too many decisions were being made at board meetings without consulting the membership. The old members didn't like the new membership policy and didn't like the way the leadership handled the issue with Nuestra. They were also uncertain about the procedure used to select some of the new members of the board. People had come on the board without a mass meeting to elect them.

When a group of dissidents attended the coop's board meetings to see what was going on themselves, they were not welcomed. Their hostile accusations were greeted with hostility. It was far different from the days when the leadership refused to allow unhappy members to separate themselves from the group and called mass meetings to solve issues. The long-time residents felt like they were not being treated with respect and were being excluded from the decision-making process.

The dissident group decided that the leadership had to go. In the absence of an open process to deal with the problem, they decided to disrupt the meetings until the leadership resigned. Conflict, sometimes physical, began to break out at meetings. Rather than opening up to the dissidents the leadership of the board unsuccessfully tried to close its meetings. It became impossible to conduct the business of the cooperative. At a final meeting in this period about forty of the dissidents came and demanded the leadership's resignation. After much yelling, the leadership of the board resigned and walked out. Some of the ejected board members became disconsolate and refused to cooperate with the cooperative. Some started sabotaging the units so they would not pass inspection and withholding rent. Some of these members including the leader left the coop under threat of eviction. Fortunately the period did not last long.

The basic premise of the interest-group pluralists is that all individuals are "self-interested" (O'Brien 1975, p. 5). In the classic economic model these individuals compete for success in the marketplace. When the theory is applied to the political arena, it is assumed that there are self-interested groups that compete for political power and resources. The theory focuses on comparing the interest of one group with another and not on the factors that hold groups together. The assumption is, of course, that collective self-interest holds the group together. Less is written about how difficult it is to maintain this self-interested consensus.

Leadership skilled in fighting for collective self-interest in the outside world may not have the same level of skill in resolving internal self-interested conflict. If consensus fails, the group may dissolve into many factions or fragment completely into individual differences. When the consensus based on collective self-interest fails, some device other than raw self-interest must come into play to hold the group together. The pluralists only exacerbated their problems by excluding the majority of the population.

The populists attempted to use their inclusive process to hold the group together by finding a new consensus in a meeting of the whole group. The clientelists were more inclined toward coercion and the threat of exclusion.[22] As is discussed in the next chapter, the realization of the limits of self-interest has caused a modification of the Alinsky's self-interested theories of organizing to include the notions of community the new populists seek.

This flurry of activity had its parallels in other cooperatives and a number of the pluralists also left the other cooperatives, many by way of eviction. Since then violent conflict over issues of community has decreased, although issues of community still arise. There is no sign that the process of evolution in the concept of community has ended. The departure of the pluralists left a void that some of the clientelists have filled. The recent leadership has been influenced by their experience of Route 2 politics and residence in the United States. In some cooperatives the leadership favors the community of the new populism; in other cases it favors a more representative form of democracy than the populists seek. More detail on the clientelist leadership and the evolution of the concept of community will follow in later chapters.

Conclusion

Critics of new populism often cite the centrality of the concept of community as one of populism's greatest weaknesses. They judge the populist concept of community with its many meanings to many people as ambiguous and as an insufficient base for a theory. Certainly community has had different meanings in the Route 2 project for the various people who have assumed leadership positions. It, however, has not been an ambiguous term. Each group has had a well-developed sense of the community they sought. The Route 2 story is a story of classic conflict over the meaning of the term. It may be true that the proponents of new populism must be clearer about which visions of community qualifies a group as new populists, but as the Route 2 case demonstrates, the alternatives are clear.

The new populists tried to establish an inclusive political community in the housing cooperatives based on the principles of participatory democracy. Their vision has been tested to the limit on numerous occasions and has seemed to weather the many storms. The new populists also began their process of hegemony, but they did not complete it. Their process and their vision finally gave way to another concept. They did not successfully create a culture that survived their leadership. When the populist leadership stepped aside, the pluralists were able to substitute, in part, a different vision of community.

The pluralists' community was less defined by the boundaries of the housing cooperative than by the total needs of the groups whose cause they championed. They saw the cooperatives as yet another arena for the conflicts they had fought in the larger society. The cooperatives were a place to continue the struggle of poor, minority, and oppressed people in a society that did not meet their needs. The pluralists also were able to partially hegemonize the population. They managed to reformulate some of the populist institutions and unleashed some of the latent factionalism. They failed, however, in holding the community of the housing cooperatives together and in addressing the larger needs of the membership or the larger oppressed population. Most of the pluralists left the cooperatives after great uproar.

The clientelist story is told in detail later in the book. They had a very different notion of community based neither on participation nor on interests. Instead they envisioned a structured community based on family. They have also only had partial success in hegemonizing the population. It is safe to say that the process continues. Given both the internal pressures and external forces in this society, one dominant concept of community will not remain stable throughout the future of the cooperatives.

The experience of the Route 2 residents reveals that it is difficult to create community in isolation from the society in which it exists. As will be seen in other instances later in the book, the external world and its ideas penetrate any attempt at new populist community formation. Even when a degree of autonomy is obtained, forces from the external world continue to penetrate the community and pose new challenges which must be faced and overcome.

The experience also indicates the difficulties in creating and maintaining counter hegemony. Hegemony needs continual renewal. In the larger society the very fabric of the society, the media, education, and the family reinforces the dominant ideology. When the organic intellectuals of the new populist hegemony withdrew, institutions within the community failed to sufficiently reinforce their ideas against the invasion of other ideas. My talks with the residents of the Route 2 corridor, however, reveal that the populist ideology has not been entirely forgotten.

Notes

1. For example, they did not want what befell a divorced woman in the Route 2 project. While living in an area heavily populated by recent Latino immigrants, she had sexual relations with a neighbor's relative. When it became known, her neighbors labeled her a fallen women, and other men in the area approached her for sexual favors. The other women in the area felt she was getting what was coming to her. Needless to say she was very unhappy about this turn of events. As she put it, she had come north to escape this element of the small town, and it had followed her to her new home.

2. I recognize that this conception of community is my personal choice (bias if you will). There are many definitions of community. George Hillery (1955) set out ninety-four definitions that covered a very broad spectrum of conceptions. Raymond Plant (1978) makes the ideological character of one's definitional choice very clear. I believe what is set out is consistent with the radical populist tradition. It was consistent with the original leadership of the Route 2 project and is much of what attracted me to them and has caused me to spend 10 years of my life studying, and working with the effort.

3. A blanket mortgage is a single mortgage that covers the entire property owned by the cooperative. The blanket mortgage binds the members of the cooperative together because the failure of members to pay their monthly carrying charges (rent) could cause a default on the mortgage and a foreclosure that would result in the displacement of the entire membership of the cooperative.

4. See discussion of Padilla's work in Chapter 5.

5. See critique of Dalh's position in Lowi (1969).

6. The question of family and community is dealt with in detail in Chapter 6. Among the issues discussed are the family as a model for community. It is true, however, that there are many extended family circles in the Route 2 population. Often members of families are not speaking to one another because of one or another family feud. Sometimes they can talk about coop affairs because this is not the subject of their feud.

7. For a discussion of dual labor markets see Edwards, Reich and Gordon (1975), Gordon (1972), and Doeringer and Piore (1971).

8. See report of similar incident at Milton-Park in Montreal (Helman 1987, pp.125-137).

9. Interestingly, this was the same lawyer who was making a living suing the Santa Monica Rent Control Board over its policies. He had great success disrupting the Rent Board's operations.

10. Hinson (1966).

11. *Laissez faire* is perhaps too mild a term. More than a few Route 2 corridor residents were legalized squatters. Caltrans' management was so lax that it would be unaware of vacancies. People would move into vacant units, and when the agent came around, they would legalize the residents.

12. In a later discussion in Chapter 5 we will see that the waiting list was lost and how troubles began to emerge in selecting new members when the choice became between friends of active members. This accentuated the ethnic differences among the members.

13. The applicants for the Section 8 units must make less than 50 percent of the county median income for their family size. The applicants for the units without Section 8 subsidies attached cannot make more than 120 percent of the median and cannot pay more than 30 percent of their income in rent. This creates both a maximum and minimum income for the applicants.

14. I have not identified the country to increase the level of confidentiality.

15. One of the membership committees interviewed a mentally disabled person for a rather drab small basement unit. After the disabled person left the interview, the committee began to discuss whether to rent the unit to the individual. The committee liked the person. The only mention of his disability was in the context of concern over the drabness of the unit. The worry was that it might depress the person. The committee decided to choose the person and leave the decision of whether the person wanted the unit to the applicant.

16. Some people have argued that unitary democracy is a particular part of Latin American traditions. See, for example, Dealy (1982).

17. See, for example, Padilla (1985) which is discussed at length in Chapter 5.

18. Americano does not mean Anglo. Both families who disliked the person in question were ethnically mixed families and included a Chicano member.

19. See discussion in Held (1987, pp. 291-292) with regard to having the option not to participate.

20. Whether such a strategy would work would of course depend on what happened at the meetings. Belenky, et.al. (1986) argue, for example, that in the case of women particular processes would be required to bring women out. See also, Colfer (1983) regarding communication among unequals.

21. This is reminiscent of the finding of Felix Padilla that conflict-based organizers defined Latino based on activism and not simply on the basis of shared tradition, i.e., language (1985, pp. 75-78). This will be discussed further in Chapter 5.

22. They were similar in many ways to the leadership of the Santa Monica activists who attempted to use ideology and psychological intimidation to hold the membership together. Their tactics were related to the small-town politics of traditional community.

3

Empowerment and Disempowerment

Very few words are as important to the practitioners and theoreticians of community organizing as the word empowerment. Yet in the early going in the Route 2 project the word was rarely heard. Empowerment is usually thought of as the process by which people organize, obtain a collective objective, and learn about their own personal power. The new populist leaders understood it would take organization and power to form the cooperatives in the midst of a hostile environment, but they did not focus on developing personal power. They were more concerned with the problem of exercising power, theirs and others. As one of the leaders told me when I talked about how organizers used the word empowerment, "I don't like the word empowerment. Power is power. It's not a process. You either have it or you don't. You win your fight or you loose it. The question is what do you do with it once you have it."

When the term empowerment was used early on, the residents generally used it as an synonym for self-actualization. It meant the process by which the individual develops to his or her fullest potential through participation in the community. In this sense the community empowers not by giving or revealing power but by providing the opportunity to members to participate in, to own, and take responsibility for the community. In the inclusive community of the new populists, personal power can divide, threaten, and exclude individuals within the community.

Later the pluralists in the project often used the more common meaning of the word empowerment in their discussions of the direction the project should take. They were people focused on power struggles and on conflicts of interests. The populists were quite aware of the potential for personal interest-based conflicts in their midst. They did not seek to repress, deny, or avoid them. Conflicts were seen as opportunities for individuals to find a way to learn about themselves and each other, to a more common good. The "us and them" of the pluralist form of community were to be interpenetrated into a collective "us" through a linking of "public and private interest" formed in open and public dialogue. The pluralists did not believe this to be possible. "We" or "they" win or lose or at best compromise.

The clientelists usually did not use the term empowerment. In their world power is important, but it is not as malleable as in the pluralist world. The clientelists world is a much more fixed structure where people are empowered through a reciprocal relationship with those in charge. Power changes when reciprocity breaks down. It is replaced not by an empowerment in the pluralist sense, but by a new hierarchy that may be more reciprocal. Clientelists live in a unitary rather than pluralist environment.

In this chapter the concept of empowerment will be examined in the theory and in the experience of the residents of the Route 2 project. First the populist-pluralist difference will be explored and then the clientelist position will be examined. The problem of empowerment intermixes questions of structure and agency. The community must be structured to permit participation, and the individuals within the community must be willing and able to utilize that structure. Because the requisite structure and the presence of will and ability may be temporal, disempowerment is also discussed. The populists view empowerment as the process of forming an empowering community and disempowerment as the process by which the empowering community is lost.

For the populists who focused on the formation of community the empowerment problem of structure and agency began when residents decided to try and wrestle their homes from Caltrans. If community was to be the outcome of the fight, the community had to be the one to fight. This seemingly contradictory position is shared by the communitarian Martin Buber who wrote: "The feeling of community does not reign where the desired change of institutions is wrested in common, but without community, from a resisting world. It reigns where the fight that is fought takes place from the position of community" (Buber 1955, p. 31).[1]

The populists resolved the "simple" questions of power internally in the project by giving away whatever formal power they amassed in the fight for the property to as many of the residents of the corridor as possible. They did this initially by changing the board of R2CHC from a self-appointed, centralized group to a voluntary federation of the cooperatives with a board selected by the residents and then by forgoing the interim ownership of the property in the corridor. The decision to forgo title to the property was particularly important to their strategy.

The state statute authorizing the sale of the property to the residents provided for a development corporation to act as an intermediary between the state and the residents. The development corporation was to obtain options to the property, rehabilitate it, and help in the organizational development of the cooperatives. It could have held on to the options until the cooperatives met R2CHC's criteria and, therefore, kept a great deal of power over the formation of the cooperatives. Instead, to keep the power lines clear and make the federation a true federation, when R2CHC obtained options to buy the property from Caltrans, the corporation immediately transferred the options to the individual cooperatives.

Of course, dispersal of power does not mean that R2CHC had no power. Although the leaders involved the mass of the people in important questions through mass meetings, they had a great deal of control because they determined what questions were important and when and how the questions would be asked. Many decisions were made in the federation meetings after long hours of debate and taken back to the individual cooperatives for what was more like ratification than independent judgment. The leadership and technical functions of the development corporation gave it a great deal of informal power. It was tempered, however, by the formal lines that would have allowed any cooperative to break off when it chose. During the development period there was much maneuvering by the coops, but no break.

The new populists' ideas about forming an empowering community are not new. They echo Jean-Jacques Rousseau's ideas. For Rousseau the dialogue of direct democracy leads to a common good that takes into account the welfare of the individual citizen as much as the welfare of the community as a whole. The individual in such a dialogic community of his or her choosing while free to express dissent at any point, is bound to yield to the common will unless the majority in the community violates its process or does not reach its decision in "good faith."[2] In either of these cases in the theory of direct democracy the dissenting minority has the right to refuse to go along with the will of the community -- the right of civil disobedience -- a perceived right that was exercised more than once in the Route 2 project.[3]

This is exactly where the pluralists finally break with the populists. The pluralists, believing that interests necessarily are in conflict, question the possibility of empowerment taking place through dialogue. They argue there exist systemic inequalities that make such empowering dialogue impossible because within such communities not everyone is equally prepared to enter into the dialogue. If an individual in a supposedly inclusive community is not empowered but is still bound to Rousseau's common will, the collective takes on a decidedly undemocratic, disempowering character.

Freedom of Will

The new populists' position in the Route 2 project is best stated by Martin Buber. Buber believes everyone has the capacity to participate in the dialogue of the community. Participation is a question of will, of commitment, not capacity or ability. There are "no gifted and ungifted here, only those who give themselves and those who withhold themselves" (Buber 1955, p. 35). The struggle is not to free the bonds that limit capacity to participate; it is to free oneself "to responsibility," i.e., responsibility to the community. John Stuart Mill foreshadows this sentiment by finding the roots of empowerment (individual growth) in, as Mansbridge puts it "taking as much responsibility as one needs or can handle at a given moment, not on being given a quantitatively equal dollop of power all the time" (Mansbridge 1980, p. 245). This approach, however, leaves unanswered the question of who decides how much responsibility one needs or can handle.

Alienation

Many authors, who agree with Buber that the problem is one of will, are not as convinced as Buber that the problem of will is such a personal problem. Alienation, for example, has been seen as suppressing people's sense of their ability to participate and thus their willingness even to try to take on the degree of responsibility in the community that Mill envisions.

Building on the work of Emile Durkheim and Robert Merton, Richard Cloward and Lloyd Ohlin believe that even with a change in the opportunity structure, alienated individuals have to "pass through a complex process of change in attitudes toward themselves, other persons, and the established social order" to end their anomic state and come to believe they can participate (Merton, et.al. 1960, p. 110). Individuals have to feel competent to participate; that they can accomplish that which enables them to deal with their own needs. The anomic individual needs help in this passage from alienation to competence. Calling on the work of Saul Alinsky, professional organizers see themselves as guides through the process of social and personal change. These helpers are catalysts to successful action in which the individual learns competence. With a sense of competence, alienation ends and no longer remains an impediment to participation. In theory, leadership is developed among the newly competent, replaces the professional organizer and continues the process (Henig 1986).

The literature is less clear on the relationship of this process to the formation of community. Both powerful collective and empowered individuals emerge in the process articulated by Cloward and Ohlin, but whether the collective is a community is not usually stated. Alinsky's work was largely silent when it came to questions of community. In his fashion, he would likely have said that if community is important to people, then they should work toward it.

The descendants of Alinsky in the organization he founded, the Industrial Areas Foundation, have explicitly included community in their theory (Cortes 1986, pp. 122-123). They separate the community-destroying notion of selfishness from the idea of self-interest. With the value of community assumed, the organizing process is thought to strengthen individuals and their communities and allow the spirit of community to flourish.[4]

Although sharing the value of community, Buber pursues community not through self-interest, but through a renunciation of self. This somewhat mystical sounding formulation is elaborated in practice by psychologist M. Scott Peck who describes the process of community formation as requiring that each individual "empty" (Peck 1987). This process means giving up individual preconceptions of the other and accepting others on their own terms, much like the relational, I-Thou approach of Buber. The desire for community comes not out of a material-based collective self-interest but the need people have for relationships.

Consciousness

Other theorists describe the problem of the will to participate in community not as a problem of alienation but of consciousness. Paulo Freire, a leader of this approach states that in situations of highly unequal power, the powerless become dependent, and "are prevented from either self-determined action or reflection upon their actions" (Friere 1970).[5] In this situation a culture of silence develops that adds an air of legitimacy to the domination of the individual. Antonio Gramsci wrote about the same problem in slightly different terms. For Gramsci the dominant ideological hegemony of society creates such a contradictory understanding of society among people that it leads to inaction, to "a condition of moral and political passivity" (Gramsci 1971, p. 333).

Like the alienation theorists, the consciousness theorists see the need for the individual to go through a "catharsis." In this case the catharsis is required to move beyond collective self-interest to an activating and liberating counter-hegemony, an understanding of society that permits coherent action. In Freire's theory, liberating teachers lead people through this catharsis with the application of his pedagogic method. Gramsci's concept is somewhat more complex. His "organic intellectuals" are intellectuals aligned with an oppressed class who lead that class as it engages in class struggle through a series of "negations" to lessen the bounds of the dominant ideology and then help the class to develop a new structure of meaning, a new hegemony that better serves the class' interests (Boggs 1984).

In Freire's model and that of the renowned U.S. organizer Miles Horton, catharsis comes through a partial withdrawal from the world into an empowering community (Haas 1982). The community exposes the individual to collective empowerment and makes the surrounding disempowering society intolerable. The classic example of this pattern is Rosa Parks whose participation in Horton's Highlander Folk School raised her consciousness to the point where she could no longer tolerate the segregation of Birmingham, Alabama. Many see her refusal to sit in the back of the bus as the event that sparked the boycott that launched the civil rights movement of the 1960s.

The Freirian and, perhaps even more, Gramscian notions come closest to describing the approach to empowerment of the new populists in the Route 2 project. They intended to create a structure that would permit, even require in a structural sense, participation, and through their leadership within that structure, assist in the transformation in consciousness to encourage participation. It was the binding, participatory and moral (self-interest limiting) elements of the limited-equity cooperative that made that form of ownership especially attractive to the leadership.

Creating and maintaining an empowering community structure is not easy. Jane Mansbridge concludes in her study of local democracy that the successful approach toward community may depend on the situation presented (Mansbridge 1983, p. 300). Even if the correct path is chosen and community is formed, it may not last. Changing circumstances may result in the opportunity for participation being diminished. The changing demands of community maintenance may result in capacity waning. Alienation may grow and consciousness fail.

People, then, can be empowered, and they can be disempowered. The structure of the community may contain flaws that can lead to its destruction. Also the structure of community is contained within the larger structure of society. A community that remains whole is a safe place protected from what may be the disempowering forces in the society and may even be a generator of forces that can transform the society.

The community may lose its protective shield over time and may be interpenetrated by the disempowering forces of society and again be destroyed. This interpenetration may be from without, a direct attack by forces outside the community, or it may be from within, from the collective response to exterior attack or from the failures of the community to maintain itself. Although disempowering elements of the state may be held at bay, the hegemony central to Gramsci's theories cannot be entirely resisted until a counter-hegemony is fully established within the community. The dominant hegemony is carried unintentionally by the residents of the community, and only a counterhegemony strong enough to transcend that hegemony can protect the community from it working its logic on the community in destructive ways.

Empowerment Through Participation

The development process of the Route 2 project itself involved a great deal of participation both in decision making and in complying with coop decisions. Rehabilitation committees of each cooperative met with individual residents and decided what should be done to the buildings. Relocation committees of the coops likewise met with individual residents and decided who would have to move. There were also corridor-wide committees to handle problems between the cooperatives. Relocation was particularly important to the project because the Section 8 program requires that no one be overcrowded.

As discussed in Chapter 1, at first there was a great deal of overcrowding, but as Caltrans emptied units and residents moved out of the corridor, a significant number of vacant units accumulated. The problem became how to use the vacant units to relieve the overcrowding. Ideally the vacant units would be joined to the occupied units to make large apartments. An entire half of one of the buildings that Caltrans had attempted to empty was consolidated into one six-bedroom apartment. In most cases overcrowding was not this easy to relieve because the vacant units were not in the places where they were needed.

A great game of musical chairs was required. About a third of the residents had to move either temporarily or permanently to eliminate the overcrowding. The decisions of who was to move where could have been made quickly by a centralized group and its staff, but the problem was that the people had to be willing to go along or the whole process would collapse. The alternative was for the committees to make decisions about the moves with participation of the affected residents. In this case not participating could be risky. The head of one of the committees didn't like it when people didn't show up. He was often quoted as saying, "If you don't show up. You don't get ----!!" Although appreciating this spirit, the leadership tried to temper his participate-or-else approach. The process worked. Only a few people said they didn't want to move. They agreed to forfeit the Section 8 subsidy and pay the full rent.

The technical staff was very nervous about giving the process over to the people. Relocation had to be carried out quickly or the project might lose its subsidies and financing. They also opposed the immediate assignment of the options to purchase the property to the cooperatives. The professionals wanted to train the people and wait until they were ready. The populist leadership was not opposed to training, but they saw much of the training taking place in the residents' experiences of taking responsibility for the cooperatives, for example, in solving the relocation problem.[6]

The populists also tried to actualize their Buberian approach to the question of will. Their approach was to try and create structures such as the relocation committees that encouraged, even required (from a structural point of view) participation of as many people as possible. They had great difficulty fully removing all the structural impediments to participation especially those inherent in the language barrier between the English-speaking and Spanish-speaking populations. As is discussed in Chapter 5, this failure was to come back to haunt the project.

A Test of the Approach

No better example of the populist's approach could be found than in the case of what was known as the invasion. Because the Route 2 corridor is made up of pre-existing properties, the disparity between amenities at various properties is great. In this particular situation a twelve-unit apartment building with virtually no back, front or side yard abutted two duplexes with very large front and back yards. The people in the twelve-unit building complained for some time that they had a major parking problem (because of a high rate of vandalism against cars parked on the street) and sought access to a part of their neighbors' backyard for parking.

The families in the duplexes saw their yards as safe play-space for their children and did not support the idea of yielding part of their space for automobiles. The plan to provide parking was acknowledged in the rest of the coop as having some merit given the amount of space, but the press of other business in the coop delayed the consideration of this particular problem.

One day four men in the twelve-unit building consumed enough beer to conceive and execute a forced takeover of part of their neighbors' backyard. They passed around a hastily drawn up petition among the residents of their building that would have been the pride of any anarchist band. It claimed that since the property was collective property and not private property, it should be more equitably distributed. Under this banner they uprooted plants and moved fences one Saturday afternoon as their neighbors screamed and the police came and left with their heads shaking.

The leader of the invaders was a very active member of the board of directors of the coop. He was Anglo as was another member of the invaders. One of the other men was Latino and the other Asian, in true Route 2 integrated fashion. Unfortunately, the invaded were all Latino and the issue was colored by the ethnic conflict between the Anglo board member and the Latino residents.

Not surprisingly the incident generated an emergency board meeting of the coop. It was a difficult meeting because the other members of the board believed that the idea of redoing the backyards had merit and had substantial attachment to their very active, fellow board member. On the other hand, no one could argue that the invaders went about their business properly or that the invaded families had not been wronged. The invaded families came to the meeting demanding relief.

The first action of the board was to declare the disputed territory a no-persons land, posting signs that declared that its occupation would lead to immediate eviction, their ultimate sanction. The second act was to remove the invasion leader from the board and replace him with the Latina spokesperson for the invaded. It was felt that this would be a strong message to their former colleague that he had not acted properly; and they knew he would be terribly disappointed by his exclusion from the board. It would also ensure that the decision-making process that followed would be fully open to the injured parties and demonstrate to the community at large that the board would not treat its own members as above "the law."

The board's third act involved scheduling a series of meetings in which the parties involved and representatives from all other parcels in the coop (30 parcels) that wished to participate would meet and negotiate this and any other distribution disputes. The meetings culminated in an agreement that parking spaces would be made available from the invaded backyard in return for the construction of a fence by the invaders in both the back and front yards so that the children would have sufficient, secure play space.

The board had sought to distribute the resources of the coop equitably, to maintain the integrity of their process, and to involve as many people as possible in that process. They were satisfied that they had been fair, the community appeared satisfied, and peace was restored although it would be an overstatement to say that harsh feelings between the invaded and invaders about the incident had been completely dispelled.

This case seems to illustrate what is meant by Benjamin Barber when he writes that conflict, rather than being repressed, must be used to "transform conflict into cooperation through citizen participation, public deliberation, and civic education" (Barber 1984, p. 135). The board took advantage of the issue to deepen the community involvement in the coop, broaden the existing democracy, and educate the membership in the process. The essence of direct democracy is not the documents legally binding participants but common participatory activity. The board expressed the essence of direct democracy when they immediately reformulated their own membership by internalizing the issue within their membership while opening the decision-making process to representatives of all parcels in the cooperative. The matter was not to be resolved by legalisms nor in closed sessions, but by a wide dialogic search for an equitable resolution in the community at large.

A Shift to a Power Approach

As the rehabilitation-relocation process was drawing to a close, a number of the leaders who had gone through this educational process and internalized many of the rules of open process on which the project was based withdrew from leadership positions. Some of the initial populist leaders decided they had accomplished what they had set out to do and that they should withdraw to look after their own lives. Some of the early leaders chose to move out of the project to take advantage of opportunities elsewhere. At the same time, as was discussed in the last chapter, a group of interest-group oriented people with histories in issue organizing moved into the coops. These are the people who helped organize the Latino caucus.

The caucus first analyzed the structure of power in the Route 2 project. They specifically sought the centers of power. New resident members of the caucus collected all the documents they could and asked many questions about how things worked in the corridor. The lack of a center seemed to confuse many of the investigators. Nuestra had absorbed the federation, and the development corporation had been sent off to do other work. Although Nuestra was a central body, it like R2CHC, had no power in the formal sense. Any coop that was unhappy could withdraw, as happened later, and obtain management services elsewhere.

In the coops the boards had power of the kind the new leaders were seeking, but it was limited. The rents of two-thirds of the residents were set by the Section 8 program, and individuals could only be evicted for good cause. The budgets for maintenance were limited, and most of the money went to repair items required by the Housing Authority, particularly in this early period. Perhaps the boards' most important decisions concerned who could move into the vacancies that occurred from time to time. These decisions, however, were largely given over to membership committees in the various cooperatives. As will be discussed in Chapter 6, a number of the caucus members made their way to the coop membership committees that interviewed and recommended people for admittance and the corridor-wide membership committee that helped set membership policy.

External Disempowering Forces

Each constraint on the choices open to the cooperative was intensely disliked by the populists. Limiting the choices of the cooperatives limits the scope of the potential growth of internal democratic processes. The populists wanted to remove as much as possible of the state, in the larger sense of the word, from their project.[7] They did not want outside experts telling them what to do, to have to borrow money from a bank, deal with a contractor, or get involved with the Housing Authority. They wanted their own development corporation and got it. They also wanted to use self-help rehabilitation, but the funding agencies and lenders wouldn't have it. They did not want the Section 8 program because of the interaction with bureaucracy it entails, but the one-for-all approach and a refusal by the state to give the property without charge to the residents or rehabilitate the multifamily property at state expense made this necessary.

In many ways the restrictions have created responsibility without control.[8] The lack of pairing responsibility with control has generated a continual stream of disempowering challenges to the community. The challenges have transformed political questions for the political community into technical questions more accessible to experts. People can more easily dispense justice as they did in the invasion case than interpret HUD regulations.[9] The reorganization of the Housing Authority generated an excessive number of such disempowering technical questions.

The Housing Authority had relatively few units funded under the Moderate Rehabilitation Section 8 program and even fewer cooperative units under its aegis. It repeatedly misapplied the regulations including how the rents should be calculated. It also had difficulty coming to grips with the cooperatives as institutions distinct from the conventional rental projects with which it works.[10] During the reorganization Housing Authority personnel continually changed. Each change meant a rerun of fights previously won. In effect, the cooperatives had to train each new administrator. This process required either the use of expertise in emergencies or long and repeated training of new leaders for what were otherwise unproductive tasks.

The Capacity Approach

The pluralist leadership's focus on power was not a focus on control and autonomy vis-a-vis the Housing Authority in the fashion of the populist leadership. The new leadership did not share the self-help, collective responsibility ideas of control held by the early leadership. Nowhere was this more clearly expressed than in the decision to expel Nuestra from the cooperatives and make it an expert-dominated external agent that could be dealt with at arm's length. To the populist leadership the expulsion was an act of collective disempowerment. To the pluralist leaders expulsion was central to their focus on getting others to do what they wanted (Parenti 1978, pp. 5-6). Where the populists regretted the use of experts to fight with the Housing Authority, the pluralists insisted upon it.

The difference in leadership was also evident in the decision to create R2FHC. The early leadership was wary of the creation of R2FHC in part because of a sense that it was impractical and in part for conceptual reasons. They believed there was not enough energy in the group to engage in this new venture when the old ventures, the cooperatives and the management company, were not fully established and when federal funding for such new ventures was being cut back. It was not the heyday of the poverty program when capital for new ventures abounded.

The pluralist leadership used the word empowerment regularly when organizing R2FHC. Again, however, the new leadership held a different idea than the populist leadership. Aside from a continued emphasis on a pluralist view of power, they focused much more on the capacity element of the term. People had many more needs than housing and until these were addressed, the group could not expect people to participate. People needed services. One of the more vocal supporters of R2FHC, who was unhappy about having her monthly charges increased, liked to say, "A coop has to do more than raise people's rent." By services, the new leadership meant professional services, not collective self-help services.

One of the early leaders responded to the idea of creating the new organization by suggesting that the coops start a food-buying club to save money or a baby-sitting collective to start the process of providing childcare. The response of the new activists was that they did not want these. They wanted a food store and a childcare center. They did not share the early leaders antipathy to the state. The state was a potential provider of services, empowering services. The problem was not to escape from the state and to create a zone free from state domination, but how to get the state to address "the people's" needs.

This position seems to me very much part of the classic, Alinsky power school of organizing. It also seemed inappropriate to the situation in the cooperatives. The project did not have the base from which such an effort could be launched. With the very mixed demographic base (age, single, family, children) of some 300 households, the cooperatives could not muster sufficient power to compete in the pluralist arena. Such an effort would more properly be area-wide or issue-based.

In addition, from my more populist view, this approach to capacity building through social services reflects a contradiction. Pluralists seek to use power to force the state, the agent of domination in society, to do something for individuals to make them more prepared to compete in a structure of domination. A sense of power then comes from what is really a very competitive moment of domination and not from any real sense of developing self.

Consistent with the old saw that power begets power, begets power, etc., the effort to provide services ended with divisions among the new leadership and passionate fights among individuals. The new leadership had a propensity to stop and fight that was in sharp contrast to the early leadership. The early leaders never stopped. They had a clear goal to buy the property and form the coops. If they were blocked, they would instantly search for an alternative path. I don't know how many times I heard one of the leadership group remark after receiving bad news, "Well, let's try this next" or "what do we try next?"

There was a short period when the two groups had a direct confrontation. It was one of the few times the old leadership used power. The reaction of the pluralists was interesting. The conflict arose over the funding of a camping trip planned by the youth organizer for gang members in one of the cooperatives.

A Power Struggle

Near the end of the development process, R2CHC, which had non-profit tax status, had obtained a grant to pay for a youth organizer to work with the gang problem in the cooperatives. Once the development was over, R2CHC, with some of the early leadership, went off to see if there was other housing to develop in the neighborhood, but it still had a portion of the youth money. Before R2FHC was formed, Nuestra, with many of the new leaders, took over the youth project. This meant that during the transition, the board of one group ran the project and the board of another group had the money.

The president of R2CHC had been trying to get a budget that would describe how the youth project funds would be spent for some time when the request for money to rent a van for the camping trip came in. She wanted both boards to approve a budget so she would know what expenditures were authorized. When she was asked for money shortly before the camping trip was to take place, she reiterated her discomfort with the lack of a budget and also asked whether insurance had been purchased for the outing. She was told that it had not been purchased. Her response was to refuse to issue a check for the outing from the youth money until she received a budget and assurance that insurance had been purchased. She did not want to risk R2CHC and the coops on this outing.

The R2CHC board later backed her up, but the new leadership was angry. A discussion of passing the hat to raise the money or people using their own cars, trucks, or vans took place at an emergency Nuestra meeting, but, to my surprise, none of these solutions to the immediate problem were chosen, instead the trip was cancelled. I am not sure why. It may be that the group decided the insurance was essential or that people's anger and the power question presented took precedence over the trip. What followed was a call for an investigation of how R2CHC got away from the federation and for R2CHC to give up control over the money remaining in the youth project grant.

The decision to create Nuestra and send R2CHC out to look for additional development opportunities was long and complicated. It included many R2CHC meetings and mass meetings in each of the cooperatives. The creation of Nuestra and the reorganization of R2CHC had definitely been the plan of the most populist portion of the early leadership (at this time, myself included), and it had been talked out and broadly accepted.[11] Of course, the new leadership had not been part of that decision.

In the end a budget was prepared for the youth project and an agreement was made to pass the money on according to that budget. Meetings began to form R2FHC, and there was talk of trying to take R2CHC back, but nothing came of this talk. Lots of accusations and hard feelings ensued. For a significant period of time, the focus on human needs was shifted to the question of power. The power question had to be resolved before any further progress could be made on the needs front. There were plenty of questions of power before in the history of Route 2 both externally and internally, but this was the first time that action stopped. Debate, moreover, moved out of the public arena into the private.

No one called for a mass meeting during any of this conflict. An organization was begun (R2FHC) and two died (R2FHC and Nuestra) without a mass meeting to discuss the birth or death.

Clientelism Emerges and Evolves

As was discussed in Chapter 2, following this flurry of activity, many of the pluralists left the cooperatives. Their departure left a void filled by some of the clientelists. Clientelism entails a face-to-face relationship of reciprocity formed between people of unequal power. The notion of empowerment as discussed above does not enter into this concept. The issue is rather whether the level of reciprocity is adequate to rationalize accepting the unequal relationship without protest.

In Latin America clientelism has evolved into a seemingly unchangeable relationship between the landed patron and the peasant. The patron is a "gatekeeper" who stands between the community and the state and connects the peasant to the larger market (Powell 1970). John Powell indicates that the patron's "basic function is to relate to community-oriented individuals who want to stabilize or improve their life chances, but who lack economic security and political connections, with nation-oriented individuals . . . ." (p. 413). The test of reciprocity is the ability of the patron to improve the life chances of the individual or more likely the family. Empowerment in this context is a term often used to evaluate the ability to survive and not, as the pluralists use it, to compete (Friedmann 1988, p. 116).

Many people in the cooperative's population brought their clientelist understanding of social relations and politics with them in their migration north. Latino residents would on occasion, for example, bring gifts to the president of a cooperative and ask that a relative be given the available unit next to theirs. In their eyes a president took on the role of the patron. The populists were very uncomfortable with these gestures. In at least one case that is discussed in detail in Chapter 6 a Latino leader fully accepted the patron role and attempted to play the part to the fullest extent possible. To some in the Latino population this was not necessarily inappropriate behavior. The question was whether the patron was a good patron or a bad patron, i.e., could he deliver what the people needed or not?

After the revolt against the patronish president discussed at the end of Chapter 2, I interviewed some of the Latino residents of the cooperative who took over control of their cooperative. I asked them why they took such forceful action. They replied using the bad patron imagery to explain the action they took. They explained to me in detail how the patron system in Latin America works with the peons, the patrons, and the bosses. They saw the defrocked president as having taken on the patron role or maybe even the role of a boss. In their minds they were forcing out the bad patron or boss. It was also clear that for some of the Latino population the concepts of clientelism had begun to change during their stay in the United States.

I asked the new Latino president whether he was now the patron. He aggressively denied he had assumed that role. It was clear that while he thought in clientelist categories, the cooperatives were to be different from the way things were done back home. As the conversation continued the president created an amalgam of the democratic form of the cooperatives and the imagery of clientelism that began to look a lot like representative democracy. He reiterated that he was not the patron. Instead he said that the board of the cooperative was to be the patron. It should have the reciprocal relationship with its members central to clientelism.

I pressed the president further to discover how far this imagery could be carried. I asked him whether R2CHC was a patron. He first said yes and then changed his mind. His new answer could serve as an introduction to Chapter 6 on gender. He said R2CHC was more like a mother that gave birth to the cooperatives than a patron. This is consistent with the clientelist's focus on family and women's role in the family. It is hard to tell, however, how much the fact that much of the leadership of R2CHC were women also contributed to this choice of words.

The same amalgam of democracy and clientelism is in practice in another of the coop boards that has become almost entirely made up of immigrant Latinos. The board of the cooperative discussed the possibility of refinancing the cooperative's mortgage to take advantage of a significant decline in interest rates. It considered at length the terms the board should seek for the cooperative. The members called on some of the old populist leadership that lived in the cooperative for information on the history of the structure of the present mortgage and advice. The populists' immediate reaction was that a mass meeting of the membership should be called to make the decision about the terms of the refinancing.

The board members were not enthusiastic about the idea. They were having a hard time understanding the options, and they believed that the membership would not understand unless more time and energy was spent on explanation than the board had at its disposal. The populists' position was that people in the cooperative would never begin to understand if they were not involved in making such decisions. The board responded that not many people would come to the meeting. The populists saw this statement as proof of their position. If the leadership didn't give people chances to be involved, they would never be involved. It didn't matter if no one showed up. The opportunity for participation had to be provided. Without the opportunity the residents would not be involved. The board reluctantly agreed to schedule a mass meeting.

The primary populist spokesperson was not at the next meeting. Between the meetings the refinancing terms changed slightly to make the question of options somewhat less critical to the future of the cooperative. The board quickly cancelled the mass meeting. When he was asked why, the president of the cooperative responded with a speech right out of a representative democracy textbook. He returned to the position that the residents would not understand. The board knew more about the issue, and besides it had been elected to handle such matters. The issue was the board's responsibility.

Just as the populist leadership had difficulty establishing its full hegemony because of the constraints on the decision-making powers of the cooperatives, clientelists had difficulty because of the constraints on their ability to establish the necessary power and stability to establish reciprocity. In Chapter 6 an example of this problem is discussed. Given the rules and regulations of the Route 2 project it is not likely in a diverse project like Route 2 that clientelism will ever be fully established. The movement of clientelism toward representative democracy is not surprising.

Further change should be expected. At this writing some of the populists in the cooperatives are reemerging from a long rest in reaction to the clientelist and representative approaches. In several of the cooperatives the populists are trying to open up the representative process. They have called for the distribution of material about the affairs of the cooperatives to the membership on a more regular basis in an effort to encourage the dialogue of a direct populist democracy. Whether they will succeed remains to be seen. As I wrote in the prologue, the process is a continuing one.

Conclusion

Much of my interest over the past few years has shifted from organizing people to obtain power to identifying what people must do with power once they obtain it. This interest has kept me fascinated with the Route 2 project over the ten years I've gone to meetings and conversed with people about the project. The populists were good fighters. They knew about power and how to reach their goal. They were not, however, very interested in keeping or exercising power in any ordinary sense of the word. This seems contradictory, but in a society in which this form of democracy and community is not prevalent, it takes power to create a space in which power is no longer an issue. The power they sought was the power to have an open democratic community where public talk and not power is supreme. To the populists existing society is class-based with one class exploiting and repressing another. Their class image contains a large dose of U.S. self-help populist imagery. Their good society would liberate the potential of the individual from this oppression and exploitation.

The pluralists did not have this same vision. They saw a never-ending fight for an equal chance to participate in a pluralist society that excluded certain racial and ethnic groups from the benefits that the society had to offer. They had thought long and hard about their and their people's struggle and were clear about the rules they sought. They had thought less about the nature of the populists' liberated autonomous communities or any form of society in which power would no longer be the central issue. They wanted the power and resources necessary to make it a fair fight, not the end of the fight. For the pluralists an end was impossible. The populists wanted empowerment through liberation from an oppressive state. The pluralists wanted an equal chance to participate in the power the state had to offer.

The clientelists acted on yet a third image of empowerment. To the clientelists struggle did not involve liberation from an oppressive society or fair competition for the benefits society had to offer. They were largely immigrants from societies where liberation meant armed resistance and where there was little surplus to divide. Empowerment related more to survival than an end to exploitation or equal distribution. They did not seek the end to inequality as much as the resources to make their way in this life.

Each of the groups found that their ideas had limited success. The populists were not able to gain full autonomy. They were not, for example, able to win the right to engage in self-help rehabilitation. Constraints of the Section 8 program continually interfered with the possibility of exercising choice. The pluralists' approach simply seemed inappropriate to the confines of a cooperative. Their need for arms-length transactions and for an adversary to pit themselves against led to continual conflict and factionalization. The clientelists, as will be discussed later, had their own problems with trying to function in an environment where bureaucratic rules are taken more seriously than in Latin America and often replace the primacy of social relations.

Notes

1.   There is, of course, not a total match between what Buber meant by community and what the Route 2 project leadership of this period meant by community. Buber's more total view of community is often encapsulated in the kibbutz. See Buber (1958, pp.139-149). I believe the point is still valid in the more limited functional, political community.

2.   Rousseau (1973), see particularly p. 132. For an interesting discussion of Rousseau on this point see Loewenstein (1970 pp. 42-52). This point is discussed from an anarchist point of view by Robert Graham (1989). Graham sets forth Proudhon's, Bakunin's, and Godwin's varying points of view on this issue of the wisdom of a binding social contract. He then sets forth Carole Pateman's (1985) solution to this problem. Pateman's position was very much like the radical populist position in the Route 2 project. Pateman says that an individual's obligation is to express their disagreement at the point they come to disagree. This is what was meant by keeping the process open in the Route 2 process. As will be seen there were limits to this openness when members sought to threaten the "community" itself either directly or through undermining actions. At some point the individual had to choose to be part of the group or outside of it.

3.   See discussion of this point in Pateman (1985, pp. 161-162).

4.   See Raymond Plant's (1978) excellent discussion of the difficulties such an approach encounters.

5.   For an excellent discussion of the issue see Colfer (1983).

6.   This view is very much like Bookchin's (1987) discussion of the Greek identification of participation in the political affairs of the polis as crucial to the education of the citizen (pp. 59-60).

7.   The state includes all the aspects of domination both governmental and corporate in this usage. See Carnoy (1984).

8.   This bind is common to many U.S. housing programs. See *The Empty Promise*, Urban Planning Aids (1973).

9.   The transformation of problems from moral to technical is in many ways a central theme of the last century. It is either representative of the advance of science or a self-interest class act of the professional-managerial class that has disempowering effects on other social classes, particularly the working-class. For a historical discussion of this point see Wiebe (1967). This point is discussed at length in Chapter 4.

10.   One continual disagreement focused on the policy for the relocation for overcrowding and under-housing. Section 8 rules require a minimum and restrict the maximum occupants in subsidized units.   If the family comes out of compliance, it has to be relocated to another appropriate unit or the cooperatives lose the subsidy. In a cooperative families are homeowners who are encouraged to invest a great deal of themselves in their home. Being moved from place to

place as your family changes works against this element of cooperative ownership. Originally the Housing Authority wanted to move people out of the cooperative to other available units in the city if they became out of compliance. This would have totally undermined the cooperative building effort. A compromise was reached that required relocation only within the cooperative, but the problem continued to be destructive in particular situations.

11. The decision to start Nuestra was not unanimous. Some residents felt the creation of a management corporation gave too much responsibility to the cooperatives when they were not ready for such responsibility. The majority was very upset with the existing management company and was willing to take the gamble.

4

Class

The Route 2 project took place during a dramatic restructuring of the world economy.[1]   Governments across the globe were forced by changing economic, political, and spatial conditions to stop major projects in midstream (Hall 1980). In the U.S. tax revolts restricted the ability of government to act and, along with localized growing political resistance to such projects, forced the end of projects like the Route 2 freeway (Schwadron 1984). At the same time real estate prices began to escalate making any public activity involving real estate very expensive and government's existing holdings increasingly valuable. Agencies like Caltrans, having been stopped in their efforts to build and having suffered a decline in federal funding, wanted to take advantage of their real estate holdings. Caltrans wanted to sell its property on the open market.[2]

Because of these structural changes the Route 2 project varies from the typical working-class/state conflicts that fill much of community planning history.[3] Typically the state, meaning all the institutions that support the *status quo* including government, wishes to displace working-class residents to build its supposedly public serving project.[4] In the Route 2 story a first round of displacement took place with Caltrans' purchase of the housing for the freeway. A second round was threatened by the sale of the Caltrans "surplus" property. Caltrans sought to act without a public purpose other than to replace lost revenues. The corridor residents characterized this as speculation and used this characterization of Caltrans often, with great success. They fought the second round of displacement, as working-class people often do. In the Route 2 corridor, as rarely happens, they won.[5]

Although many of the residents were heroic in this struggle against the state, the fight was not won without allies, chief among whom were professionals including planners, lawyers, and architects. They helped in the fight against Caltrans, and once the property was obtained, more professionals helped rehabilitate the property. Still more professionals have assisted in the management of the cooperatives. It is not unusual for professionals to help groups like the Route 2 residents, but in such cases the relationship between working-class clients and professionals is not unproblematic. The professionals are often caught in a contradictory position between the interests of their clients, their class position, and the interests of the state.

This chapter will consider the issue of class.[6] First the question of the relationship between the professionals and their working-class clients will be examined. As with other issues faced in the Route 2 project, the different ideological groups varied in their approach to professionals. The populists were very suspicious of professionals, perhaps even anti-professional. They challenged professional advice and sought to exercise great control over the professionals they employed. The pluralists and clientelists were not anti-professional. The pluralists tended to see professionals as their allies in their continuing struggles and clientelists, accepting the notions of hierarchy, and did not question the professionals' role but instead judged particular professionals as either supportive or un-supportive.

The second part of the chapter will focus on class conflicts within the corridor population. These conflicts are complex in character because they are intermixed with issues of ethnicity and race in the project and are primarily intra-class conflicts between class strata. The immigrant status of much of the population plays a key role here. In the immigrant process the Latinos are channeled to the secondary labor market whereas the Americanos in the corridor function mostly in the primary labor force. The question of the relationship between class, ethnicity, and race is introduced in this chapter and examined further in the next chapter. Route 2 provides a view of this subject that is not often available.

The Professional-Managerial Class

Herbert Gans, in his famous 1962 study of urban renewal in the Italian working-class West End community of Boston, argues that most professionals act according to middle-class value patterns that have been institutionalized "in the recruitment and training of professionals, in the creation of a professional image and self-image, and most important, in the structure of professional-client relationships." He calls for planners to abandon their traditional methods for new approaches and relationships catering to the working class, who live in a "strange and hostile culture" (Gans 1962, pp. 306-308).

Gans has not been alone in these findings. Authors such as Fellman (1973) and Repo (1977), examining other later working-class planning experiences, reach similar conclusions. Two general solutions are offered to the problem. Some authors call for greater sensitivity on the planners' part to the "cultural" gap (Brooks and Stegman 1968) and, in the extreme, for equal dialogue between planner and working-class clients (Friedmann 1973). Others view the call for sensitivity or dialogue as insufficient and advocate a re-alignment of the professional-client relationship itself, for community control (Arnstein 1969; Altshuler 1970).

The class position of professionals is extremely complex because professionals, as a class, stand between the dominant and the working classes (Ehrenreich and Ehrenreich 1979; Fellman 1973). Professionals are charged with the class project of organizing and managing society.[7] They occupy positions within the social structure that require them to intercept and mediate social conflict as well as implement policies that are antagonistic to working class interests.[8] Professionals who, in attempting to align themselves with the working class, reject this role and participate in the empowering process discussed in the last chapter are, in effect, denying their class.

Class denial or the revolutionary extreme, "class death" creates two problems (Chabal 1983). First, the mere denial of class does not solve the "cultural" problem Gans describes. Although dialogue, one of the solutions proposed for the Gans problem, is a good metaphor for its resolution, it is easy to underestimate the complexity of the forces within the class and state that continually reinforce the cultural differences between classes.

Second, professionals who attempt to bridge this gap and align themselves with the working class are subject to the pull of their own class and the state toward their original class position. If they yield, they become agents of the state in conflict with the working class. If they don't yield, they risk ostracism by their class and the state and the loss of their value to the working class.

If the professionals become employed by the working-class community, i.e., subject to community control, they do not escape these problems. First, community control is never totally possible given the many external forces that impact on any community. Second, in addition to the problems of class denial discussed above, community control generates its own class dynamics. The professional, when truly subject to community control, becomes an employee of the community, a worker working for workers. The employee-professionals, however, still carry their class advantages. The confusion of class roles and the class advantages of the professional have often led to the charge that supposed community organizations are "staff dominated."

Class conflict then penetrates the solutions to the class conflict problem and is continually renewed throughout the community planning process. This is perhaps most obvious and intense in community-controlled situations. When the working class has a degree of control, its class interests are more fully articulated than in most situations. Typically, however, the interests of the working class are quickly overwhelmed by the dominant classes and their ally the state.

The Two Dimensions of Class Conflict

It is, perhaps, best to analyze the interaction of the working class and professionals in two dimensions: the cultural, a term used by Gans, and the structural, the institution of professionalism and all those elements of society that support that institution. It is the converging of these two dimensions that make the problem of cross-class cooperation so difficult.

The Culture of Class

In order for professionals to fulfill the destiny of their class origins and occupy the administrative and organizational roles they play in society, they must undergo an extensive socialization process differing significantly from that of the working class. Socialization entails extensive internalization of specific values, personality traits, social skills, and attitudes in an individual's formative years and their continual reinforcement in later occupational roles.

The professional-managerial class (PMC) is introduced to, educated, and acts in a world of economic opportunity where class actors must appear to be "rational," "theoretical," and "articulate." Professionals insist upon the necessity of maintaining autonomy in their lives so that they may exercise "independent, expert judgment." Work, to the PMC, is not just earning a living, but is a means for personal expression and fulfillment (Hochschild 1979; Kallenberg and Griffin 1980).

The working class is born, educated, and exists in a world that lacks much of the calm veneer of PMC life. It is a world that also lacks much of the opportunity for "fulfillment." Work is usually more detached and instrumental but can become all absorbing, particularly during the intensity of a strike. The compulsion of the "appearances of reason" does not have the same central importance, and "articulateness" is many times replaced by other modes of communication. Conflict at work and economic pressure at home result in either silence or confrontational, blunt and direct communication (Halle 1984; Kohn 1976, 1969; Rubin 1976; Levinson 1974; Miller and Reisman 1964.).[9] Problems can quickly lose the supposed "objective" distance of the PMC world and be defined in terms of cause-and-effect with individuals ascribing blame to others

(Miller, 1979). In the working-class world, personal autonomy is rare and interdependency common (Gans 1962; Komarovsky 1962; Handell and Rainwater 1964; Patterson 1964; Sennett and Cobb 1973; Ehrenreich and Ehrenreich 1979).

Quite obviously class socialization, like the distinctions between classes, is complex, with a multitude of exceptions and overlaps. Ethnicity, class, and gender, for example, are deeply intertwined, and some people do move between the classes. Yet, despite their complicated nature, very distinct class-related cultural tendencies do exist.[10]

Structure

Professionalism emerged as a major social force in this country during the progressive era after the turn of this century (Wiebe 1967). Rapid industrialization of the United States created opportunities for people with technical, mediative, and administrative skills who could rationalize industry, manage the emergent industrial working class, and advantageously insert themselves in the social structure.[11]

Within this structure, as Larson found in her seminal study of professions, "the monopoly {corporate}, state and academic sectors . . . define the organizational contexts within which professions find new instruments for self-organization and self-expression." These large, bureaucratic organizations, which are dominated by the interests of the upper classes, "provide the climate of ideological legitimation for both old and new professions; they also provide models, sponsorship, equipment, and resources" (Larson 1977, p. 145).

Over time, the class interests of the PMC have increasingly become tied to the perpetuation of the state. For the PMC to maintain the high living standards, great work autonomy and prestige associated with professional status, it must lend its prestige, support, and loyalty to the various government and corporate bureaucracies whose policies are usually antagonistic to working-class interests. Although the class interests of the PMC often place it in conflict with some of these policies, the class has usually yielded to the pressures placed on it by the state to serve upper-class interests.[12]

The problems generated by these cultural and structural contexts are not easily overcome even by professionals who willingly subject themselves to community control. The deep socialization of class cannot be overcome simply by intentions. If a professional finds a method of bridging the gap, the state pressures the professional to abandon such attempts and resume the original, conflictual class behavior.

The problem of bridging class conflict is best explored in the concept of dialogue that has been suggested as a solution. Dialogue requires equality between the two actors in a dyad (Buber 1970). The class positions of the professional and working-class clientele are clearly not equal. Athough, as discussed in Chapter 3, Buber limited the problem of establishing dialogue in the formation of community to giving oneself, he revealed the importance of the class dimension when it comes to professionals having dialogue with their "clients" (Buber 1965, p. 176). When professionals engage in a helping relationship with their clients, the professionals are seen as competent helpers and clients as helpless needy recipients. The help flows one way and the relationship is not mutual. Neither party in this characterization of the professional-client relation-ship can give him- or herself in Buber's sense and the relationship, therefore, cannot be dialogic.

Paulo Freire has focused on problems of language in attaining dialogue (1970). Speech is clearly class-laden, with the professional having socially-defined effective speech and the working class socially-defined deficient speech. These values make dialogue very difficult. Carol J. Pierce Colfer in her study on communication among socially defined "unequals" found that people given lower status were inhibited in the "free expression" of their ideas and that this interfered with any mutual learning process (Colfer 1983, p. 278).

The Populist Period

Professionals Working for the State

Class conflict emerged at a very early stage in the project when the residents and the professionals grappled over who was in control of the project. From the residents' point of view, the resolution of the issue was clear; from the bureaucracy's the issue was far from resolved. The HCD professionals working in the field and having day-to-day contact with the tenants were often converted to the tenants' position on the fate of the property. They aligned themselves with the working-class community, in effect abandoning their class role, and sought ways to support the tenants' efforts.

When they returned to their main office to represent the residents' position, they were often criticized for abandoning the bureaucracy's position on the project in favor of what was seen as a fanciful position of the residents, i.e. "going native." The professionals, under pressure, would sometimes yield and return to the residents "to get control of the situation" and assert their professional dominance. This act, in turn, prompted the residents to criticize them for abandoning the residents' efforts, and another cycle of conflict would begin.

The conflict over control came to a head when the tenants decided to withhold a portion of their rent against the wishes of HCD. The tenants wanted Caltrans to repair their homes while negotiations for the purchase of the property proceeded. They felt a rent strike was the only way to force Caltrans to repair the conditions that had developed while the property was awaiting first demolition and later sale. HCD saw itself as the broker negotiating the purchase of the property for the community from Caltrans and felt a strike would eliminate any chance it had of success.

HCD responded to the tenants' action by threatening to abandon its negotiations and stop funding the community organizing effort. No one outside the project residents, including HCD, had looked closely at the condition of the property. When the tenants organized public tours of the problem buildings, HCD was shocked back into the process. The strike was won and negotiations to buy the property continued.

Before this crisis many professionals in and out of HCD had attended the development corporation meetings. At times they outnumbered the residents. The Route 2 project was technically interesting, and the professionals hoped to test out their ideas. After the strike action, most of these professionals disappeared. The question of direct control was now resolved.

The remaining HCD staff did attempt to gain indirect class control. They asserted class hegemony by first making every effort to put professionals on the board of directors of R2CHC and when that effort failed, conditioning the sale of the property to R2CHC on the creation of a professional advisory board to assist the development corporation. When the bureacracts sent professionals as potential board members to the early R2CHC meetings, the community managed to find reasons for rejecting all but one of the outsiders. Eventually the professionals got the message and gave up. When the bureaucracy insisted on the creation of an advisory commission of professionals, the community didn't resist. The commission was formed, never met, and played no role in the process.

Professionals Working for R2CHC

The development corporation, once formed, obtained funding and hired a professional staff. This staff was clearly sympathetic to the tenants' interests. With professionals now working for the tenant-dominated development corporation, class conflict was turned on its head. Workers who formerly took orders from the PMC now found themselves on top. Drawing their models from their own life and work experiences—typically routinized, harsh, and heavily supervised labor—the leaders replicated those experiences with the professionals of the project. Very little discretion or autonomy was given the corporation's staff. No one was hired, even temporary workers, without board interview and approval. All checks, regardless of the amount, had to be signed by officers of the corporation.

Accustomed, in working-class fashion, to conceptualize phenomena more in terms of observable cause and effect relationships, the residents did not accept the current vogue of separating the responsibility for making policy for the board and leaving administration to the staff (Mayer 1983). The board undertook a meticulous, painstaking and challenging review of every proposed plan and nearly every proposed document in the project. The residents, in order to prevent the professionals from "talking circles around their heads," moved to slow the professionals down and insisted upon understanding every step in the process as a condition for its being taken.

To further rein in the professionals, periodic meetings were held without staff members, called "no-staff raps." The residents felt the presence of the staff sometimes inhibited their free discussion. These no-staff raps usually dealt with questions relating to the goals of the project and served to keep residents on their own path rather than yielding unthinkingly to professionals' advice on what "had to be done."

There were also moments when individual residents attacked what they saw as overpaid professionals for not working hard enough, although the professionals worked long hours in overcoming technical obstacles to putting the cooperatives together. The residents saw the staff sitting around the office talking to one another or to other professionals on the telephone. It didn't look like work to these residents used to working-class jobs, and they expressed their views (Halle 1984).

The residents' expressions of their views were often rough, on occasion almost leading to physical combat. Professionals accustomed to work situations that call for more dispassionate, rational, and polite forms of communication were unprepared for the bluntness of the complaining residents. With their autonomy constrained, their actions slowed, and being subject to occasional personal attack, much of the staff developed an embattled mentality.

Staff members responded by collectivizing. Acting on their own, they abandoned the hierarchical staff structure set up by the board, held their own private meetings and tried to develop strategies to get their way. Some of the staff attacked the credibility of particularly troublesome residents (bosses) and once threatened a strike after an employee was fired. Interestingly, they also found class solidarity and support from outside professionals who urged them to assert themselves. All of this was very worker-like. Indeed the interplay of these conflicting behavioral tensions moved the situation more toward class conflict typical of working-class occupational settings than toward dialogical understanding and equality.

The Key to Working-Class Control

The basis of working-class control came not just from the contractual relationship between the corporation and its employees. It also came from the stance of the leadership in R2CHC. Although the literature describes the working class as more instrumental and more cautious than professionals, there are occasions when the working class takes extraordinary risks well beyond those usually engaged in by the PMC. As a number of researchers who have examined strikes have found, the pent-up desires for dignity, respect, and some degree of control over alienating working conditions, underlie the wage demands of many strikes (Hyman 1977; Lane and Roberts 1971; Cliff 1970; Gorz 1965; Kornhauser 1954).

The residents of the Route 2 corridor, living on the margins of society and experiencing only limited control over their home life, similarly desired more than simply avoiding displacement. They wanted what is most difficult for working-class people in this society to attain, dignity and control. They were willing to risk the homes they were fighting for to get it, much as workers risk the jobs they seek to improve in a strike. Their willingness to take risks prompted not only the rent strike, but also led the populist leadership in R2CHC to repeatedly reject any professional advice that might threaten its loss of control despite the apparent risk to the overall project.

For example, the professionals seeking financing for the project had difficulty finding a lender interested in loaning money to scattered-site limited-equity cooperatives. They began to recommend syndication of the property to raise what they thought was needed capital. The leadership demanded to be taught about syndication before it made a decision and after having its questions answered, took a position against syndication. Syndication involves the sale of ninety-nine percent of property ownership to people who can make use of the tax deductions available in a real estate purchase while one percent of the ownership is kept by the cooperative along with vestiges of managerial control.[13] Although a syndication can be structured so that the residents can buy back the ninety-nine percent interest in the property they sold when the tax deductions are functionally exhausted, the uncertainties of the process carried too much risk of loss of control. The residents had come too far to give up what they wanted more than their housing.

The counter-hegemonic elements of the leadership set a tone which dominated the process. The president of the board articulated the R2CHC response to the ultimate professional threat of technical infeasibility: "We have been poor all our lives. If this project works or not, we will still be poor. You have got to understand that to us this project is not worth doing if it is not done right." This willingness to risk failure always unnerved the professionals. It put them on the defensive many times throughout the project and blunted the normal sharp dominating edge of expertise.

Heightened Class Conflict

The resistance of the board to syndication and other similar schemes put added pressure on the professionals to solve the financing problem. The options to purchase the property lasted for only two years. Local lenders had no experience with lending to cooperatives, much less scattered-site limited-equity cooperatives. As the option time passed without financing success, tension grew and created more intense conflict between the staff and the residents.

The next focus of the class conflict was over the question of whether the property should be organized into one large or five smaller cooperatives. The study by the Los Angeles Community Design Center found that the 2.25-mile-long project passed through several separate geographic neighborhoods. The residents agreed with the finding of the study and, early in the process, decided to divide the corridor spatially into five separate cooperatives to facilitate democratic participation and community control.

The professional staff supported democratic participation and community control and realized, along with the board, that participation and control would be greatly enhanced if the project was packaged as five separate cooperatives. Yet, they also had to confront the reality that the institutions with which they had to operate were unresponsive and even hostile to the success of the project. For example, when staff members approached financial institutions to obtain financing for the five cooperatives, they were typically met with skepticism by loan officers unfamiliar with cooperatives. On occasion the staff was literally laughed out of lenders' offices.

By the time they began their search for financing the professionals also felt overwhelmed by the intensity of the participatory process. They remembered all too well the meticulous and painstaking reviews the board of the development corporation had undertaken of their work in the past and the emotional battering they had received in those sessions. To move from the board of the development corporation to the boards of five separate cooperatives would mean repeating those types of sessions five more times.

The staff members felt that they and the project would not survive such a process, particularly given the limited resources available to organize and package the cooperatives. Consequently they proposed that the cooperatives be merged into one big cooperative. Like workers in a factory facing impossible production quotas, they tried first to reason with the board, and when that failed, they resorted to resistance and conflict.

Conflict dominated a series of stormy meetings on the subject. The professionals presented their plan for one big cooperative and argued that this was the only way to maintain some degree of democracy, retain the options, and secure financing within the resources and time available. The board, for its part, responded that whether the staff was right or not on the question of what was possible given the constraints, one big coop would simply not work socially. Also, as is typical of employers, the board members had doubts about what was, in effect, the staff's complaint of an unreasonable "speed up" of the work. They would not yield and insisted that the staff find a better alternative.

The federation solution that emerged indicates how open conflict can result in creative solutions. In this case the conflict created qualitatively different organizational forms and relationships. The board and staff found the solution to the impasse in the classic idea of federating the cooperatives. In the federation the leadership of the separate cooperatives joined together for decision making that would affect each individual cooperative. Specifically the board of the development corporation was transformed from a board made up of the remnants of the R2TA leadership into a board made up of the officers of each cooperative. This meant that the staff still had to package and arrange financing for five cooperatives, but that on many matters, they could find agreement at a single meeting rather than five.

The solution provided for community control and technical feasibility. It emerged over time and through the pressures that each side brought to bear on the other. Original opposing elements were synthesized into a new form. The technical feasibility concerns of the staff were embodied in the single, interlocking board, while the concerns of the board that the project be pursued at a democratic level were met by maintaining the independence of the five cooperatives through federation.

The Pluralist Period

The federation served its purpose, but it, along with all such "solutions," generated other tensions within and between the cooperatives, the federation board, and the staff. As discussed in Chapter 2, the pluralist leaders saw the federation as a flawed model permeated with conflicts of interest. They also did not see the staff like the populists. They were not anti-professional, but saw professionals as allies or opponents in their struggles. A professional on your side fought those on the other side.

The manifestation of this shift was the reformulation of Nuestra. The populists and staff always had difficulty presenting the federation in schematic form. Some had drawn a radiating wheel with R2CHC at the center, but that wasn't right because R2CHC did not hold a central position. The group had settled on the image of an umbrella for R2CHC, but that didn't really fit either. When the populists were replaced by pluralists, the staff accustomed to the populist approach was replaced by staff more accustomed to traditional work environments. The new staff of Nuestra with its pluralist allies set about dismantling the federation structure. Its members had a completely new vision. They wanted a much more traditional organizational structure that could be schematized clearly with boxes and lines of authority that fit the pluralists' need for clarity in power relationships. The transformation was completed with a reformulated Nuestra and the creation of R2FHC when the clientelists inspired the separation of the business from the social aspects of the project.

The reformulated Nuestra under pluralist leadership emerged as a staff-dominated organization. The relationship between Nuestra and the cooperatives was more individualized and distant. Nuestra was not at the center of the circle of coops nor an umbrella that sheltered the coops, it was a satellite at the side of any chart. Competition for attention rather than a collective struggle for control became necessary, a competition that could be manipulated by the staff and pluralists. Many private loyalties were developed and exploited. Many private talks took place that included the phrase "Don't tell . . . but." In general the flow of information, the life blood of democracy, became greatly controlled.

The Clientelist Period

During the clientelist period, the staff began to fill the patron role. This began with the interviews for executive positions in Nuestra. The interviews were heavily attended by immigrant Latinos. The populist leadership sat back feeling it was time for the reins of the project to pass on to the emerging activists. What took place in these interviews, however, surprised the populists. After the candidates, including people from aristocratic Latin American backgrounds, made their presentations, few questions were asked. Instead the upper-class applicants were praised and thanked for considering the possiblility of working for the residents.

The clientelist leadership did not question the patron role, but rather began to ask, in effect, if staff members were good or bad patrons. The issue was whether the staff members cared about the people or did not care about the people. The conclusion was they didn't care. This question had been present before, but now it was encouraged. The populists were not interested in the question and focused on resident control and the end product. The pluralists made a power alliance with staff members, and as long as they were on the same side, did not question either outcomes or sentiments.

Some of the clientelists responded much as James Scott set forth in the book *Weapons of the Weak* (Scott 1985).[14] They publicly assumed a noticeably subservient posture in the presence of staff leadership while privately engaging in passive resistance, slowdowns, withdrawal and attack by rumor. Others became openly hostile and attacked the staff to their faces for not caring. Much of what happened in this period is discussed in Chapter 6, but the end result was that it became increasingly difficult to gather a quorum for a Nuestra meeting. No one wanted to be outside the collective and "take care" of the business of the cooperatives only to be subject to criticism of not caring for people. With people withdrawing, Nuestra became even more staff dominated.

When Nuestra was clearly failing, various organizational innovations were tried to reassert resident control, but they failed in the exhaustion of the period. With the focus on the staff, communication between the cooperatives declined. One cooperative sent a threatening note to the staff of Nuestra stating it would leave if its problems were not addressed. It sent a copy of the note to the president of Nuestra, but it was misaddressed and wasn't delivered. The cooperative's representatives stopped attending meetings, but it was not clear under the new form of organization whether this was necessary. No Nuestra board member took steps to find out why the cooperative's attendance stopped, and the staff of Nuestra did not inform the board of the threat to leave.

When the cooperative's problems were not addressed, it left Nuestra. Nuestra's board first heard of the withdrawal when the staff circulated a copy of the letter stating the cooperative had found a new management company. The withdrawal provoked a crisis. It worsened the already fragile economics of the company. Something had to be done. In an extraordinary expression of disempowerment, the board of Nuestra gave up and chose to dissolve the organization rather than to try further reorganization or replace its staff. They had tried and failed. They decided it could not be done. Mejo Repo's writing about a community planning effort in Canada warns that the working-class is not always ready for self-help efforts and that failure can teach them the wrong lesson (Repo 1977). Consistent with Repo's fears the residents took responsibility for the failure and assumed their own inability to master the task.

Class Struggle Among the Residents

Class conflict was not limited to conflict between the residents and professionals. There was also class-based conflict within the corridor population. The corridor population, while overwhelmingly working-class, is composed of various strata of the working class. Certainly the leadership tends to be skilled workers with many union members. A few of the leaders have moved into administrative positions and are approaching membership in the professional-managerial class. A great deal of the corridor population, however, works in the secondary labor market with garment workers, domestic workers, and contract labor in significant numbers.

The split between the primary and secondary labor force in the leadership and general population also roughly matches the division between Americanos and Latinos in the project. Because of the tendency of labor market membership to be coterminous with ethnicity, many of the class-strata-based conflicts in the corridor are perceived by residents of cooperatives as ethnic or race conflicts. Ethnicity and race are the primary subject of the next chapter, but the remaining pages of this chapter will examine the elusive issue of the relationship between class, race, and ethnicity.[15]

In the Route 2 project ethnicity is a major issue if for no other reason than language, a primary element of ethnicity which divides the population and prevents full direct interaction. Race, on the other hand, is an issue that seems to have been superimposed on the setting. Within the diverse Americano population it had rarely been an issue. It appeared as a programatic issue only as the immigrant Latino population was integrated into the racialism of U.S. society.

Ethnicity or race as analytic categories do not perfectly fit the Route 2 project situation. Examples of the misfit are found in the sometimes frayed relations between Chicanos in the project and the immigrant Latinos, and the fact that the Latinos in the project come from fourteen different countries including a range of types, in racial terms, from white to black or, in ethnic terms, from European to African. As is discussed elsewhere, many Latino immigrants take the view that if Chicanos cannot speak Spanish, they are no longer Latinos. The categories the immigrants used, Latino and Americano, while having significant ethnic content, more clearly divide immigrant from non-immigrant than ethnic or racial groups from one another.

The emphasis on immigrant status represented in the Americano/Latino categories in the Route 2 project echoes a distinction described by Robert Miles (Miles 1982). Although Miles is writing about England, much of what he has written seems to apply to the Route 2 project.[16] He argues that race (as opposed to racism) has no objective basis in the current historical period and is, therefore, an inappropriate category to be employed in understanding social relations. He sees race instead as a social construction of the racial state that is employed through the practice of racism to divide the working class.[17] Ethnicity on the other hand has material characteristics such as language and presents a real, rather than ideological, category. This has certainly been the case in the Route 2 project. Ethnicity and language are a major focus of the next chapter. Beyond this Miles argues that the immigrant process itself is central to understanding social relations, particularly its role in the fractionalization of the working class.

The central role of immigrant status is demonstrated in the Route 2 project. The tendency for the Latinos and Americanos to have different positions in the labor force introduces a number of structural elements into the project beyond the obvious one of variation in financial resources.[18] Workers in the primary labor force usually work nine-to-five, five-days-a-week jobs. Workers in the secondary economy have much more irregular hours (Sassen-Koob, 1985). Some of the more marginalized workers in the cooperatives are day laborers who cannot easily control their work hours or plan their free time. In this setting establishing meeting times is difficult. The Americanos usually want to meet on week-day nights. The Latinos are often unavailable on these nights and prefer instead either Friday night or weekend meetings. Friday night meetings are a particular anathema to the Americanos.

Scheduling meetings is not the only problem. Autonomy in the work place is also a factor. Having access to a phone during work hours is important to conducting the business of the cooperative. Since the Housing Authority is primarily a nine-to-five office with phone hours between 10:00 AM and 12:00 PM and 1:00 PM and 4:00 PM, the opportunities for communication are limited. Many of the Latinos work in very regulated environments with little opportunity to communicate with the outside world or take time off for meetings. Workers in the primary labor force have more freedom during working hours. Certainly those members of the cooperatives with administrative positions have a great deal more freedom.

The role of class emerged clearly within the Latino population. Different countries have sent various classes to the corridor or sent more people with rural rather than urban backgrounds. For example, the Cubans in the project tend to be from major cities with petite-bourgeoisie or professional-managerial backgrounds and college educations. The Mexicans in the project tend to be rural and have minimal educations. The class educational divisions have resulted in language fights over the style of Spanish to be used and in other episodic conflicts. More than once the charge of racism has been leveled by one Latino against another.[19] The charge suggests that the offender has seperated him- or herself from the group and considers him- or herself better than other Latinos.

Class difference was a major factor in a conflict that emerged when a group of very low-income Mexican residents, who lived in overcrowded quarters without open space, felt deliberately snubbed when they attended an organizing party held in a much higher-income Cuban neighbor's backyard on a hot summer night rather than in the hosts' spacious house.[20] The party was held outside due to the heat and because the varnish was drying on the newly refinished floors inside. The Mexicans had held meetings in their modest apartments and didn't understand why they were meeting outside. The reasons did not satisfy the offended. Why did the host have to refinish his floors that weekend? Weren't they good enough to be invited inside?

It may be that a class mix is necessary to make the project work. The cooperatives certainly require both mental and manual skills. Finances have to be managed, HUD regulations have to be interpreted, and buildings have to be maintained. It might be possible through training to create the necessary mix of skills within a single strata, but the time and resources this training would require have never been available in the Route 2 project.

The next chapter will show how the Americanos and Latinos expressed their strata positions by focusing more on either mental or manual skills in the selection of new residents. In part this is an expression of class differences in the population and as yet unresolved class/ethnic/ideological conflicts within the cooperatives.

Conclusion

The populists saw themselves in a class struggle. They believed that although they won their battle against Caltrans to gain control of their homes the class struggle continued. They treated the professionals as potential class enemies and sought to assert their control over the professionals' work process. The professionals fought back in part as workers and in part as privileged members of the professional-managerial class. They failed during the development phase in loosening the bounds placed on them. Community control with its internal contradictions was asserted.

The pluralists did not share the focus on class and did not see the professionals as class enemies. Professionals held power which the pluralists sought to harness. In the search for power the pluralists were consumed in part by the power of the professionals to control the flow of information and the course of events. When together with the clientelists they freed Nuestra from its community bounds and set it on a course of professional control, they, in effect, disempowered the community. The result was unfortunate. Nuestra was too difficult an undertaking to be turned over to the professionals without the aid of the energy and good will of the community. It died an unfortunate death and taught the community a lesson it is taking time to unlearn.

Class conflicts within the Route 2 population have also been a factor in the life of the project. They have not, however, been clearly seen as class conflicts. As is discussed further in the next chapter, class is masked by the ethnic and racial categories that seem inevitable given the multiethnic nature of the corridor population. Only recently has the role of class begun to become clear to the residents. Whether they can sort out the basis of their conflicts and find a solution to them remains to be seen.

Notes

1.   Restructuring is a complex concept. It is best discussed in the sense that it is used here by my colleague Ed Soja (1989). The Route 2 project is a product of restructuring in many ways. The change in government capacity, the change in the economy that contributed to the in migration of many of the project residents, and the real estate market in which the project developed are all in part products of the restructuring.

2.   Asset sell-off has become a usual part of governmental budgeting including that at the federal level (United States General Accounting Office, 1988). This has raised many issues including as in this case the inherent functions of government.

3.   See Hartman, C. et al. (1982).

4.   Martin Carnoy (1984) sets out seven primary theories of the state, two liberal, one corporatist and four class based theories. The first liberal group, the "populist conservative" sees the state as increasingly lead by corrupt and autonomous bureaucracy that unduly interferes with the free market. The second is the "pluralists" reflecting the will of the majority. The "corporatists" believe the state can rationalize society. The class theories include "instrumentalists," "logic of capital," "autonomous," and "relative-autonomous" theorists.   The instrumentalists view the state as instrument of the ruling class. The logic of capital theorists see the state's role as maintaining and stimulating capital accumulation in the face of a falling rate of profit. The autonomous theorists see the state as responsible for accumulation, but also see the state as an independent mediator of class struggle posed between capital and labor.   The relative autonomous theorists believe that "the dominant class is a conscious class and attempt to influence and control the State as an object of its socioeconomic power, but at the same time, because of the existence of class struggle, the State must appear to be autonomous from dominant class power in order to retain its very legitimacy as a state." In this theory class struggle takes place in the heart of the state (pp. 253-254). My position is closest to the later view, and the term state is used in this sense in this book.

5.   For an excellent account of a similar successful, working-class controlled planning experience see Fraser (1972).

6.   Much of the first part of this chapter is adapted from Heskin and Bandy (1986a; 1986b).

7.   See Walker (1979) for a thorough debate concerning the issue of the professional-managerial class (PMC). Regardless of whether professionals are conceived of as constituting an independent class, as the Ehrenreichs see it, or are considered a sector or fragment of the working class due to their lack of ownership of the means of production and the need to sell their labor power to their capitalist bosses as others would argue, it is clear that the class position of professionals is a contradictory and middling one that places them in an antagonistic relationship with the working class.

8.   The PMC also plays an important ideological role within the structure of society. According to McKenny (1981) and Larson (1977) professionalism serves to divide the working class and justify the class-based inequities in society as the "natural" result of differences in individual abilities and determination.

9.   Research on the working class should be employed with caution. Much of the research in the U.S. has been flawed with inappropriate, class-biased methodologies that have relied too heavily on survey research (Spencer 1977; Broadhead and Rist 1978). Research into the class structure of the U.S. has been imprecise, overstating the size of the "middle-class" and overemphasizing the study of superficial status ranking variable (Huber and Form 1973; Levison 1974;

Parker 1972). The attempt here is to draw on research that has avoided these methodological flaws.

10. Jackman and Jackman (1983) claim to have found in their research that "in feelings of group identity, interpretation of group differences, and in the perception of group interests, social class is at least as strong a factor as race and is often stronger." Levison has pointed out that most minorities are working class and much minority poverty is working-class poverty (see also Greer 1977; Fredrickson 1982). Additionally, some activists in the women's movement have found that despite a common oppression, the issues of working-class women are different from those of women from other classes and that class continues to be a major issue within the feminist movement (Red Apple Collective 1978; Sidel 1978; Luttrell 1984).

11. According to the Ehrenreichs (1979, p. 16), "The accumulation and concentration of capital which occurred in the last decades of the nineteenth century allowed for an extensive reorganization of working class life - both in the community and in the workplace. ... The net effect of this drive to reorganize and reshape working class life was the social atomization of the working class: the fragmentation of work (and workers) in the productive process, a withdrawal of aspirations from the workplace into private goals, the disruption of autonomous working class culture and its replacement by 'mass culture' defined by privatized consumption of commodities (health care, recreation, etc.)." It was into this process that the PMC inserted itself and emerged as a class.

12. For a thorough review and discussion of the literature on this issue see Derber (1982).

13. Syndication is employed to raise capital. Outside investors buy a large portion of the housing project as "limited partners" in order to obtain the tax benefits from the depreciation of the buildings (Coulter, 1983).

14. Scott's conclusion is that his findings of resistance among the poor to mistreatment argue against Gramsci's position on hegemony. I do not agree. Hegemony is a deeper phenomenon than the level Scott measures. Hegemony would express itself in the acceptance of clientelism as a model and the recreation of a new patron should a particular patron be overthrown.

15. There is certanly voluminous material on the subject of ethnicity, race, and class. See for example the excellent collection of articles in Rex and Mason (1986).

16. The global phenomenon of restructuring contributes to making this juxtaposition possible. See Soja (1989, p. 188).

17. For a further discussion of this point and its implications see Fields (1982). It is important to note that Miles sees *racism* as important if not central to societal analysis. If, however, I am correct that racism is not a primary internal factor in the Route 2 project, then racism itself does not come into play. The extent to which racism exists in the project is a subject of discussion in the next chapter.

18. This is somewhat offset internally by the subsidization of the monthly carrying charges of the lower income residents. The housing in Route 2 is sometimes treated as transitional housing on the way to unregulated ownership and is employed as part of the immigration process. Over the years that Caltrans

owned the housing many immigrants moved on as they successfully integrated into the economy. This process contributed to a collection and over-representation of those who did not have this success. The Americanos have also gone through a similar process of passing through this housing on their way to unregulated ownership, however, they tend to have a head start in the process.

19. Interestingly I rarely heard the charge publicly made against an Americano although as the interviews discussed in the next chapter indicate, the feeling existed in the Latino population.

20. Nationalism is also a factor in Route 2. Long held national animosity clearly played a role in what is called motivation in the next chapter. How one approaches a problem is a result of history. Nationalism in this context shares a great deal with racism.

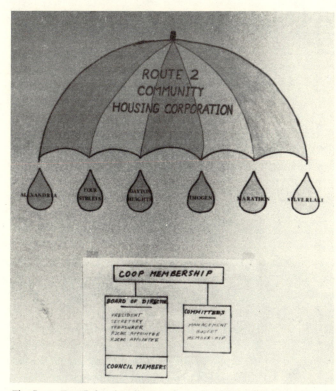

The Route Two Federation diagram drawn by the cooperative residents (photo by Mel Chavez).

The Route Two Cooperative residents (photos on this page and the following page by Mel Chavez).

5

Ethnicity, Language, and Racism

Los Angeles is very much a segregated multiethnic city (Research Group on the Los Angeles Economy 1989). Latinos from various countries concentrate in East Los Angeles, the inner ring around downtown and the eastern portion of the San Fernando Valley; blacks concentrate in the south-central part of the city and the eastern portion of the valley; and Asians concentrate in various ethnic enclaves bearing the name of their nationality. The multiethnic character of the city's population has increased due to an in-migration of nearly two million people from third world countries over the past twenty years (Soja, Heskin, and Cenzatti 1985). The national racial minorities have become a local majority (Adler 1983a, p. 482).

A few areas in Los Angeles differ from this general pattern. Many of these are transitional zones where ethnicities mix and intermarriage is common. These open areas also often serve as ports of entry for different national groups. Schools in these zones typically report that their student population speaks more than fifty languages and dialects. The Route 2 corridor is in one of these uniquely diverse and internationalized zones.

During Caltrans' ownership much of the Route 2 corridor housing acted as port-of-entry housing. The primary in-migrants have been Latinos from some fourteen Latin American countries who make up about sixty percent of the population. Other parts of the world are also represented in smaller numbers. The remainder of the population is Americano equally divided between whites and a mix of native-born minority groups. Monolingualism is common across the population including both large numbers of English-speaking-only and Spanish-speaking-only individuals.

The project has an exceptional multicultural image.[1] This has attracted the liberal politicians and professionals who supported the project. Internally, issues of ethnicity, language, and racism have been omnipresent. They are endemic to multiethnic environments and denote that interaction is taking place. At their best these tensions are representative of a dynamic process of creation.

As in other matters, the various ideological groups that dominated the Route 2 project had different reactions to the project's multiethnicity. The populist approach to the multiethnicity of the project can best be characterized as multiculturalism. Multiculturalism is a form of social relations in which different ethnicities "maintain their identities, but engage in extensive interaction and mutual influence." When multiculturalism occurs, "relations between single minorities and the dominant culture are complemented by organized interaction among minorities," and members of ethnic groups become "able and willing to communicate and cooperate across cultural boundaries" (Heskin and Heffner 1987, p. 526). In the process each group's identity is continually enriched and reconstructed.

This progressive populist approach must be distinguished from the color blindness claimed by current-day conservatives sometimes referred to as "authoritarian populists."[2] The Route 2 populists are quite aware of ethnic differences and celebrate the differences rather than ignore them. To many of the populists multiculturalism is not an approach to a problem, the problem of multiethnicity, but an attraction that keeps them living in and working on the project. In their view the coops with many mixed ethnic families as members should be an oasis from the racial state outside the project.[3] As discussed in Chapter 2, a nondiscrimination pledge has been repeated over and over again in the project, and the relations among the Americanos of all ethnicities reflect its intention. The relations between the Americanos and the immigrant Latinos have not been as healthy. The gap has proved more difficult to bridge.

Reacting to years of experience with racism, the pluralists see minority ethnic groups as bases of power for fighting historical and continuing oppression. They emphasize the importance of communication between groups rather than between individuals. Multiethnicity or multiculturalism is not valued *per se*. Pluralists believe multiethnicity should be managed with full consciousness of the needs of each ethnic group. In their focus on needs of competing groups, however, the needs of outside groups are not of primary concern. Some theorists characterize this primary focus on the needs of one's own group as nationalism or cultural nationalism (Omi and Winant 1986, pp. 103-108).[4]

Another twist in the particular approach of the pluralists in the Route 2 project is their requirement of activism for "true" ethnic membership. This allowed the pluralists to form the Latino caucus and at the same time delegitimize non-participating Latinos in the cooperative where old members were divided from new members.

Felix Padilla discusses the active requirement for ethnic identity in his book, *Latino Ethnic Consciousness* (Padilla 1985). Padilla divides the Latino approach to ethnic identity into two camps, traditional and emergent. The traditional group identifies Latinos by their shared culture focusing primarily on the groups' common language. The emergent group focuses on conflict and limits Latinos to those who "come forward and identify themselves and get "involved in the issues" (p. 76). The organizers who moved into the Route 2 cooperatives and formed the pluralist group were in this emergent group.[5]

The clientelists' approach to the issue of ethnicity is heavily influenced by their immigrant status.[6] Their national identities can push them apart, reflecting old feuds and more recent class conflicts, but they also find commonalities in their pasts and in their current experiences in a strange land. Clientelists emphasize the obligations of immigrants to family members also undergoing the immigrant process. Strong elements of what may in other contexts be called nepotism come into play.

The clientelist immigrants undergo a process of identity reformulation as they integrate into this country.[7] They learn about racism in this country, their position within the racial state, and the country's racial rhetoric. In the process they develop common ground with the pluralists. According to Padilla, however, they are far more in the tradition of Latinos in the United States than the pluralists. Ethnic solidarity offers the clientelists a means of coping with the process of immigration but is not necessarily a base for political action. As is seen in Chapter 6, the immigrant population, while not as politically focused, can be organized and act with considerable effectiveness. This difference in focus, however, sets up points of friction between the pluralists and clientelists that play themselves out in the Route 2 project.

In this chapter the issues that arise from multiethnicity will be examined. The first part of the chapter will consider the barriers to communication the populists discovered in their efforts to achieve multiculturalism and the role the pluralists played in encouraging wider participation in the project. The populist emphasis on openness and participation received its greatest test here. The second part of the chapter addresses the more difficult issue of racism as it is raised in the multiethnic environment of the corridor. In the diverse Route 2 corridor population many of the issues of our increasingly multiethnic society are being worked on hopefully to a successful resolution.[8]

Communication[9]

The R2TA and R2CHC and the cooperatives share much with other forms of organization. They can only function if they successfully achieve a formal arrangement for interaction toward common goals. To be effective the participants in these organizations must communicate; to communicate, they must have both the *ability* and the *motivation* to do so (Taylor and Simard 1975). Interpersonal conflict, or class and culture-based rivalry and differences in norms, values, and perceptions can all interfere with communication. As will be seen in the second portion of this chapter, perceptions of racism can certainly contribute to the motivation problem.

The issue of effective communication held particular importance in the organizing and development phases of the Route 2 project because of the dominant populist leadership. The populists insisted that problems ordinarily lightly passed over in the name of expediency be confronted and solved. Solutions could not be imposed from above (Adler 1983b, p. 362; Harris and Moran 1979). They insisted upon having an open debate and relied on it as a check on their actions. Individuals affected by issues were expected to participate. Language and culture can disrupt the smooth working of this process. They do in the Route 2 project.

The early leadership approached the communication problem in two ways. First, they sought to operate as bilingual an organization as possible by providing all notices, newsletters, and key cooperative documents in both English and Spanish and providing translation between English and Spanish at meetings.[10] Second, they hired Latino and Chicano bilingual organizers to work with the residents. The organizers would not only do their jobs as organizers but would also act as translators and multicultural mediators when needed (Taft 1981). The leadership was not very sophisticated about the meaning of this scheme in practice. Little was known about the requirements of bilingualism and interpretation, and few organizers were available who had experience in the type of organizing needed in the corridor. More organizers know about conflict-oriented organizing than about populist multicultural community building. Further, it is difficult for a multiethnic group to attract many of the best Latino and Chicano organizers. Many of these organizers are nationalists and, therefore, want to make their talents available to support their own group.

Ability

In the multiethnic-monolingual world of the Route 2 resident cross-cultural interpretation is certainly an essential element of communication. Cross-cultural interpretation requires a greater skill level than is usually available within groups such as those in the Route 2 project. Interpretation requires more than switching the words in one language for those in the other. The interpreter must convey a speaker's tone and gestures, and the context. Interpretation is situation-specific, and requires considerable familiarity with all the differences of culture, class, and gender contained in the audience (Seleskovitch 1976). In a technically sophisticated project like Route 2 it also requires technical proficiency with the language not readily available.

In the search for situational and audience-specific equivalents, an interpreter must call on a knowledge of the contextualization cues that allow listeners from different backgrounds to sort out the ambiguities inherent in all language. Disastrous confusions of meaning can result from misuse or misunderstanding of (1) non-verbal signals such as posture, gaze direction, facial expression, and body movements; (2) paraverbal signals such as intonation, tempo, and loudness of speech; and (3) the implicit semantics of technical jargon or dialect. The sum of these cues, together with strictly verbal content and presuppositions drawn from the context (physical location, social setting, history of encounters between the participants), will determine the specific meaning drawn from what is said (Gumperz 1982, 1976; Conklin and Lourie 1983, p. 262-76; Brislin 1980).

Over and over again this reality has been demonstrated in the project. Publishing a newsletter is extraordinarily difficult. On one memorable occasion four separate translations of a newsletter were completed before an acceptable version was obtained. Translators for the articles were sought from the Route 2 population. Several residents who volunteered claimed to be fully bilingual, but these individuals proved to be only partially bilingual and not up to the task. A supposedly professional hired translator was also unsuccessful. Finally a professional was located who could do the job. This was not an isolated incident. It took time to find people with sufficient skills to do similar tasks.

There was also a running debate about what style of Spanish should be used in the project. At one point the debate erupted into a near violent argument over whether the formal urban Spanish of the Cubans or the more informal rural Spanish of Mexican peasants should be used in fliers and newsletters. The Cubans felt Spanish would be defiled by the rural style. Others worried the mass of the residents would be unable to read the more formal Spanish text. Periodically committees of

Latinos from different countries were set up to decide what style of Spanish should be used and what words should be employed for the very technical terms of the housing cooperatives. Usually the the board would have to intercede by asking the committee to come to a resolution so the project could proceed.

In the early organizing period of the Route 2 project before funds were available to hire translators, the groups had no choice but to use members with varying degrees of bilingual skills to interpret at meetings. The job usually fell upon one of the bilingual members on the steering committee of R2TA. The person who usually translated also joined the R2CHC board and inherited the interpretation job for that group's first meetings. When organizers were hired, they often took over the job.

As was later learned, the organizers' skills at interpretation also varied greatly. In the life of the project ten people held organizer jobs, only one of whom had ever served as an interpreter before. In this period interpretation was often by summary or by whisper to a group on the side of the meeting. In large meetings sequential translation was provided to the best of the translator's ability. Much later in the process professional interpreters capable of simultaneous translation were hired for meetings. Even later in the process translation equipment (head sets) was sometimes employed.

Motivation

The Route 2 corridor population is no different than many other groups. Some people are eager to participate and others are not. Also some people who are willing to participate will make the extra effort required to communicate across cultures while others will not. An effective organizer must be able to bridge the intergroup biases and differences contained in the organization and bring the membership to active participation while recognizing and developing organic leadership. Various authors have described organizers as stimulants, catalysts, mobilizers, enablers, and trainers (Alinsky 1971, 1969; Fellman 1973; Kahn 1970; Molina 1978; Twelvetrees 1982). There is always a danger that the population will become dependent on the organizer and that the organizer will be drawn into a leadership position. In theory once the political/managerial skills are imparted to the residents and experience begins to accumulate, full responsibility for the organization devolves upon the resident leadership.

The multicultural mediator role that the organizers are expected to fill only further complicates the organizers' task. Mediators must understand expectations about the behavior and roles appropriate to given situations and resolve issues such as who approaches whom, whether an appeal is to reason or sympathy, whether demeanor is assertive or humble, whether etiquette is formal or casual, whether topics are intimate or impersonal (Taft 1981, p. 56). Errors in communicative deportment of this kind are especially serious, because they will be seen, not as simple misunderstandings, but as breaches of conduct attributable to attitude or character.

The mediator is the person who determines the intentionality of a cultural *faux pas*, as in the case of the outdoor party, and leads the group either in rage or friendly laughter in such moments. It is not enough to abstractly appreciate that a remark is an insult or a joke. The mediator must feel the insult or get the joke and ensure that everyone understands its meaning. It is this ability that allows the mediator to bond with all elements of the membership and bring them closer to bonding with each other (Taft, 1981).

The job of a multicultural mediator is to grasp and convey meaning beyond the limits of an interpreter's competence. Equivalents for everyday objects, events, and stereotypes that depend on shared experience require the mediator's intervention. To find semantic equivalents for metaphors or allegories requires the mediator's knowledge of the actual conditions of living in a specific culture, as distinct from the interpreter's knowledge of its linguistic conventions (Sechrist et.al. 1982).

The Organizers

The first organizer in the Route 2 project was not hired until shortly after the formation of R2CHC. The first money given directly to the development corporation was a small grant from the HCD to hire an organizer, called a coop education specialist. Two likely candidates applied. One was an Anglo man with limited organizing experience who had spent time in Latin America and was bilingual. The other was a Mexican woman, educated in this country, with about the same level of experience. The man had more technical knowledge of housing, but the woman was chosen for the position. It was felt that both her gender and her ethnicity would help her do a better job.[11]

Over the next five years the group obtained additional funding from various foundations to hire additional organizers. At one time there were three paid people serving as organizers. The organizers came from various ethnic backgrounds: the next two people hired were Chicanas; two later people who worked part-time were Cubanos; and then a Puertorriqueno was hired. These organizers were followed by a largely monolingual English-speaking Anglo woman and a Salvadoran man. Two Chicanos were the last full-time paid organizers in the project.

Only the Anglo woman was a professionally trained organizer although several of other organizers had held jobs that involved organizing. The Latinos were capable of varying degrees of bilingualism with some stronger in English and others in Spanish. The degree to which they served as bridges between the groups, and cultural mediators also varied. Some of the organizers were better at this function than others, although evidently as a group they did not successfully serve this function. The technical complexity of the project as well as the intercultural dynamics discussed earlier made this role difficult. Some of these organizers also seemed to see themselves more in pluralist terms, as monocultural advocates and brokers, rather than mediators.

Learning About the Requirements of Communication

The initial board of the development corporation was primarily made up of members of the R2TA steering committee who lived in multifamily housing. As has been discussed, although the board remained multiethnic, it was primarily made up of Americanos. Most of the Latino leadership lived in single-family houses that were not to be part of the cooperatives. This left a largely English-speaking, non-Latino board leading a majority immigrant Latino, largely Spanish-speaking population.

In this period the leadership was expanded, with the help of the organizers, but very few Latinos were among those added. Residents were organized into boards of directors of the individual cooperatives, and the cooperative boards were federated into the board of the development corporation. As the development corporation purchased and rehabilitated the property, the Latino population, in the main, went along with the process, but at a distance.

The most vocal Latinos to emerge in the early period were leaders of the dissent group described in Chapter 2. The experience of fighting off the revolt by this group began to acquaint the English-speaking populist board members with the means to involve the Latinos. As is discussed in Chapter 2, several Cuban residents along with a black resident of the multifamily property led a largely Latino dissident group that wanted the same private property rights as the people who lived in single-family property. The leadership decided to hire a professional translator for the meeting that grew out of this conflict because of its importance and expected complexity. A court-certified interpreter was hired and contributed extraordinarily to the well-attended and intense meeting, creating clarity and calming people down to the point that communication was possible.

The leadership noted the value of having a "real" interpreter and lamented not being able to afford such a person at all their meetings. Once with the encouragement of an organizer, a Latino resident came to a meeting to ask that an "independent" translator be provided at meetings. Unfortunately, the board reacted defensively to the request and did not seek to find out what the person really wanted. They had hired Latino organizers to do the translation and didn't know what else to do. They did not control what the organizers said in the translations and felt they had gone more than half way in reaching out to the Latinos. They felt unjustly accused of somehow biasing the translation. The organizer who encouraged the Latino to come to the meeting was silent and did not mediate the misunderstanding. It took some time for the board to gain a full understanding of what the Latinos wanted and change its position.

The everyday problem of language at development corporation meetings was complicated by the populists' approach. They insisted that every detail of every element of the process be reviewed. The federation/development corporation board took hours to gain a word-by-word understanding of every document, lease, contract, or regulatory agreement that was to be involved in the project. As the board became more knowledgeable, newcomers had an increasingly difficult time understanding the discussions at the meetings. Some English speakers did overcome this hurdle through patient listening and asking questions; Spanish speakers did not.

It must have been very difficult for the Spanish speakers attending the meetings to tell whether their lack of understanding was due to technical and language barriers, personal inability, or deliberate exclusion of Latinos. Tenacity and faith in the process was required to stay long enough to overcome both the technical and language barriers. The discussions required a high level of technical sophistication with both languages. The lack of trained knowledgeable interpreters made the Latinos' task unsurmountable.

Given the barriers to Latino participation, mediation was necessary to assure the Latinos that they were not being deliberately excluded and that Americanos were doing their part to bridge the cultural gulf. As in the case of the request for the independent translator, the organizers were not able to provide the mediating element and doubts about the intentions of the non-Latinos went unchecked.

Interviews with Latinos in the project during this period disclosed much confusion and suspicion about the development of the cooperatives. For example, many of those interviewed were very upset that their children could not inherit their homes. As one person put it, "her children would be put out if she died." In fact, children were not excluded from inheritance. A lengthy debate had been held at an R2CHC meeting on this subject early in the process, and it had been agreed that children should have the right of inheritance. The documents affirmed inheretance rights, but the affirmation was buried in many pages of technical legal documents. The word did not get down to the members. About half of those interviewed attributed some problem either real or rumored to anti-Latino bias in the project.[12]

As the cooperatives began to take on more operational substance, the lack of Latino leadership became more serious. The rehabilitation and operation of the cooperatives presented complex policy questions that directly affected the residents' lives. There were hard choices to be made, and much resident participation was necessary to make them. In two almost entirely Latino groups, one of the cooperatives and Imogen, stable leadership did not develop. The growing belief that the two leaderless groups would fail as coops and the increasing operational burden on the non-Latino leadership in the other four groups created an atmosphere of crisis. The leadership put increasing pressure on the organizers to solve the Latino leadership problem. Under this pressure, one of the organizers, a Chicana, left the project. It was a critical time, and the board was becoming desperate for someone who could do the job.

Working on the rehabilitation staff as a bookkeeper was a trained professional organizer. Although she was Anglo and had little facility with Spanish, she had worked for a multiethnic organization and had successfully organized a Latino neighborhood community in Los Angeles.[13] She was committed to multiculturalism and felt the responsibility to solve the problem. Under the urging of staff and board, she was pressed into service.

The former bookkeeper and the remaining Puerto Rican organizer, who had started with the organization as a rehabilitation trainee, responded to the pressure for success in organizing the Latinos with a demand for higher pay and the professionalization of their function. In addition to their organizational and leadership development responsibilities, they had been involved in many minor tasks generated by the rehabilitation, such as getting signatures on documents or arranging for temporary relocation during fumigations. The organizers wanted to be freed from this responsibility so that they could concentrate on organizing. The board acquiesced to both demands, raising the organizers' salaries and creating a new position to carry on the rehabilitation work.

The board intended, at this point, that the English-speaking organizer would work with the four ethnically-mixed, functioning cooperatives.

The Puerto Rican organizer, with support and training from the new, professional organizer, would concentrate on the two troubled, primarily Latino, Spanish-speaking cooperatives. It soon became obvious that this strategy did not sufficiently address the needs of the two troubled cooperatives and pressure to solve this problem was, again, brought on the organizers, particularly the Puerto Rican organizer.

The response to the pressure was, again, a demand for more money for the Puerto Rican organizer. This time the federation board lost its temper and fired the Puerto Rican organizer, who, in the eyes of the board, had not successfully switched from his position as a rehabilitation trainee to a professional organizer. His firing generated a crisis that proved to be another important step in learning how to solve the problem of communication.

The fired organizer attempted to rally the people he had been working with against his firing. Many of the Latinos were afraid of what would happen to them when he was gone. As one person said, "He was our only link to the corporation." Once again the leadership responded by calling a mass meeting. Again, the professional interpreter was called in to translate. The Latinos supporting the organizer demanded that he be reinstated pending a full evaluation of Latino participation and the organizer's performance. If this were not possible, they demanded full participation in the selection of his replacement.

The meeting was very painful, but productive. In the anger of the meeting, yelling and shouting, the English-speaking leadership felt that for the first time they had participated in a direct conversation with the Latino residents. They saw, again, the value of the professional interpreter. They did not want the organizer to be the Latinos' only link to the corporation. They became concerned that the organizers, by virtue of their monopoly on interpretation and cultural mediation, had been playing a gatekeeper role not proper to the organizer function. They wanted a mediator, not a broker, and more than that they wanted to talk directly to the residents.

The board refused to reinstate the fired organizer, but willingly accepted full participation of the Latinos in hiring the next person. During the hiring process, conversations between the Americanos and Latinos began to take place. It was learned that one of the problems with the past organizing was that the organizers were not good translators. Some of the Latinos were sufficiently bilingual to know that what was said in Spanish was different from what was being said in English. This made them suspicious of the organizers and the overall cooperative process.

The board learned that when the Latinos had called for independent translators, they were not attacking the board but the low quality of the organizers' translations. What the Latinos really wanted was competent translators. As a result of what it learned and its increased desire to talk directly to the Latinos, the board, for the first time, created a translation budget. Perhaps in anger and somewhat out of necessity it took the money from the organizing budget and adopted a policy requiring that professional interpreters be present at all "significant" meetings.

A primarily Spanish-speaking Salvadoran, who had recently moved into the cooperatives and who had been a labor organizer in his country, was recommended by the interviewing committee and hired by the board. The work of the two organizers was no longer divided along language lines. The new plan was for the two organizers to work as a team. Working this way, they began to make headway. They exploited the organizational potential of small and large crises that took place in the cooperatives by holding building meetings and teaching the people about how to take charge of their situation.

In the dramatic case of the invasion discussed in Chapter 2, the organizers played an important role. They saw the situation as an opportunity rather than a problem. They encouraged and assisted in setting up the committee of representatives of the twenty-four properties in the coop to analyze the distribution of space, recommend a solution for the immediate crisis, and head off future problems. The cooperative was two-thirds Latino, and there was heavy Latino participation on this committee. The incident initiated more active Latino participation in that cooperative.

Latino participation was increasing in all the cooperatives and organic Latino leadership was being identified in the four functioning cooperatives, but the leadership problem in the two troubled groups did not materially improve. The organizers assembled boards that held together temporarily, but in both coops family problems overwhelmed the elected presidents, and they dropped off the boards. The problem was greater than mere instability in Imogen. Unlike the cooperatives, Imogen had a federally required deadline for purchase of shares and formal conversion. The deadline for sale of the shares and the conversion to a cooperative passed without the required sale.

The Imogen residents suffered from years of failed organizing and Latino isolation. The firing of the Puerto Rican organizer split the group between those who had come to trust the leadership and its process and those, still suspicious, who did not. There was not enough time for the new organizing effort to heal the wounds of the past, and at the time the sale was required, each faction approached the development corporation board with the desire to buy the other out. Since this was not possible, the project remained a rental.

The failure of Imogen to convert drove the organizers even harder to find a solution to problem of the the remaining leaderless cooperative. The organizers concluded that internal leadership development was not possible under the urgent operational pressures facing this cooperative. They believed that the educational level of the particular immigrants in this cooperative was too low and their economic marginality too great for them to carry out the tasks needed to operate the cooperative without years of preparation and training. Their solution was to look outside the cooperatives for potential leadership.

There were about fifty vacancies in the five cooperatives after the rehabilitation was completed, including half a dozen in the troubled coop. The organizers began to encourage organizationally active Latinos they knew to get on the waiting list. A number of these people signed up. Next, the organizers focused on membership selection, particularly in the troubled coop. Their efforts and the choices made by the cooperative boards brought in a significant number of people with the leadership skills and the educational background to understand how to operate the cooperatives. Several of these people were organizers themselves. Quite a few had full bicultural Latino-Americano membership and were fully bilingual. Although the goal of the organizers had been to find caretaker leadership, they had, in fact, recruited people into the ranks of the residents who for the first time had the qualifications to act as multicultural mediators.[14]

The recruitment of these multicultural mediators provided a major missing element in the achievement of multiculturalism. For a period of time it looked like the strategy would work. The pressure of operating the cooperatives transformed the Latino caucus from a primarily political body into an educative body. The group focused on how to get the job done, and the initial Latino advocacy focus was moderated by a concern for who was a good worker and who wasn't, regardless of ethnicity.

In this period the policy to employ paid professional interpreters was implemented. Many individuals were tried but did not prove up to the job. Each interpreter selected different equivalents for the coop words and confused the process further. Finally, a capable individual was hired regularly to translate as many evenings as he could, with other paid translators and volunteers filling in where necessary. With the addition of the new bilingual leadership, this seemed to work.

The bilingual activists monitored the quality of the translation and ensured the uniformity that had been missing. But they did not want to translate; they wanted to participate in the meetings, and could not do both. However, they often interrupted the translation with discussion of how to translate various concepts. Sometimes the translator would shout out for help, and one of the bilingual people would make a suggestion.

Besides assuring uniformity and correctness in translation, the new activists made the discussions accessible to different cultural groups, in particular the less-educated and rural Latino immigrants. They were able to illustrate and explain technical concepts by reference to agrarian metaphors and stories from local oral traditions. They could find the cultural equivalents for jokes, puns, and role references. They could detect the intention behind a clumsy phrase, a potential insult, or an inappropriate gesture, and ensure understanding on all sides.

In sum, the bilingual activists performed the whole spectrum of functions that the theoretical literature assigns to the cultural mediator. Unfortunately, this period did not last. Two problems emerged. First the imported leadership became impatient with its caretaker role and began to exclude long-time residents as is described in Chapter 2. This problem was accentuated by their inability to solve long-standing problems faced by the cooperatives and some unfortunate decisions that worsened the situation. Second, the new leadership began to fight among itself.

Currently the ease of communications with the cooperatives varies. As will be discussed in the next portion of this chapter, deep-seated feelings of separation and racial difference still exist. There is, however, more communication between the Latino and Americano population. Membership committees have begun to favor bilingual applicants, and direct communication within the multiethnic population has increased. Time has also passed, and people have become more familiar with each other.

Racism

The very existence of multiethnicity in the project coupled with its location within the racial state gives rise to the question of the existence of racism among the corridor populaton. Certainly the fact that the leadership of the development phase of the project was Americano created the suspicion of racism. This situtation should lead any researcher to ask whether one group is favored over another? Does the structure of the project result in an unequal distribution of benefits or burdens? Is that look of disapproval or other action racially motivated? Every time a significant question is answered the answer is subject to scrutiny for racist behavior or result. Who was elected to the board? Whose unit was repaired or improved? Who was selected for a vacant unit? The issues never end. After discussing these and similar questions in general, the remainder of the chapter will examine a case involving the selection of a new member of one of the cooperatives.

Discrimination can be intentional behavior or the unintentional product of the particular structure within which an act takes place (Feagin and Feagin, 1986). There were isolated incidents of intentional racist behavior in the project, but these were not the rule. Overt racism is not acceptable behavior in the project. At one point in the development of the cooperative a group of Anglo residents approached the board and demanded their cooperative be divided into two areas with one largely Latino and one largely Anglo. The Anglos rationalized the split would provide internal cohesion. The largely Americano board of R2CHC saw the Anglos' request as racially based. Moreover, the failure to include the two areas in the cooperative would have made the purchase of the largely Latino area financially infeasible. The leadership insisted that everyone should benefit and no one should be displaced. The coop was not divided.

The issue of structural racism is more complex, but by the most obvious measures one would have to say that the Latinos received more of the benefits of the project than the Americanos. Certainly an analysis of subsidy dollars would lead to that conclusion. All families in need received Section 8 subsidies, but the Latino families tended to have a greater need for these subsidies. All overcrowded families received units appropriate to their family size, but the Latino families tended to be more overcrowded than the Americano families. A high percentage of rehabilitation funds were spent creating large bedroom apartments out of smaller ones. Four, five, and six bedroom apartments were created for specific Latino families. These benefits, however, also indirectly benefitted the Americanos. They made it possible for everyone to avoid displacement and become part of the cooperative.

The analysis is also complex when the burdens are considered. The Americanos did most of the work that made the project possible even though they received less of the direct benefits. These burdens, however, are balanced by the fact that the Americanos tended to have nicer units than the Latinos to start with. This contributed to their greater willingness to participate. Also the Americanos suffered less of the inconvenience of the rehabilitation including the inconvenience of moving. Americanos are more likely to pay a monthly charge that while higher in a dollar amount (the maximum) represents a smaller percentage of their income than the members on Section 8. They are less likely, moreover, to suffer the indignities of participating in a subsidy program. Research has shown that some people value their privacy over housing quality and affordability (Hollingshead and Rogler 1963). A researcher could find this sentiment in the Route 2 corridor. Although the Latinos gained the most they also had to give up more of their privacy to the Housing Authority and HUD regulations.[15]

Any unevenness to benefits and burdens in the project cannot be isolated from the greater variance in the larger society. The structural racism of the larger society penetrates the project creating inherent inequalities in the corridor population that no project by itself could overcome. One of the most salient elements of this is that the United States is not officially a bilingual nation. English speakers have an extraordinary advantage over non-English speakers in the society. The lack of bilingualism in the larger society has created a constant pressure to have a native English speaker as president so that person can represent the cooperative to the outside world. In dealing with the politicians or the Housing Authority on complex matters such as Section 8 regulations, English is virtually a requirement. Recently the Latino majority on the board of an eighty-percent Latino cooperative pushed to have Americanos be president and vice-president of their board. Only at the insistence of the Americanos did a Latina unsure of her English, who is the acknowledged leader of the cooperative, assume the presidency.

The advantage conveyed by the ability to speak fluent English exists when dealing with cooperative business as well as in each individual's economic life. Monolingual Spanish speakers are likely to be shuttled to the secondary economy while the English speakers are more likely to find a place in the primary economy. As is discussed in the last chapter, this secondary place in the economy carries with it other structural disadvantages in dealing with cooperative business.

Who is the Racist?

Residents addressed the issue of racism in selecting a family to occupy a two-bedroom non-Section 8 unit vacated by an Americano family in one of the cooperatives. The cooperative had to choose between three families: a Chinese family consisting of a mother and teenage son; a Latino family consisting of a husband and wife and two young children; and a mixed family consisting of a pregnant Anglo wife and a Latino husband. The Chinese woman was an accountant with a substantial income although still within the moderate income requirements; the Latino husband was a sheet metal worker; and the Anglo wife, the spokesperson for her family, was a bilingual school teacher with an organizing background in Latino communities and her Latino husband was an artist. The Latino family was a friend of a Latino member of the board and the Chinese and Anglo applicants were friends of an Americano member of the board.

In the demise of Nuestra and the shift to a private management company the waiting list for units in the cooperative had been lost.

Applicants became a mix of people who walked into the management company when a unit was available and friends and relatives of residents of the cooperative. Several members of the board had taken the opportunity to admit their friends and relatives. No one was happy with what was taking place. Because for some time a majority of the cooperative and its board were Latinos, an increase in the Latino population in the cooperative had ensued. The Americanos were worried about the cooperative losing its multiethnic character and saw the process as a Latino problem. When Americanos were successful in moving one of their friends in, the Latinos saw it as an Americano problem and there were murmurs of racism. The non-Section 8 case brought the issue to a head.

Three Latino and three Americano members of the cooperative acting as the membership committee and the two Latino neighbors of the vacant unit interviewed the applicants. Of those present four people were on the board, two Latinas and two Americanas. Only one person at the meeting, an Americano, backed the Chinese family. He argued that the accountant had skills the cooperative desperately needed and that over the time the cooperative had been interviewing no one with this skill level had applied. A Latino member replied that the family didn't need the apartment since the woman had plenty of income and could live anywhere. The Americano said that was exactly the point. The accountant wanted to live in the cooperative and would work for it. If need was the primary criteria, particularly in non-Section 8 cases, the cooperative would soon be without the skills to operate.

All the Latinos in the room including the neighbors backed the Latino candidate. The friend of the Latino applicants had been on the phone recruiting support and brought another friend to the meeting whom she had previously and successfully supported for admission to the cooperative. Since this person had not attended a meeting for several years, her presence at the meeting angered some of the Americanos who felt the meeting was being stacked. The Latinos argued that the Latino family needed the apartment more than the other families and that the husband's skills would be valuable in supervising the maintenance of the cooperative. He had also promised to do the repairs himself, a promise that had been heard before from applicants but was never kept. The husband and the family's friend said the wife in the family had secretarial and accounting skills, but the wife was very quiet and spoke very little in the interview.

The Anglos reacted by saying that they had heard the man's speech before and that very few of those making this speech ever kept their promise to work. The cooperative had a lot of men with manual skills who failed to be active. This made the applicants' friend angry; she declared she knew the family and promised it would work for the cooperative. She put her credibility on the line. Underlying the Americanos' reaction but unspoken, however, was the memory of two friends of this member who had previously been admitted after promises but who had not kept their word.

The remaining two Americanos (one Anglo and one not) backed the mixed Anglo/Latino family. They believed that like the Latino family the mixed family needed housing. In addition, however, they saw the organizing skills of the wife in the mixed family as more important to the cooperative than any other skill. Active cooperative members needed help encouraging participation in the cooperative. The women's bilingual and teaching skills could be employed to prepare a newsletter. The cooperative had wanted a newsletter for some time, but few people had the skill to prepare a bilingual newsletter and none of them had made it their priority.

An Americana populist at the meeting believed the Anglo woman applicant would also encourage multiculturalism in the cooperative and act as a multicultural mediator. The Americana did not see the husband in the Latino family in that role although he was also bilingual. In the Americana's mind the Anglo woman's marriage to a Latino and her long-time involvement in Latino communities confirmed her abilities for the role. She regarded the husband in the Latino family as part of the Latino culture and not likely to be a prime mover towards multiculturalism. Since the Chinese family was not bilingual, it also could not bridge the gap between the cultural groups.

The tense meeting became tenser when one of the Americanos reacting to the perceived attempt to stack the meeting asked whether the Latinos at the meeting were voting for the Latino applicants because they were Latino. The Latinos answered the question negatively and reiterated their reasons for supporting the family. The family was the most in need, the family's skills would be useful to the cooperative, and they were the neighbors' choice.

The Latino family received a majority of the votes at the meeting, but among the attending board members the vote was split two to two. Consequently the three members of the seven-person coop board who did not attend would have to make the final decision. Two of the three remaining board members were Latino. It was decided at the committee meeting that the highest ranking member of the board in attendance, the Americano vice-president, should hold a meeting with the absent board members the next night to make the final decision.[16]

One of the Latino members could not attend the meeting. The other two members came at different times and ended up talking individually with the vice president. She described the three applicants. Both of the board members voted for the mixed family, and the family was awarded the unit.

The Latino member of the board who had supported her friends was clearly upset at the decision. She felt she made a mistake allowing the Americana to convene the meeting and that pressure had been put on the other Latino member to vote for the mixed couple. She withdrew from activity in the cooperative, but after several talks with the Americanos involved (talks that would not have likely taken place at an early point in the development of the cooperatives) resumed full involvement. The board resolved to create a new waiting list for the non-Section 8 units to reduce the chances of such a problem reoccurring.

Almost everyone involved in this event believed initially that racism played a part in the interview meeting. There was no agreement about the nature of the racism. The Latinos saw the Americanos as anti-Latino and voting for their own, and the Americanos saw the Latinos as biased in favor of Latinos and voting for their own. The Latino members viewed the Latino member who broke ranks and voted for the mixed family as a "dupe" of the Americanos, a term which had been applied before in the history of the project to Latinos who consorted with the Americanos. They were regarded as tokens or only Latinos on the outside. In the most dramatic incident a Latino distributing fliers in his cooperative had been accused of being paid by the Americanos. He had to go home and get his pay stub to convince his accusers that he had another job and was just volunteering to help the coop.

What the charge of racism means in a multiethnic organization like the Route 2 cooperative is not entirely clear.

If the Intentional Bias Charges Were Both True --

In the larger society Anglos are the majority and as a group the purveyors of the racial state and racism. Minority groups who suffer from racism and the racial state are seen by some as having a legitimate right to assert their group interests in the larger society and to demand affirmative treatment to redress past and continuing wrongs (Omi and Winant 1986).[17] In the cooperatives the division between the majority immigrant Latinos and minority Americanos confuses the usual societal debate.

National minority groups that are subject to discrimination in the larger society, including Chicanos, form a minority Americano population in the cooperatives. Can the immigrant Latinos claim an affirmative action preference for Latinos within the project without being seen as racists? To a U.S. black member of the cooperative, for example, the preference for Latinos can look like a new version of the same racist game. The Americanos claimed not to be anti-Latino but pro-multi-cultural. Can Americanos support a claim for affirmative action for Americanos on the grounds that they are seeking multiculturalism in the cooperative? If they are saying in effect that the Latino quota was filled by past practices which increased the percentage of Latinos in the cooperative, that this unit was an Americano unit, and vote against a Latino for that reason, are they being racist? Can a bias for multiculturalism be seen as racism?

If Nepotism Controlled Judgment --

It may be that intentional bias had nothing to do with the decision and that one or both sides were simply favoring their friends and received the support of their friends in their effort. The reality of the situation in the project and in the larger racial state is that each ethnic/racial group is likely to have people of their group as friends. Trying to help a friend and friends helping friends who are helping friends is likely to have a biasing effect. The activity may have no racial motive, be unintentional, but have the effect of creating biased results. It has been argued that nepotism in this form, the "good-old-boy network," is the basis of racism (Feagin and Feagin 1986). Here the story is only complicated by the presence of numerous groups that suffer from exclusion from these networks.

If Different Criteria Controlled Judgment --

The Latinos stressed the applicants' level of need in their discussion. As one of the Latinos put it, "helping people in need is what the cooperative is all about." The Americanos emphasized the skills of the applicants and the needs of the cooperative. Their position is that once eligibility is established, skills need to be considered primary or there will be no cooperative to help people in need. Here the issue becomes one of structural racism. Structurally Latinos have less economic and educational opportunity than Americanos, particularly Anglo Americanos (Barrera, 1979). If the Americano criterion of skill level is used, then selection is likely to favor Americanos. Conversely if the criterion is need, the opposite is true. Selection results are less clear when national minority groups are brought into the picture.

Given the limited number of vacancies in the cooperative there is no external reason for structural racism to express itself in the cooperative. Here, however, the issue was not just skill, but a particular type of skill; the Latinos saw manual skills as important while the Americano stressed mental skills. When the type of skill becomes a criterion and a choice is made from an applicant pool largely representative of the present representatives in the cooperative, the likelihood of this structural tendency to express itself is greatly enhanced. The claimed importance of mental skills is certainly subject to skepticism by the listener whose group will be negatively effected by its application.[18]

The issue of skill level as a criterion also raises the question of training of members of the cooperatives. Whose responsibility is the training? Who designs the training and who does the training? Do the residents with greater skill levels have a special responsibility to train the less skilled members or is it an overall cooperative responsibility? Training has taken place from time to time. Members who participate are becoming more sophisticated over time. The issue is partly one of short-term versus long-term participation. In the long term people can be trained. In the short term the skills are needed.

If Stacking the Meeting and the Reaction Controlled Judgment --

In the cooperative majority rules. The populists, however, believe the rule of the majority should be part of an open process where decisions are based on meritocracy.[19] Can the societal history of racism justify stacking the meeting? I have been in groups where it has been argued when there have been complaints against such tactics that "its about time Anglos understood what it feels like." Can the Americanos' definition of meritocracy be seen as biased in itself and justify stacking a meeting? What is usually argued is that merit is only a proper criteria up to that necessary to do the task. Beyond that affirmative action can come into play (Maquire 1980). If the meeting were stacked, can the Americanos justify violating their own rule of meritocracy and vote against the stacker's friends? This would seem to corrupt the process even further.

Conclusion

The residents of the Route 2 project faced the necessity of solving the problems of bilingual, multicultural organizing. Through persistence and good fortune, they discovered a partial solution to their problem. They learned that an organizer's dedication to multiculturalism may be more important than bilingualism or particular ethnic membership. When it came to interpretation, they learned how loosely the term bilingual is used and that their situation called for a very high level of bilingualism. In a multiethnic situation with a substantial number of monolingual individuals, great care must be taken to ensure that the person assigned this role has the requisite ability.

Residents also realized that in multicultural organizations there are both practical and organizational risks in combining the organizer, translator, and mediator roles. On the practical level, it is difficult to find a person with this multiple competence. On the organizational level, the organizer may not be able to maintain the neutrality necessary to satisfy the requirement of interpretation. Moreover the gatekeeper potential of the roles may inhibit direct contact between ethnicities and undermine the development of democratic institutions within the organization.

The residents also discovered the central importance of resident multicultural mediators. They learned how fragile multiculturalism can be. Without mediating individuals in the community to build trust between ethnicities many misunderstandings can overwhelm good intentions. They also learned about the dangers of injecting mediators into a community devoid of such resources.

Even with this knowledge, however, the residents have learned how difficult it is to create true multiculturalism. The implication of bias is possible in nearly every significant act. The whistle cannot be blown, and everyone cannot simply agree to avoid behavior that could be interpreted as racist. The suspicion and distance created by the racial state cannot easily be overcome. The existence of racism in the racial state is omnipresent and tears down the community constructed within the cooperatives. As will be discussed in the final chapter, time may be the most important factor in overcoming this problem. As people get to know each other, the words for communication are found and distance is reduced.

Notes

1.   This statement should be qualified. The multicultural image was largely in the Anglo world. Among Chicano activists in the city, the project was often characterized in the early days as a Cubano project because of the original Cuban leadership.

2.   For a discussion of the authoritarian populist rather than progressive populist approach, see Omi and Winant (1986, p. 120).

3.   For a discussion of the racial state see Omi & Winant (1986). Omi and Winant set out the long history of racism in the United States and discuss the role of the state in the establishment, maintenance, and redefinition of racial categories, what Miles (1982) calls racialization. Their position is similar to those theorists who see the state as the locus and product of class struggle and, therefore, relatively autonomous from the bourgeois (Carnoy, 1984). Omi and Winant see the racial state as a focus of "racial" conflict in which distinct state institutions intervene in a contradictory fashion as pressures are placed on them.

Overall, however, as with the relative autonomy theorists position on class, their position is that racism underlies the state's actions.

4. The racial state and the attack on ethnic groups requires self-defense. The stress on one's own needs is an inevitable result. The creation of the category "race" and the fractionalization of the working class is the result (Miles 1982).

5. Padilla sees the traditionalists as pluralists and the emergent group in another category. On this point we disagree. I see the difference between the groups being a matter of tactics. They both seek benefits from the state. What is different is that the traditionalists play more within the rules and the agenda set by the state than the emergent group.

6. There are Americanos who also share a clientelist approach, but they are in the minority in this group.

7. This is true even with immigrants who believe they will return to their country of origin. To some extent they have to adjust to conditions in the United States.

8. "Organizations as a separate, competitive monocultural group or bloc have not always offered a completely satisfactory alternative route to full social entitlement: externally, racism limits entry into the central arena of power, while internally, ethnic groups are divided by socioeconomic class, national origin, citizenship status, length of residence in the U.S. and degree of assimilation to the dominant Anglo culture.

For Angeleno Latinos particularly, the mechanisms for assimilation to the dominant culture have been weak: language and cultural maintenance are supported by ethnic segregation, the physical proximity of Latin America, the continuous inflow of migrants, and by a dense network of Latino businesses, communications media and social institutions of all kinds (Conklin and Lourie 1983; Giles, Bourhis and Taylor 1977).

Importantly, many of the goals of low-income groups (such as crime prevention, adequate housing and access to public services), are shared with the contiguous or intermingled communities of other ethnic groups. Organization along strict ethnic lines means fragmentation, and competition for scarce resources. Each minority must direct its demands, in isolation, to the dominant culture, thus minimizing minority interaction and contributing to the maintenance of the status quo. To be truly effective, in a multiethnic environment such as Los Angeles, organizing must have the capacity to employ multiculturalism.

Active community organizers have stated this new multicultural imperative quite dramatically, and generalized it to the national scale. Jose M. Molina (1978) writes that "as a breath of fresh air blowing throughout the organizational field, a new trend is now in motion in this country -- in San Francisco, Los Angeles, Cleveland, Arkansas, North Carolina, Connecticut and elsewhere. I am referring to multiethnic, multiracial majority constituency organization." Other organizers, such as Miller (1974) and De Leeuw (1974), concur" (Heskin and Heffner 1987).

9. Much of this section of the book is adapted from Heskin and Heffner (1986).

10. The reference to key documents indicates the structural limits of what a group can do in a non-bilingual environment. For example HUD does not provide its material in multiple languages. To translate all HUD regulations and appropriate statutes to Spanish would have been an impossible task. Corporate documents, rental agreements, disclosure statements and the like were translated. Handouts and training material were also translated.

11. Most of the initial organizing would be done at the residents' homes. Women were home more than men, and it was felt women residents would be more comfortable with a woman. It was also believed that a woman would have a better chance of getting in the home to talk to the residents.

12. Interviews with 20 active and inactive Latinos from a variety of countries were conducted by Lupe Compean between July and August of 1984. An example of a real problem that existed was the overt racism of the some employees of the contractors hired to rehabilitated the property. Several incidents took place of verbal attacks on Latino coop members by these workmen. Complaints were filed with the contractor by the R2CHC staff and the problem lessened.

13. The organizer was trying to get away from that kind of work and develop professional skills that would allow her to make a decent living. Organizers are traditionally under-paid.

14. Part of the organizers job in a multiethnic situation is to identify and develop "natural cross-links" in the population (Molina 1978). They could not find these people and instead recruited them into the project.

15. One of the biggest issues in the research and in the Route 2 project involves how many people live in a home. The Section 8 program has regulations on overcrowding and being underhoused. Those in the Section 8 program can be forced to move from their existing homes to an "appropriate" sized unit.

16. The other board members at the interview said they were too busy to come to yet another meeting that week.

17. For a discussion of the affirmative action debate see Maguire (1980).

18. There is some basis for the argument that need alone will detrimentally affect coop participation. The boards of the cooperative tend to be made up of people who are either non-section 8 residents or people towards the top of the Section 8 income criteria. In the cooperative in question, for example, the majority of the residents on the board are non-section 8 members. Among those who are Section 8 eligible all but one are in the higher income group . That one person just suffered a personal tragedy which greatly reduced the family's income. Whether mental versus manual skill is preferable is more debatable although clearly both mental and manual skills are required to make the cooperative work. It should be made clear that the Americanos are talking about skill and not capacity. However, either interpretation could be made by a listener to the argument.

19. See discussion in Chapter 2.

6

Gender

In this chapter the role of gender in the Route 2 project will be examined. Significant gender issues have laid beneath the surface of the Route 2 project throughout its history, but they have rarely been articulated, as such, in the debates that have taken place.[1]

As the reader can see from the pronouns employed in the text thus far, both men and women in this predominantly working-class group have served in the leadership of the Route 2 project. A man was president of R2TA and women were vice-president and treasurer of R2TA. Women have served as president, secretary, and treasurer of R2CHC, and men as vice-president and secretary of R2CHC. Women as well as men have at one time or another been presidents of all the cooperatives and prominent on all the cooperative boards. Many of the staff of HCD were women. A woman was director of R2CHC and so were numerous other staff. Men acted as the president and director of Nuestra with women also participating.

Both women and men figure prominently among the leadership of each of the ideological groups discussed in this book. Women are the dominant figures in all the groups although at one point a man was the most dominant figure among the pluralists. The prominent if not dominant role of women among the activists in the project seems to confirm findings of others.[2] What is new here is the differences that have emerged among the active women in the course of the Route 2 project. The relevant literature on gender tends to focus on differences between men and women or the differences between working-class and third-world women and white middle-class women considered to be mainstream feminists. The literature usually does not focus on differences among working-class women.[3] This chapter takes this step by considering how populists, pluralists and clientelists explain gender roles in the project.

There are many ways to categorize varying theories of gender. It is common, however, to argue that a division can be made between those who stress concepts that support the inherent equality of men and women and those who see an inherent or systemically generated difference between men and women.[4] The first group focuses on establishing equality between the sexes particularly in the public arena. The second seeks to end the separation of the public and private parts of women's lives and promotes the assertion of women's unique qualities. Central to the latter position is the statement "the personal is political" and the critique of western societies and thought for their inherent patriarchal character. Among feminists the first category is often characterized as liberal feminism and the second as cultural or radical feminism (Donovan 1988).

This mainstream scheme has been the subject of intense criticism by theorists speaking from a working-class and third world perspective. Authors such as Bell Hooks argue at length that this organization of ideas is one of white middle-class feminists and does not speak to the conditions in which working-class and third-world women live (1984). Hooks argues that working-class and third world women must struggle with their men against external oppressive forces and therefore, cannot emphasize conflicts between the genders. They also cannot as easily call for the ending of the separation of public and private in middle-class terms. The private arena of the family where men and women interact is a center of survival which must be kept separate from the threatening public arena.

Sexism in Route 2

Although everyone was quite conscious of the prominent role women came to play, the project was not internally seen as a women's project and gender *per se* did not present itself as a conflictual issue in the project's public life. A non-sexist atmosphere was established early on. The very first leaders of the Route 2 tenants were Cuban men. The professional women from HCD and these men worked well together. The Cuban men were soon joined by Route 2 project women. An early Americana woman activist worried that the Cuban men would not work with an Americana woman, but told me she relaxed when, somewhat to her surprise, she felt accepted.

The prominent leadership role women played undoubtedly contributed to gender not becoming a public conflictual issue in the development of the project. There were plenty of classic examples of sexism and patriarchy in the life of the Route 2 project but sexist behavior is often isolated as a "private" matter in this society. Gender has not yet achieved the public status of race and class. Although the feminist movement has made great strides, in most organizations cries of racism or elitism, a form of class cry, are expressed and heard long before the cry of sexism.

The first staff help the residents received was from the Department of Housing and Community Development. Like Caltrans, HCD was part of the California state "super agency," the Business and Transportation Agency. Locally, the two staffs were gender divided. The HCD staff that initially worked on the project was female and the Caltrans staff was male. In the early going the Caltrans men would from time-to-time try to chase the HCD women away. As one of the HCD staff put it, "We were becoming time-consuming impediments to Caltrans' plans. Caltrans staff would treat us as if to say, 'Why don't you be good little girls and go away.'" The women sometimes joked about the division. "Building roads was men's work and caring about housing for low-income people was women's work." The HCD women never directly confronted the Caltrans men, but it is more than likely that the sexism added energy to the women's efforts.

One of the women coop presidents had a husband who acted as if he was very jealous of her position and status in the cooperative. Although at one level he encouraged her participation in the cooperative, he would from time to time demand that she follow his advice in running the cooperative and "forbid" her from doing otherwise. Both partners in this marriage were seniors, and they had spent a life together. The husband was ill, and the wife worried about his health. In other environments women have banded together to confront husbands who behaved similarly, but this did not happen in the Route 2 project.[5] The other women did not intervene in part because of the particularities of the couple, but also, as will be discussed later, because of the type of community they sought in the project. They sympathized with the woman's problem and chose to wait until she and her husband resolved their difficulties and she returned to the business of the cooperative.

In the Latino population the early coop meeting attendees were noticeably women. Their presence followed in the tradition that holds the home and issues surrounding the home as women's responsibility (Oakley 1976; Bookman and Morgen 1988). It also seemed to be an exemplar of sexism. Some of the Latinos thought that talk of buying the property and forming cooperatives was "silly," but decided to keep track of the progress of the project by sending "their" women to follow the action. There were stories of Latinas stating at meetings that they had to consult their husbands on matters before they could cast their family's vote on any issue being discussed. When, to these men's surprise, the property was purchased, the men started attending, and the women stayed home. This dominant male presence, however, only lasted a few months. Finally, Latino attendance at meetings and membership on boards of the cooperatives became more gender mixed.

Populist Working-Class Feminism

Most of the early women leaders of the Route 2 project worked or had worked and also maintained traditional gender roles as wives and mothers. Both the public and private lives of these women gave direction to their leadership. The president of R2CHC had studied theories of human development and ran a neighborhood child care cooperative. Her approach to child care spilled over into the project.[6] One of the leaders had two children. The children and their friends were in and out of her house all day long when school was not in session. She seemed to always have something cooking on the stove in the event one of her children or a neighborhood child wanted something to eat. When visitors came to her house the smell of the cooking was the first thing that greeted them. Discussions about the project ensued between tastes of what was being prepared. Increasingly the staff people chose to drop in at meal time for their discussions.

The populist women were proud that women had played such a prominent role in the project, but insisted, when asked, that their gender made little or no difference.[7] As has been seen in earlier chapters, systemic differentiation of any sort was rejected. If I pointed out a woman's special ability, for example, the ability to mediate disputes between men, I would be told that this characteristic was a personal skill rather than a systemic gender trait.

The black woman president of R2CHC was particularly adamant on the point. Her reason for rejecting the approach of feminists who see the genders as inherently different is shared by many third world feminists. The members of the Combahee River Collective, a black women's collective, stated that black women "often find it difficult to separate race from class from sex oppression because in our lives they are most often experienced simultaneously" (Moraga and Anzaldua 1981, p. 213). Moreover the members of the collective saw an inherent danger in the difference approach. The emphasis on the distinction between male and female suggests biological determinism. Biological determinism often becomes a basis for racist arguments (p. 214).[8] The president and the other populist women saw the community formed in the Route 2 project as a place of equality where sex and ethnicity were not to be issues. Particular racist and sexist incidents might evoke a reaction, but to these women, the collective issue of the Route 2 population was class.[9] Bell Hooks could have been paraphrasing the Route 2 populist women when she wrote that women must exercise their power in ways that "resist exploitation and oppression and free them to work at transforming society so that political and economic structures will exist that benefit women and men equally" (Hooks 1984, p. 92).

As discussed in Chapter 3, the early populist women leaders were far from believing that all people were the same. This belief prompted one of the women populist leaders to argue strongly against having a single criteria for participation in the project. People all had different skills to contribute to the project whether they were male or female.

Some of the younger white women who joined in the leadership in the development phase of the project held the position that men and women were different.[10] They did not, however, manifest this position through feminist organizing. No attempt was ever made, as in the case of the Latinos, to form a women's caucus. In part this absence may have been because the early activists would not have supported a separatist form of organizing. It is also likely, as is discussed later in the chapter, that many of the women with other ideologies and ethnicities would not have joined the effort.

The early women leaders were working class and in some cases members of ethnic or racial minorities. They were generally in their forties or older.[11] Among these women were some extraordinary people who had to cope with heavy doses of sexism, racism, and classism in their lives. In the process they had become very strong capable people. One leading senior woman had graduated from law school in her youth but gave up the possibility of a law career to follow her husband throughout the country in his search for success in show business. She had many jobs before spending the last nineteen years of her work life in California as an executive secretary for a major corporation. Another woman leader grew up in Harlem in the care of a guardian, lived in a foster home in her teenage years, had a child when she was still a child, and moved to California with that child. After working many years, she won a college degree with the benefit of life experience from a local alternative university and now held a responsible administrative position. These women were vocal, active, visible, and, as one woman put it when talking about herself, "terribly aggressive." Not all the women who participated in the development of the cooperatives were as dynamic as these women. Many women fit much more into the shy, private image portrayed in some women's literature (Belenky et.al. 1986). Some of these women went through a personal transformation as a result of their participation. Some had never been active outside the home and were slowly recruited into active positions in the cooperatives, took responsibility, found a voice, and were brought fully into the world outside the home.

I remember the joy of one of the early woman leaders when she told me that an Asian woman who had become active in her cooperative had gone beyond being active in the cooperative to find a job outside her home. The leader took pride in the transformation of her "sister" from a shy housewife who rarely spoke into a public person and a working woman.

In my conversation with this woman about her conception of the differences between men and women I brought up her joy in this woman's growth. She said her pleasure was not evidence of an assumption of a basic difference between men and women and reminded me of a male example which gave her the same pleasure. In this working-class population of tenants there were men who rarely spoke in public before becoming active in the project. One such man, a Chicano cabinet maker, after much prodding took on the job of secretary in his cooperative. He scribbled the minutes of the meeting in a little notebook he always carried for that purpose. It was a painful job for him, but he did it. In the process he gained a public voice and organizational skills and later became president of the cooperative. He told me once in his laconic style how much he had gained from his involvement in the cooperative.

Some feminist literature argues that relational skills as well as other such social and organizational skills are a particular trait of women (Nodding 1984). Women are said to have developed particular "warmth, trust, dialogue, [and] uncompetiveness" in the home that males tend to lack (Donovan 1988, p. 77).[12] Or, more basically, as disclosed over the course of human history, "[t]he basic feminine impulse is to gather, to put together, to construct; the basic masculine impulse to scatter, to disseminate, to destroy" (p. 46).[13] This distinction brings to mind the contrast between the populists under female leadership and the pluralists under male leadership although as was pointed out to me over and over again, both genders were involved throughout the process. The clientelist women as will be seen later fit less well in this dichotomy.

When I discussed the skills characterized as "women's" skills with the project's early populist women leaders and the professional women active in the project, they rejected them as women's traits. They pointed out to me that many men who were active in this period had these and other "women's" skills and that some of the women didn't. They preferred to see the positive qualities of people who were active in this period as the characteristics of individuals rather than as gender characteristics.

Some of the Route 2 populist resident and professional women I talked to about this explained the prevalence of "women's" skills in the project through an analysis of the social structure in which the project operated. They thought perhaps the uniqueness of the project and its high risk created an opportunity for professionals with these characteristics. The women who chose this job may have been marginalized from the mainstream, in part, because of their gender. Both the men and women, however, may have been marginalized because of their approach to professional work. A similar structural observation was made by a Route 2 woman leader, who when asked directly about women's propensity for community activism, noted that there were plenty of men active in politics which she saw as the upper level of community work. In her mind women were confined by sexism to the grass roots.

There were Route 2 project male leaders and professional men who worked in the project with relational skills, and there were also women without them. Just looking at the professional women, one would find great stylistic differences. Some were very technical and formal and didn't care much for the messy process of the project, others were very emotional and sometimes lost control of themselves inappropriately, others were very open to process and yet others were very non-directive, what one observer of the cooperatives called "democratic fetishists." Similar variations could be found among the male professionals and in the resident population.

One of the woman leaders had notoriously poor relational skills. She had an ego of very large proportions and was on her way to offending as many people as the relationally skilled women attracted when a life change took her away from the project. With this and other individuals in mind one of the woman bluntly stated her sense of equality; there were "jerks with skirts as well as jerks with pants" involved in the project.

The men who were active early also did not think gender was a telling factor in community activism. In one line of feminist theory "caring" is seen as a central characteristic of women and a basic element in women's propensity for community work (Noddings 1984).[14] When asked about why people participated in community work, one of the early male leaders spontaneously gave the answer that "caring" was the important governing factor. When probed, he asserted that caring is not gender related. His sense of caring came out of a deep religious commitment to loving his neighbor.

One of the staff men who the women identified as a man with skills some feminists identify as feminine moved on to a male-dominated development corporation after his job with the Route 2 project. In his new job he was from time to time referred to as the "woman" of his new office because his relational approach set him so far apart from the other men in the office. Some feminists argue that certain men have more developed feminist sides and are exceptions to the difference rule. Maybe these men gathered in Route 2 and these theorists are correct.

A Case of "Women's" Skills

The female populist leadership focused on goals of the project and consciously gave men "a lot of slack" if they helped in the process. One of the most telling incidents of this focus and forgiveness occurred when one of the female board members of R2CHC and I visited a local politician's aide to talk about the project. The meeting took place during the period when Caltrans, under pressure from the state legislature to repair the property, was trying to move people out of and abandon buildings rather than repair them. Caltrans complained that the tenants' were stalling and would never buy the property. In the politician's view the project had been dragging on. He was beginning to lose confidence in the tenants' ability to perform, and he wanted some action.

The woman leader tried to explain why the project was not going faster and what the politician could do to help. The aide, who had been very supportive but was clearly on a mission to get things rolling, appeared perplexed. The more she tried to explain the situation, the more perplexed he looked. I interjected myself in the conversation after many uncomfortable minutes of non-communication and began to repeat verbatim what the woman was saying. The aide responded to me, and we proceeded in this fashion with me doing English to English translation until the meeting was successfully concluded. Afterwards the resident leader and I had a laugh about it and moved on.

In a meeting with another male political aide that I attended with the same woman leader, the aide and I got into what seemed to me as a "male" ego confrontation with the first words out of my mouth. I shut up. The aide warmed to the same woman the other aide could not understand, and she took over the meeting. In the first case, I became the contact person from then on. In the second the resident was the contact person.

Some streams of feminism focus on personal power as part of the idea that the personal is political (Evans 1980, p. 99). Consistent with that emphasis, feminists sometimes choose to confront directly a diminution of their personal power. By allowing me to interpret and be the contact person with the political aide in the first story, the woman gave up some of her personal power in a fashion that would cause some feminists to stop and consider the tradeoff of personal power for results. This is not a trade off the woman in question made.

When I asked the woman leader a direct question about the issue of personal power, her response was that to take his and my action as a diminution of her personal power would have been to allow him and me to define her. She felt comfortable with who she was and was not personally affected by his or my actions.[15] As discussed in Chapter 3, the populist women of Route 2 were not focused on power in this sense.

This woman leader was particularly noted for regularly giving away power. It was the secret, if you will, of her populist success within the project. She focused on obtaining the results she desired for the project. She made it clear that anyone who wanted could have all the credit and all the responsibility he or she wanted involving the project as long as he or she was working for the goal of establishing the cooperatives. Whatever power she had was there for the taking. Interestingly she was seen as the most powerful person in the project and was revered and even feared by some of the residents.

The force of this woman's presence was demonstrated by a rather bizarre event I by happenstance observed. One of the pluralist woman involved in the conflictual and unsuccessful attempt to form R2FHC moved out of her house under threat of eviction for nonpayment of rent. I was present when she drove away from her coop unit for the last time with her belongings in tow and heard her scream out her car window "no more cooperative" and, with particular emphasis, "no more (name of the individual woman leader)." As a general proposition, this early group of leaders and professionals was very conscious of social relations and the role they play in working with people. Initial meetings with people would always be in groups. After the meeting the people who attended talked about the ability of one or another person in attendance to communicate with those on the other side. Whoever could communicate best with that person continued the contact.

Gender Not a Public Issue

Aside from the populist womens' leadership and their position of the equality of the sexes, there were other reasons that gender did not become a public issue in the project. In part, it was because the populist leaders focused on the job at hand and decided pragmatically not to raise the issue. Raising gender issues could have sidetracked the cooperative organizing effort by either alienating men who were helping the project succeed or causing fights within families that would have required a lot of attention once the fights began. Also the women leaders were clear about keeping their public and private lives quite separate. As is discussed in Chapter 2, these women saw the community in Route 2 as a public community. They were not seeking a totalizing community where the distinctions between public and private would end.

It may be, however, that the non-expression of the issue may also represent a deeper sexism in our society. Several hints of racial differentiation in the project were noted and attacked. Gender did not have the same status. The difference is illustrated by several incidents that took place in the project.

The first incident involved a fourplex which was to be remodelled into a triplex to relieve overcrowding. This meant that one family in the fourplex had to be relocated. Two of the families in the building were Latino, one was Black and the fourth was a single-parent White woman. One of the Latino families was out of the country when the first decision was made, and that family was chosen to relocate. When they returned, the two Latino families approached the mixed gender-ethnic cooperative board asking that they both be allowed to stay and that the White single parent be asked to move. They got along fine with the Black family, but they didn't like the single parent. In classic stereotypical terms they described her as having men coming to visit at all hours of the days and night, i.e., of being a prostitute and being a bad mother. Their characterization of the woman was not greeted the way such a stereo-typical characterization of a Black or Latino person would have been greeted. People's hackles were not raised. It was simply something to look into and consider.

Another incident involved some of the populist women and some of the male Latino staff members of Nuestra. The populist women came to believe that some of the male Latino staff of Nuestra were sexist. They felt the men were patronizing them and didn't like it. There were some clashes between these men and the women which the men explained away as being personality conflicts. (A polite form of the typical characterization of the "hysterical women.") I asked them why they did not press their confrontation with these men further. They noted that they were disengaging from active participation in the project at the time. It was obvious that the women in question were very tired from a long political and development struggle. One of the women, however, said it was not only that. The ethnicity of the men also played a role. She was not Latina and felt that she would have to take on the whole culture of which these men were a part to change the behavior which upset her. Whether she was right or not, it disclosed that in her mind gender did not have the same status as ethnicity in such matters.

Pluralist/Clientelist Working-Class Feminism

There were other very influential women in the project who were less openly vocal, active, and visible than the early populist leaders. These women were more in the pluralist and particularly in the clientelist camp. They were very much like the "center women" discussed by difference theorists in Ann Bookman's and Sandra Morgen's *Women and the Politics of Empowerment* (1988). The term center women refers to women at the center of social networks who have power in political settings because of their networking skills. In particular, the article by Karen Brodkin Sacks in Bookman and Morgen's book describes what I observed in the Route 2 corridor (pp.77-94).

The center women and their networks in the project were found primarily among the immigrant Latinas.[16] As Sacks describes, the women had dominant roles in these networks. They formed consensus on votes for candidates and on various issues that they saw as important. Some of the more prominent women joined the boards of the cooperatives, but, as Sacks found, they usually helped install men as president and spokesperson for their group (Sacks 1988). It is important, however, to understand that election to office is a result and not a cause of the women's central position. Center women are not elected. They emerge from a process of social interaction.

The center women's role became particularly important with the transition from new populist to pluralist leadership. In the pluralist environment of interests and power these women could more easily influence the trend of events than during the populist period. For example, the center women helped shape the Latino caucus and the decision to separate Nuestra from the cooperatives. As discussed below, the center women's model of society was based more on the model of the family than the polis of the new populists. In their minds the cooperatives should be social and familial in character. Nuestra was a business and as such had to be separated from the cooperatives. They initially supported the pluralist man who led this move and later played a major part in bringing him down.

After the formal separation of Nuestra from the cooperatives, men were left behind on the Nuestra board to take care of the business. The center women, who first congregated on their coop membership committee and then the corridor-wide membership committee, put their efforts into R2FHC, a group that was to address the social needs of the residents.

A Case of Networking

In one coop a center woman came on the board who always supported a man for president. She repeatedly stated her loyalty to her network in moments of choice over who should be admitted into the cooperative, whose units would be repaired first, or who should be evicted. If a member of her network fell behind in her rent, she would do all she could to protect the person from eviction. If a member of her network needed his or her place repaired, she would work to make that happen. She kept her own waiting list to fill vacancies, and she worked to have people in her larger network admitted into the cooperative. She would say things like: "my people are more important than the cooperative," and "I don't like it when my friends can't get their apartment repaired."

She did not ask for or get personal favors. Her fight was for her people, her family. She was a very political Latina who saw herself as engaged in a struggle for her people's survival larger than any needs of the cooperative. The needs of the cooperatives had to be subservient to her people's needs. She did not seek the personal rewards of a patron, but she very much understood the model of clientelist relationships and knew how to work with it to get support for the ends she sought.

When issues presented themselves, she behaved as a consummate networker using her skills at private talk on the phone or more often in personal visits. She understood people's biases and needs and exploited them. She did not set herself aside as a leader in the formal sense. She remained an advocate for "her people" attacking the coop, even while being on its board, and its leadership, while being a leader. The center women's role is much like that of an organizer, and you could say she was an outstanding organizer.

She demonstrated both her understanding of the Latino population and her organizing skill by unifying the left-wing Central Americans and right-wing Cubans of her cooperative into her network. She did this by convincing the board of the cooperative to pay for a mass at a local Catholic church when one of the elderly Cubans passed away. Some of the Cubans who had been aloof from the cooperative fearing it as a socialist or communist endeavor changed almost over night. They were now part of the process, and their door was open to the center woman for visits at decisive moments.

The power of the network was not limited to cooperative issues. It also had power of its own over the members of the network. Networks operate by consensus. The consensus may result from mutual reasoning or may be enforced through social pressure (Mansbridge 1980, pp. 163-182). Exclusion from the network, particularly for immigrant Latinos, can have very serious potential consequence. It can mean an individual's exclusion from his or her support structure in a strange land. In the few cases where individuals tried bucking the consensus and the center women, they were usually publicly attacked as racists. As is discussed in Chapter 4, within the Latino context, this charge meant they had placed themselves above (against) the other Latinos.

Such networks are excellent devices for fighting oppression and for fighting for survival. Whether they are such a useful device once the battle is won may be another matter. They can be tools of oppression. I talked to a populist leader about the networks when they were becoming increasingly visible in the corridor. She saw them as cliques destroying the process of forming community. The cooperatives should be inclusive; the networks were exclusive. She had been part of a multi-ethnic church when she was young. Cliques were a problem the church had to struggle against. She did not want a repeat of that experience in this multi-ethnic environment.

The Importance of the Family

The corridor-wide membership committee and R2FHC were primarily made up of women, but discussion in the groups' meetings rarely dealt directly with women's needs, and the women did not speak of themselves as women or their organizations as women's groups. The leading center women participated as representatives of their families. The family needed inexpensive food, health care, and child care, and the children needed supportive after-school activities. The cooperative, if it was to be a valued institution, had to meet the families' needs. Ideally it had to be an extension of the women's collective families. Rather than an instrumental adjunct to family life, the cooperatives had to be part of that life.

The populist women insisted on keeping the family and the cooperative separate. They wanted an instrumental cooperative community and saw the Route 2 project almost in classic Athenian terms as a polis. They were seeking a democracy where kinship ties and authoritarianism were replaced with a public society of citizens based on reason and merit and a private life of the family (Bookchin 1987; Plant 1978).

Most feminist literature has been very critical of the widespread favorable view of the Athenian polis. Nancy Hartsock is among the primary feminist critics of the Athenian model (Hartsock 1983).[17] Noting the exclusion of slaves as well as women from Athenian public life, she argues that the polis was less than history has claimed for it. In Greece of classic period, the family and the home were women's world and public institutions and politics were men's world. The populist women certainly would not have endorsed this aspect of the Athenian model.

Beyond this, however, Hartsock moves closer to the clientelist women's approach. She sees home and family as the bases of life, of the reproduction of life, and ancient Greek politics as lacking this foundation. According to Hartsock ancient Greek politics lacked substance and was without the primary relationships and eros that is necessary for a society to survive. In Hartsock's view the Athenians, who were focused on what they saw as rationality and merit, on debate, neglected survival and, as Athenian history demonstrates, had a model that could not last. Family is the model to build from, not the sterile male-dominated society of patriarchal reason.

The populist women would agree with Hartsock that family ties assure survival, but they did not see the cooperatives as necessary for survival. It was this attitude that led the populist president of R2CHC to tell the staff, as I reported in Chapter 4, that it would be all right if the project failed. Life would go on whether the cooperatives existed or not, but if they were to exist, they had to be places of equality and justice in which reason, as the Athenians would define it, prevailed.

Feminist writer Carol Gilligan stands with Hartsock on the value of family as the feminist model for society. She specifically rejects an emphasis on justice for being an expression of patriarchy (Gilligan 1982). She substitutes a female, mothering principle of an "ethic of care " for the emphasis on justice. Populist feminist Mary Dietz disagrees with Hartsock and Gilligan and argues, as would the populist women in the Route 2 project, that this dichotomy between justice and care is false (Dietz 1987).[18]

Dietz writes that Gilligan, Hartsock, and other like-minded feminists are not providing an adequate model for democratic political community. Family is certainly a model for caring relationships. In her words citizenship cannot be modelled on "the bond between a mother and her child." She writes that democratic citizenship is a unique relationship, something unto itself. "The democratic vision does not legitimize . . . the transformation of private into public virtues" (Dietz 1987, p. 14). She sees citizenship as deriving "its meaning from the collective and public engagement of peers and not the "loving intimates" of the family. The primary relation-ship of democratic citizenship is that of "civic peers; its guiding virtue is mutual respect." Dietz does believe that the revitalization of democratic citizenship is an especially appropriate task for feminists to undertake, and would undoubtedly claim the approach the populist women have selected as a partial expression of their gender (p. 16).

Hartsock's work assumes a very patriarchal world, gender segregated between home and politics. Such segregation is not the case in the Route 2 project; working-class women were in both worlds. The coops were not dominated by men, and the new populists would argue, the politics of the coops were not dominated by patriarchy. If anything, the democratic society of the cooperatives was liberating from patriarchy and eros at home. Although the women would stand with their men against the outside world, within the cooperatives where they had a modicum of control, they wanted an open, rational meritocracy, not the working-class patriarchic structure many of them faced at home.[19]

One of the early activists indicated she was "brought up and had become accustomed to the teaching that the husband is the head of the family; the father is the one who gives orders; the husband is the one who tells you what to do; the one to direct." Her education and her work had taught her otherwise, but she held to the old ways at home. If she did not want it that way, she felt she would have to get a divorce and this was something she did not want to do. When she was out of the house, things were different. She was her own person.

This woman and other women often talked about having to work around their husbands.[20] I remember being struck in a conversation with a woman interested in participating in a committee when she told me that she would have to talk to her husband about it first. There was a twinkle in her eye as she indicated that she'd find a way to get him to go along. One of the populist leaders less compliant in her home life regarded this behavior as "women's manipulation" and attributed it to the patriarchy of the home place. She believed bringing this skill into the public arena would enlarge the power of women, but it would not contribute to the formation of a just democracy or an empowering community. Whatever people "had to do" to survive at home was their business; she wanted the Route 2 project to be a place where this manipulation was not necessary.

The populist women's attitude about the nature of the cooperatives did not mean the family lacked importance for them. They were fiercely dedicated to their families. They did not believe, however, that the kind of passion they had about their families had a role in the cooperatives' internal business. For them the cooperative could not obtain the level of commitment that sometimes kept families from being ripped apart by the passion they contained.

There are many extended families in the Route 2 project. Some of these families had internal feuds of long standing. One of the populist women liked to tell people to leave their family fights behind. She clearly enjoyed telling me a story about two warring sister-in-laws she got to work together on coop business. She said they had an easier time talking about roofing material than their long-time family problems.

The populist women's instrumental approach was consistent with the existing social and geographic reality of the cooperatives. The coops were far from family groupings.[21] Some of the cooperatives consisted of from twenty to thirty parcels of property spread over ten or more blocks.[22] Even neighbors did not necessarily know each other before the coops were formed. One liked her coop because after working on the coop, she and her neighbor of twelve years had started talking to one another. Even after the formation of the cooperatives, however, if the residents were not neighbors or relatives, they often did not associate with one another outside of cooperative affairs.

The early activists were neighborly to the people who lived around them (I saw many instances of aid for someone in trouble, in the case of fire for example), but they did not see the need for a great deal of social activity.[23] Their social lives and social networks were elsewhere. It was unusual for the coops to become a center of any resident's social life, although this was the case with one of the coop presidents who was a young single woman. More than one person who moved into the cooperatives indicated that they were surprised at how little social activity there was in the cooperatives. Some of the center women, consistent with their belief about the cooperative as family written large, tried to start more social activities, but the effort was not sustained.

It may be that the new populists' reaction to the center women and networking was accentuated by the particular political-cultural content of the networks. The Latina women's networks in the corridor were permeated with clientelism. At first I thought that the networks had been part of the pluralistic power politics that briefly dominated the project, but, on reflection, I changed my mind. Whereas networks are clearly a source of collective power, as some feminist theorists argue, there is a particular relational difference between socially based women's networks and interest-based pluralism power politics (Ackelsberg 1988).

Reciprocity between the leader and the followers is an essential element of clientelism (Powell 1970). What a clientelist would see as the necessary reciprocity between a patron and a client the new populists would see as corruption. Although both parties benefit in the clientelist relationship there is no doubt that the patron benefits more than the client. The new populists held that leaders should get less, not more than the residents as a whole. The president of R2CHC, for example, insisted that her cooperative be the last to be purchased to make this point. With this stance they could not accommodate patronism.

The clientelists were very critical of the cold, direct, instrumental way the populists sometimes conducted the business of the cooperatives. I remember a Latino trying to explain to me, a sometimes very direct populist, about his unhappiness with my behavior. He said "I like what you do. I just don't like how you do it." Populists are sometimes, in clientelist eyes, too aggressive, too rude, too unfeeling to be tolerated. As was discussed in Chapter 5, the Americano's behavior in general was more than once seen as insulting by the Latinos.

It is clear that clientelism in a limited-equity cooperative in the United States would have to take a somewhat different form than in rural Latin America. There were no landed patrons and peasants. There were, however, definitely border people who linked the immigrant population to the larger society. These were not necessarily the same people who played the role of multi-cultural links discussed in the last chapter. The patron might speak little English, but have access to services for Spanish speakers in the larger Latino world of Los Angeles.

A Case of Clientelism

Clientelism emerged in the new construction project that failed to convert to a cooperative. Because of the error by the consultant the R2CHC board had control of the project. It attempted to organize the residents through a residents' association that could manage the project. Reluctantly, one after the other individuals, primarily women, were recruited by organizers as candidates for president of the residents' association. One after another, the individuals elected by the people would, upon assuming the office, be attacked by the people who elected them for separating themselves from the people and, one after another, each would resign and rejoin the larger group.

What the Americanos did not initially understand was that they had moved four women into the project who had been managers working for Caltrans in various parts of the corridor. The women had great power in the Caltrans management scheme and like petite patrons controlled who moved in and whose unit was repaired. Now stripped of their authority by the creation of the cooperatives, they were jockeying for position in the new construction project. After more than a year in residence, one of these women emerged as dominant and assumed the role of a center woman. Although as Sacks discusses, center women resist assuming formal leadership, this woman was convinced with much effort to step forward by the organizer working on the project. (Sachs 1988)

The source of the center woman's power with the Spanish-speaking immigrant population was, in large part, that she "knew" many people who could provide services in Los Angeles. She was a bridge to the outside world. For example, the people in the project wanted a fence around their development. The Route 2 leadership responded to the idea by asking the people to get bids on what it would cost to build such a fence. The leadership's idea was that this would be good training for the eventual take over of the project. The task turned out to be over-whelming.

The people who were largely maids, garment workers, and teacher's aides had no experience with bids or fences for such a large project and had no idea how to start to respond to the request for obtaining bids. A stalemate developed with the people wanting a fence and the R2CHC leadership wanting bids. After a period of time the center woman, who was not yet president, spoke up. She had a friend who did that kind of work. She would get a bid. In general if the immigrant population needed help, a lawyer, a doctor, an accountant or the like, she knew someone. She was a source of advice on many topics including how the women should deal with the men in their lives.

When the center woman stepped forward as the president of the association, she took it on her clientelist terms. She would become the patron. The problem was that just as the rules governing the larger project restricted the ability to make choices essential to populism, they largely eliminated the power to generate a reciprocal relationship between the president and the residents of the project necessary for clientelism. The center women set out to correct that problem.

She made it very clear that the federal regulations that governed the operation of the project would not be her concern. Consistent with the experience of many Latin Americans, she was very cynical about such things as HUD regulations, and if her job was to run the coop, she would do it her way. This was troubling to the Americanos who, while they also didn't like many of the regulations, did not share her cynicism about their importance. The clash in attitudes came to head when a vacancy occurred in the project. The president wanted her relative to move into her project and helped falsify the relative's application documents to make this possible. When this was discovered, the relative was denied admission. The center woman, turned patron, was encouraged to resign from her presidency by the organizer who had talked her into it in the first place. The incident was a source of embarrassment and was an indication to her that she could not run things her way. She followed the organizer's advice and resigned. This presidency was then filled by a series of short-term presidencies until the effort to organize the group into a cooperative ended. The center woman could have created the coop, but it was on terms the new populists (and HUD regulations) could not tolerate.

Conclusion

The Route 2 project is in many ways an expression of working class and third world women. Although these women have a lot in common, they are not unified on many issues of community and empowerment. As authors like Bell Hooks note, working class and third world women live in a different reality than white middle class women. What has not been made clear is that these women have differences about how to approach this shared reality which may in its own way set them as apart from one another as collectively they are ideologically set off from white middle-class women.

The populist women in the Route 2 project accept a populist approach to the project at variance to much of mainstream feminism and their more pluralist and clientelist sisters. The clientelist and pluralist women did share a theoretical base with some mainstream feminists, but they did not set gender at the center of their organizing. At times they could be seen as conservative women.

Notes

1. For a primary work that examines issues of gender in the context of housing cooperatives see Leavitt and Saegert (1990).

2. See, for example, Bookman and Morgen (1988).

3. There are books that examine the various positions of different ethnic groups. See, for example, *This Bridge Called My Back: Writings by Radical Women of Color* (1981) edited by Cherrie Moraga and Gloria Anzaldua. These books do not, however, compare the positions of the various groups in a single conflictual setting.

4. Catherine MacKinnon (1987) articulates the distinction in much of her work to establish a third path in feminist thought. The distinction is also seen in such interchanges as that between Virginia Sapiro (1981) and Irene Diamond and Nancy Hartsock (1983) and is discussed with great care in Zillah Eisenstein (1988). Natalie Harris Bluestone (1987) in her analysis of classic literature and Cynthia Fuchs Epstein (1988) in her analysis of social science research expressed the no distinction position in great detail.

5. For an example of collective action by women in such situations see Fuglesang and Chandler (1986, p. 118).

6. The child care center was organized around the theories of Piaget and John Dewey. It was run in an open but structured style. This was consistent with how the Route 2 project was organized. There was structure, but the people were free to decide. Leadership meant creating structure.

7. In 1984, Nefise Bazoglu, a Turkish sociologist, surveyed men and women in Route 2 along with other men and women in Los Angeles to investigate gender's role in activism at the community level. She has shared her work with me for which I am grateful.

8. For a full discussion of the attitudes of black women on the difference position see Hooks (1984).

9. The Route 2 effort can be contrasted to examples of women's housing cooperatives. For a description and examination of women's housing cooperatives see Wekerle (1988).

10. One of the younger white male professionals also held this view. He believed that the women were better listeners. Listening is said to be one of the skills women develop that makes them different and more effective at direct

democracy (Mansbridge 1990, pp. 134-135). The women who he gave as examples disagreed with his position.

11. For discussion of age in this context see Evans (1980).

12. Citing Susan Sontag's "Third World Women" (1973 p. 203).

13. Citing Charlotte Perkins Gilman's *The Man-Made World, or Our Androcentric Culture* (1911, p. 114).

14. See also Carol Gilligan's *In a Different Voice* (1982, p. 19).

15. For a discussion of the strength of some working class women and their difference with some feminists on this point see Kollis (1975).

16. There was a great variety of ideologies among the Latinas from very left to very right although they tended to share the center woman and, as is discussed later, the clientelist approach. There was a significant group of very traditionally conservative women in the Route 2 population. The most classic example of their attitudes is demonstrated by an incident reminiscent of rural village life. A divorced immigrant women had sexual relations with the male relative of another resident of her complex. When it became known, the men in the complex began to approach her for sexual favors. The other women in the complex rather than coming to her aid, took the position that she created the problem by her behavior and deserved what she got. The woman's reaction was that it was like she was back in the village in Latin America from which she has come. She had travelled north, in part, to get away from all that.

17. For a further discussion of the sexism of the Athenians see French (1985). Bluestone (1987), while not referring to these works, gives a different view. Focusing on Plato, she finds more gender neutrality than the above authors.

18. See also Mansbridge (1990) who states the difference position but calls for an alliance with the direct democrat theorists.

19. Several of the women had life histories that were consistent with the findings of Lillian Breslow Rubin's findings in *Worlds of Pain* (1976).

20. This is certainly reminiscent of Simone de Beauvoir's observation that women learn "to lie to men, to scheme, to be wiley" in handling men (1949, p. 243).

21. For the opposite conclusion see Leavitt and Saegert (1990). It may be that the degree of diversity in the two populations and the difference in the nature of the neighborhoods in which the cooperatives are located accounts for the difference in the findings. The Leavitt and Saegert work focuses on Afro-American residents of cooperatives in Harlem.

22. Leavitt and Saegert (1990) refer to the formation of what they call the "community household." Their work focuses on relatively large buildings as opposed to the scattered site nature of the Route 2 cooperatives. Also, while for Los Angeles the area in which the Route 2 cooperatives are located contains something akin to neighborhoods, these neighborhoods are a far cry from what this word means in New York.

23. For a discussion of the distinction see Willmott (1986). I observed neighbors coming to each others' aid in cases of fire or broken pipes and the like.

Afterword

In this afterword I will examine the Route 2 project in light of what has happened in other similar efforts elsewhere. The Route 2 story is the story of a process. It does not contain lessons of absolute right and wrong. Strategic decisions were made and actions taken in response to particular circumstances. The decisions and actions could have been different. The project could have been more successful, or it could have ended at many points in complete collapse and failure. In an idyllic world of social science a tape of the project could be altered and rerun to see the impact of alternative decisions and tease out the rules of the community formation process. Unfortunately no such technology exists. The only available alternative is to compare my remembrances of the Route 2 project story with other different but related stories remembered by other researchers. Literature on social movements and community development is relevant here and will be employed to see what lessons can be gained to help guide other community planning endeavors.

Two projects very similar in many respects to the Route 2 project are of particular relevance in this analysis. One is Milton-Park, a project somewhat larger than the Route 2 project, that took place in Montreal, Canada. The Milton-Park project is the subject of a book by Claire Helman entitled *The Milton-Park Affair* published in 1987. The other is a smaller but equally passionate project in Liverpool, England that resulted in the Weller Streets Housing Cooperative. The Weller Streets project is the subject of a book by Alan McDonald entitled *The Weller Way* published in 1986.

The Milton-Park project involved 600 plus units on 25 acres in an area three by seven blocks near McGill University and downtown Montreal. The Milton-Park project residents like the Route 2 project residents included a broad mix of peoples. The difference is that the Milton-Park project included English and French speakers rather than English and Spanish speakers and many more students and people connected with the nearby university than the almost entirely working-class residents in the Route 2 Project.

The residents in Milton-Park battled a private developer who owned all the property later involved in their project. The first round went to the developer in a battle that lasted from 1968 to the late 1970s when he began to demolish the property. The second round belonged to the residents, when after just beginning the demolition, the developer's project failed in economic collapse. The residents with the help of powerful friends, were able to exploit the opportunity this presented in the early 1980s by convincing the Canadian Mortgage and Housing Corporation to intervene on their behalf and finance the project. The end result was the creation of 14 cooperatives consisting of 339 housing units (compared to 5 cooperatives and 272 units in Route 2) and 158 units in non-profit ownership (compared to 105 plus single family houses in individual ownership and 16 units of non-profit housing in Route 2).

The Milton-Park residents had the advantage of having an established cooperative housing program in Canada and were able to raise sufficient funds to spend $50,000 per unit on rehabilitation compared to under $10,000 per unit in the Route 2 project. As of the publishing of the Helman book, however, the title to the property was still in the hands of a non-profit sponsor, and the terms on which the property ownership would be transferred to the cooperatives had not been worked out. This created friction that was avoided in the Route 2 project. In the Route 2 project the property was never owned by the non-profit developer, R2CHC, but was purchased directly by the cooperatives as a matter of choice.

The Weller Way story varies from Route 2 because it involved the construction in the early 1980s of a 61 unit cooperative as replacement housing for people in a clearance project. Weller Way residents lived in housing managed by a London-based housing association that had been taken over after bankruptcy of the owner. The residents were awaiting demolition of their homes and relocation. In the mid 1970s they became tired of waiting for relocation and began to protest for the clearance to take place immediately. The idea of the cooperative emerged after the residents were told they would have to wait ten years because there was no replacement housing and no land in the area to build new housing (McDonald 1986, pp. 30-33).

Although there is a long history of cooperative housing in Britain,[1] the idea of the construction of cooperatives as replacement housing in clearance projects was new (p. 14). Because of this the Weller Way residents, like the Route 2 residents, faced many battles in convincing the establishment of the wisdom of their idea. This also meant similar battles with professionals over implementation of the residents' ideas. The ethnic mix in the Route 2 and Milton-Park populations was missing in Weller Way, but the strong working-class tone of the project shares much with its relation in Los Angeles. When I read the reports of conversations in McDonald's book, the words, sans accent, match many of the conversations I overheard in the Route 2 project.

Neither of the reports of these two projects have much information on the operation of the cooperatives once formed. Here I will have to rely upon studies of other ongoing cooperatives. Particularly relevant are those in New York City where cooperatives are a well established housing form. Some 400 limited-equity cooperatives have been created in recent years. Their origin is different than the cases above because they are the product of landlord abandonment of buildings and resident takeovers after city tax foreclosures. The City of New York also has established cooperative development programs to try to renovate some of the large number of abandoned buildings and a long history of tenant activism to build upon. The New York programs and the dynamics of the New York City conversion process are set forth in Jacqueline Leavitt and Susan Saegert's book *From Abandonment to Hope* (Leavitt and Saegert 1990) and follow up work by Saegert (Saegert 1989).[2] Their work shows that once the cooperatives are formed, regardless of origin, the problems of operation are common.[3] One of the commonalities of community struggles regardless of their national or coastal base is that they are all expressions of the people's reality and the will to continue to resist oppression and domination. They will do so either openly and collectively as in the Route 2, Milton-Park, and Weller Way cases and in many buildings in New York City, or privately and individually as described by James Scott in *Weapons of the Weak* (Scott 1985). The process by which people jointly come to the decision to openly rebel is quite eloquently described by John Gaventa in his book on Appalachia, *Power and Powerlessness* (Gaventa 1980). His explanation relies heavily on the existence of an opening in previously overwhelmingly dominant conditions that results from an exogenously generated shift in power relations. Without this opening, he argues, collective protest movements are unlikely to begin, and I would add that if they do begin, they are likely to fail.

In the case of Route 2 such a shift in power relations was in process. A new liberal governor had been elected at a historic moment in which the restructuring of economic relations created cracks in the clarity of state power--what Jurgen Habermas calls the *Legitimization Crisis* (Habermas 1973). I doubt that it is a coincidence that the Milton-Park and Weller Way projects overlap in time with the Route 2 project. The restructuring and the legitimization crisis that left the space for the residents of Route 2 was not limited to Los Angeles. It also created an opportunity for the other projects in other parts of the western world to succeed as well.[4]

The fact that people can and do rebel, of course, does not mean they will succeed. As stated in the beginning of this book defeat is a more common result even in moments of opportunity. The complex nature of the struggle and the many potential pitfalls that await a rebellion even as partial as the cases reviewed here makes this lack of success very understandable. One is reminded of the many attempts to model elements of the political processes including Pressman and Wildavsky's (Pressman and Wildavsky 1973) attempt to model the problems of implementation of policy and Bachrach and Baratz's (Bachrach and Baratz 1970) intricate model of the political decision/nondecision channel. In these stories the problem posed is perhaps complex even beyond those analyses. The number of decision points and the necessity of appropriate action at each of them is striking.

This afterword is divided into the three stages of the project enumerated in the first chapter. The struggles could have been lost at any of the three stages. The residents could have lost the initial political struggle and been evicted; their effort to develop the property could have failed; or the cooperatives could have by now disintegrated. It is also possible that rather than being lost the struggle could have been entirely transformed into a very different story, but still one that could have been judged as success on its own terms. The key actors in the process are the residents, the state, intellectuals both within and outside the state in civil society, and capital, in these cases particularly real estate and finance capital. Conflict can exist between any of the actors and involve any of the important elements. The process is dynamic.

Stage One: Mobilization and Social Action

The Demand

The process begins with the formation of a demand. The demand can be on the state, capital, or both. The formulation of this demand can play a major role in the outcome. Internal disagreement on the contents of the demand can end a movement before it begins. The process by which the demand is formed can also be a relevant factor. It is not unusual for the leadership of a movement to formulate demands ahead of the mass of the movement. This can generate problems later in the process if the validity of the demand is challenged. Partly because of this the presence of leadership that has both the vision to formulate demands and sufficient clarity to help the group through the challenges from the internal dissention and external resistance that awaits at various decision points in the process is essential to success. All three projects had such leaders. These are the people in the Route 2 case who I've called organic intellectuals.

In both the Los Angeles and Montreal projects there was conflict among the leadership over the formulation of the demand. The issue of collective ownership versus individual private ownership existed in both projects. The conflict in the Route 2 leadership was cut-off by the decision to treat single- and multi-family property differently. A similar issue was not so easily resolved in the Milton-Park project and was a source of constant disruption (Helman 1987, pp. 109-110; 125-137). In the Los Angeles project the leadership also had to cope with the more traditionally left members' criticism of the new populist leadership. This was not present in Montreal because the contested property was in private hands and not owned by the state. The attack was with the customary left anti-anarchist logic (anarchism is disguised individualism) first expressed by Engels in *The Housing Question* (Engels 1975) and later expanded in Rod Burgess' criticism of John Turner's self-help housing work (Burgess 1982). In the Weller Way case this left position was not expressed as much within the project as it was by Labour Party local councillors opposing the project (McDonald 1986, p. 17).[5]

In the Route 2 project the left also saw the demand for ownership as potentially coopting and self-defeating rather than empowering (because the effort was absorbing the failure of the system and was itself doomed to failure) and proposed to confront the state to meet its obligation to continue to house the residents rather than demand ownership of the property. A left housing advocacy organization in New York City named Homefront attacked the cooperative organizing in New York on the same grounds (Homefront 1977).[6] The positions of either of the sides in the Route 2 project could not be compromised into the other's position. Had the left's efforts resulted in an unresolvable division in the population, the project could have ended before it started. Had the anti-self-help group in the Route 2 project become the dominant leadership the story may or may have not been a success story, but it would have been different.

In all three cooperative cases the demand for the formation of cooperatives was formed by leadership ahead of the general residents. While in all cases the overwhelming number of residents were united against the opposition, the common response to the cooperative idea was that it was "crazy." As one of the Weller Way residents who represented residents of all three efforts put it, "I wasn't keen on the idea . . . I thought it was pie in the sky. I thought it was a crazy idea" (McDonald 1986, p. 39). In the Route 2 project this worked for the leadership because the opponents of the idea did not take the formation of the cooperatives seriously until the first cooperative was already formed. The Milton-Park leadership was not so lucky. Dissenters objecting to their homes being included in the cooperatives took the cooperative idea seriously and launched a sophisticated attack to protect their interests. Even though the demands of the leadership were not uniformly held by the mass of the population of the projects, the leadership importantly was able to maintain the appearance of tacit majority support of the populace throughout their negotiations. In Route 2 this was in part because Caltrans was ineffective in exploiting the potential divisions in the population. As will be seen this again was not true in Montreal.

The Response to the Demand

The reaction to the demand is also an essential part of the demand process. The opposition can take several tacks in response to a demand. They can simply refuse to hear the demand or if it is heard, refuse to comply. They can go further and attempt to retaliate against those with the nerve to make the demand and attempt to crush the movement in its infancy. In the alternative the opposition can seem to acquiesce in whole or in part to the demand. Sometimes the appearance of acquiescence can kill a movement before it starts. The yes answer can include an attempt to coopt the leadership of the movement formally or informally into the state apparatus, and the apparent support can later dissolve in bureaucratic detail. The state, for its part, is rarely a unified whole. Because of this it is also possible for different elements of the state to simultaneously take any or all of these positions. Targeted capital is rarely as ambivalent, but capital as a whole can be divided.

In Route 2 the initial demand presented to the state was for the individual residents to be given the right to buy state-owned housing. In reaction to the state's (Caltrans') negative response, this demand was transformed into a state sponsored compromise (HCD and political) between populist and individualist portions of the project leadership for both individual and collective purchase of the property. The state's negative response forced the original organizers to broaden their base, and the common belief in self-help in the dominant project leadership permitted the compromise. Given the ideological conflicts within the core group, such a result might have been unlikely without state opposition making compromise a necessity and state intervention making the compromise plan possible. In Liverpool, as is stated above, the initial demand was for relocation of the Weller Way residents in the near term. The refusal to do so led to an indigenously-generated, unlikely idea of building a cooperative.

Caltrans and the opposition in Milton-Park took the line described by Bachrach and Baratz of denying the legitimacy of the coop idea (Bachrach and Baratz 1970). In the Route 2 project Caltrans repeatedly attacked both the general population by failing to maintain the housing and increasing the rent and the leadership by the hostile responses to their efforts. Their actions tended to unify the leadership and left the masses nowhere to go but to follow the leadership. While in Los Angeles the state's efforts at dividing the population were feeble, this was not true in Montreal. There, it is believed, a private detective was hired to infiltrate the residents' protest efforts, to cause dissension and discredit the leadership (Helman 1987, pp. 65-81). The opposition need not be so aggressive to kill a movement. Landlords in Ann Arbor some years ago used the tactic of simply being responsive to tenants' needs to break up a city wide rent strike effort (Jennings 1972, pp. 58-59). Had the opposition not been as hard line in the cooperative cases the results of the projects could have been very different.

In each of the three projects the state was divided. Without support from some element of the state all such efforts will likely fail. Both political elements and intellectuals in the employ of the state came to the Route 2 residents' aid. In the Weller Way case support came from a local office of the managing housing association that coincidentally broke away from its parent in the period the project began. While, as will be seen in the development section of this afterword, there were many disagreements between the housing association staff and the residents, the residents would likely not have succeeded without this help. This is much like the case of the residents of Route 2 and the staff of the state's HCD.

Support of the state can be garnered through external support from elements of civil society. One person who has looked at the interaction of support from civil society and the state is Michael Lipsky in his work on the "great Harlem rent strike," *Protest in City Politics* (Lipsky 1970). Lipsky argues that it is not the demand itself or the power of the demanders that causes the state to respond positively, but the support of large powerful segments of the populace garnered through media exposure that brings pressure on the political elements of the state.

In the Route 2 Project the leadership seemed to be aware of Lipsky's option to winning political support, but did not choose this path. They decided to use the media very selectively and wage a low profile campaign. The fortunate presence of sympathetic, powerful politicians, a good fortune the other groups lacked, made it unnecessary to go very public. It is also likely that the thought of potential press coverage of 1,500 low-income people being simultaneously evicted, an image the Route 2 project activists kept alive in their rhetoric, added enthusiasm to the political support. In Montreal the initial support did not come from dominant politicians but from elites in civil society.[7] The project's major allies were a prominent and exceptionally well connected attorney and the historic preservation organizations of the city (Helman 1987, pp. 103-114). The Milton-Park protest was very public and received a great deal of media coverage. Lipsky's model could explain some of the support they received, but it was the individual rather than mass support that made a reality out of the residents' demands.

Lipsky's book focuses solely on the politics of the process and not on the role of intellectuals within the state. The state is made up of politicians and intellectuals (more commonly referred to as bureaucrats if hostile, or professionals if not). It is not uncommon for reformist or radical intellectuals to seek employment within the state. Relevant here is the literature that discusses the social change strategy sometimes called "the long march through the institutions" (Dutschke 1968) or *Guerrillas in the Bureaucracy* (Needleman and Needleman 1974). This literature contains the argument that working for the state is a transformative activity necessary for social change. In the Route 2 case such intellectuals were numerous in the housing bureaucracy of the state in the wake of a liberal political success. They formed an alliance with the residents and the political elements of the state that supported the project against the other negative elements.

In the Milton-Park project intellectuals within the state also came to the aid of the residents. During the protest period, most notable was a planner in the city planning department who kept the residents informed about the moves of the city and the opposition (McDonald 1986, pp. 26-28) They also received extraordinary support, at least in spirit, from the primary architect working for the opposition. He resigned in protest to the plans he was preparing for the developer after finally realizing he could not convince the developer to mitigate any of the negative impacts of the developer's scheme (p. 50). No such gallant act took place in the other projects, but many professionals outside the state contributed to the realization of the residents' dreams.[8]

Intellectuals in the state opposed all three projects. In Liverpool and Los Angeles the entrenched local bureaucracies were not supportive. McDonald argues that new construction cooperatives were not supported because cooperatives are seen as a threat to public sector maintenance jobs (McDonald 1986, pp.16-17). The problem in Los Angeles may have been one more of inertia than intention; doing business as usual and lack of interest in responding to a new idea. In the Route 2 case it goes without saying that certainly the Caltrans staff, which saw its operations negatively affected by the below market sale to the residents, opposed the project.

An Alliance with Elements of the State and Civil Society

An alliance is not a unity. Lisa Peattie in her examination of her advocacy planning experience with Urban Planning Aids in the Boston Area makes the observation that planners tend to follow their own agendas rather than those of the clients (Peattie 1968).[9] Where the planners' agenda overlaps with the clients' the alliance is possible. This sort of alliance seems to have been formed in the three cases.

Most of the interests of the supportive intellectuals in the Route 2 project had more to do with a liberal vision of housing policy than the agenda of the residents of the project. The lack of identity of interests has within it the seeds of conflict. Successful management of these conflicts can be essential to the success of a movement. The decision not to apply for new construction funds from the federal government and the rent strike presented potentially movement ending conflicts. In Montreal the alliance with people whose primary agenda was historic preservation generated tensions in the alliance. Both the residents and supporters wanted to preserve the buildings, but this was primarily a means to an end for the residents. On the other hand the central issue for the residents was continued affordability, a secondary issue for the supporters. In both cases the conflicts were set backs but were not alliance ending. The fact that there were tenants in place and displacement was a pending reality gave both alliances a stability that other more general movements lack.

The conflicts over strategy and tactics in the Route 2 project were with the intellectual elements of the state and not the political elements. Had the politicians qualified their support in a fashion unacceptable to the residents it would have put the project leadership to a more difficult test than they faced. (Certainly they did compromise, for example, in the agreement to handle the single- and multi-family housing and the elimination of self-help in the rehabilitation process.) There was a threat of this occurring when the delays in the project led the politicians to begin to lose faith in the ability of the residents to accomplish their development plans. The residents responded in a fashion that allayed these fears and the political support remained open ended. Whether the coherence of the intellectuals among the resident leadership would have withstood a more severe test is something that will never be known. Certainly pragmatic compromise is not unusual. The intellectuals within the state knew the politicians expected happy constituents and a positive outcome. The leadership of the residents knew they had political support. Without this the intellectuals in the employ of the state might have taken control of the project. The project might still have been a success, but it might also have been very different.

Opposition by Capital and Necessary Support

One of the primary determinants of success or failure of a rebellion is often its relationship to the interests of capital. The state as a structural ally of capital will be far less likely to respond favorably to a demand which is significant in the eyes of capital than one which capital sees as peripheral. This does not mean that success is impossible even in a direct confrontation of the interests of a protest group and capital. It does mean a much larger and protracted fight. This was certainly true in Montreal where a private developer owned the contested property. In fact the initial protests were a failure on the surface. The cooperative project followed the developer giving up on the project when market conditions worsened. It is undoubtedly true that the resident protests slowed the process and contributed to the eventual abandonment of the development scheme. After this decision was made, the state-capital logic was turned on its head, and the participation of the state in formation of the cooperatives was a capital-supportive act, a capital bail out.

In the Route 2 case only local small scale capital was offended. The local realtors joined with Caltrans to fight the project and with their own intellectuals, lawyers, attacked the project. They did not make a political dent in the effort, but only managed to delay the project in the courts.[10] The fact that one of the lawyers later became head of Caltrans demonstrates how not only the project's inoffensiveness to capital but also its timing played a part the project's success. In Liverpool capital was not a major factor in the opposition to the drive for the construction of the cooperative.

Stage Two: Developing the Cooperatives

Winning the battle and gaining the right to buy and rehabilitate or build cooperatives, which in our cases involved heroic efforts, is only a small part of the task the groups set out to accomplish. As McDonald put it, along the way the "crazy idea" turned into "a bloody complicated business" (McDonald 1986, p. 43). Had not their homes depended upon it, none of the groups would likely have lasted. As a Weller Way resident put it, "the early enthusiasm . . . was based upon vision and anger, not on any rigorous sense of what might happen" (p. 39).

In classic planning terms it might be said that in such situations activists must move from protest to planning (Davidoff 1965). In these cases it would be more correct to say that the groups had to move beyond protest and planning to responsibility, a much more serious undertaking. For example, in Route 2 this meant an immediate reversal of position. Instead of attacking Caltrans, the leadership was attacked by dissidents like those Milton-Park had already experienced. In Route 2 this changing role and attacks were met with a good degree of openness and a concerted effort to hegemonize the population out of the "we and they" thinking in the political battle phase to the "us" of community based development. All the activists had to try and establish a requisite degree of legitimacy, the same legitimacy that they attempted to destroy in the opposition.[11]

Taking responsibility also means engaging in the very laborious and technical development process, an unbelievable number of meetings, and many potentially friction-filled interactions among the residents and with professionals, some trying to help and others openly hostile. It may also mean, as it did in the Route 2 project and Weller Way cooperative, having to organize the necessary resources to do the project and, in the case of Route 2, find support from finance capital.

In Great Britain and Canada once the political problems are solved, government has programs in place. This does not, of course, mean that the bureaucrats operating these programs cooperate in every respect.[12] The conditions upon which development may proceed often continue to be under negotiation throughout the life of such projects. This means changing realities have to be repeatedly explained to the residents. One of the principle rules of organizing people, of establishing legitimacy, is the requirement of consistency. In a development environment this is rarely possible. The newness of the undertaking in Los Angeles added levels of necessary learning and unavoidable chaos to the Route 2 project not present in other efforts.

In the more working-class projects in Los Angles and Liverpool the residents were girded for these tasks and conflicts by a similar very aggressive attitude. Just like the Route 2 leader who had the all or nothing attitude, the Weller Way leadership was said to have "a kamikaze attitude that we've got nothing, so we've got nothing to lose. It's a nice attitude in that you can take anybody on." (McDonald 1986, p.40) This attitude also contributed to the insistence on resident control that resulted in these two stories containing so much conflict between the leadership and professionals.

The development process is also lengthy. The span of time required, particularly if it is on top of a lengthy political fight, tests an organization's staying power. The process in Montreal and Los Angeles was affected by a lengthy struggle to get the right to proceed and in Los Angeles and Liverpool by the length of time necessary during the development phase. In all three situations only a handful of hard core residents survived what was years of political and technical activity. At one point only five or six people held the Milton-Park project together (Helman 1987, p. 93; McDonald 1986, p. 151). In Route 2 the number got down to about seven before success caused the number to rise. The result in all three projects was the same. Only a limited number of people sustained activity during the struggle and learned the political lessons of the project. In Route 2 this meant that when political support was needed later in fights with the local housing authority, the group had to go back to the original activists for help.

When the actual development began in each project the number of participants increased, but in none of the cases, even the smaller Liverpool case, was participation in overall decision making exceptionally broad. In every case the learning curve of those at the center of activity was so steep that they soon became separated by knowledge from the group.[13] This presents less of a long term problem than the lack of a political memory because there are levels of the development process which will not be repeated unless other cooperatives are developed. But the separation begins to play on the trust necessary to maintain support of the overall group in the process and project and slows the organizational development necessary for the later operation of the cooperatives. This is particularly true in mixed language situations where language gaps can add to this separation. This was less true in Montreal where there is a provincial commitment to bilingualism.

The cooperatives were all developed by non-profit development organizations. In Los Angeles and Montreal the organizations had staffs. The Route 2 organization was created and dominated by the residents; in Montreal an organization of which the residents were a part was created; and in Liverpool the development organization was the cooperative and technical assistance was provided by a consulting housing association.[14] Neil Mayer in his book *Neighborhood Organizations and Community Development* sets forth the findings from an in depth study of many such organizations in the United States.[15] He lists three relevant general categories of factors in project success: internal characteristics in the development corporation; relations with communities and outsiders; and the type of project (Mayer 1984).

In the first category Mayer included items such as: quality of the staff; working conditions in the organization; the relationship between the board and staff; and the existence of a track record. In Montreal and Los Angeles the development organizations seemed to have extraordinary professional staffs. The same seemed true of the assisting housing association in Liverpool. In all three cases, however, the working conditions seemed less than ideal. In the Route 2 project they could have hardly been harsher. Rudimentary facilities, overwork, and pressure were the usual conditions. The project had to be done regardless of obstacles within a very confined time.

The Milton-Park development organization is more typical of what Mayer studied. In both Liverpool and Los Angeles, people sought to dominate. In the Route 2 project the people in the project were the board. As explained in Chapter 4 there was a high level of board-staff conflict in the Route 2 project. This was also true in the Liverpool project. The best that could be said was that certain elements of the board and staff had cooperative relationships and that this was enough to carry on.

In Liverpool they fought both with parts of their development staff in the housing association and their architects. As was true in Los Angeles, some of the leadership saw the professionals as "the bad guys trying to pull another stunt" (McDonald 1986, p. 111). Some of the staff was seen as having the ability to "sit among us;" others were not (p. 69-73). Similar to their Los Angeles counterparts, they had an attitude that the "professionals should be at their beck and call;" or more colorfully "You've got to be on tap, not on top" (p. 79). As I observed they treated the staff the way they perceived their bosses treated them. A variation of this conflict also existed in Montreal although from the Helman report it was between resident and non-resident board members. These conflicts seemed to be more a product of control issues arising from the failure to transfer the property to the residents than the class conflict McDonald and I saw in the projects we wrote about (p. 67, 121-122).

In Montreal there was a lengthy participatory design process to obtain each resident's view of their living space. Helman's account indicates this was less an arena of conflict than the professional-staff conflicts in the other projects (Helman 1987, pp. 141-147). Design was certainly a major issue in the new construction Liverpool project. In Los Angeles design was less of an issue because it was a rehabilitation project with a very low level of funding. The conflicts that existed were more in the nature of the classic architectural conflict between form and function. On occasion the architects spent the limited funds on design features while the residents wanted to use their funds to make sure the systems of the buildings functioned.

The subject of the existence of a track record seems more a factor in Los Angeles than in the other cases. Canada has a well established system of providing technical assistance to organizations for cooperative development, and the Liverpool housing association which provided technical assistance was also well established. Certainly the residents had to establish legitimacy in the state's eye, but a track record of development was not key. In Los Angeles which doesn't have an established system, the lack of a track record was a major problem. Until, with consultants' help, the development corporation began the new construction portion of the project, the group was not taken seriously as a development organization. The attitude of many of the bureaucrats changed dramatically. It was like night and day.

In the category of relations with communities and outsiders Mayer lists community support; relations with local government; technical assistance; and links to the private sector. In both Montreal and Los Angeles the project had community support. In a time when neighborhoods resist development, especially the construction of low-income housing, anti-displacement-rehabilitation cooperatives still seem to gain support of their neighbors. This was certainly true in Los Angeles. All but one of the surrounding homeowner groups supported the project. In this environment keeping things as they are and fixing up property is a plus. In addition the home ownership character of cooperatives is more comfortable than the many rental forms of affordable housing.

The relations with local government have already been discussed. Each of the projects clearly had its friends within local government, but it would be hard to characterize any of them as having good relations with local government. They were born in struggle and each undoubtedly left its residue of discomfort in the bureaucracy. Each project received quality technical assistance. In Los Angeles the technical assistance of the Los Angeles Community Design Center and the state Department of Housing and Community Development was key. In Liverpool the project could not have happened without the housing association's help.

Links to the private sector was a more troubling area. In both Liverpool and Los Angeles the groups had difficulties finding contractors to do the work (Mcdonald 1986, pp. 159-171). No such problem existed in the Milton-Park project. Montreal has a very active and quality rehabilitation industry. The problem was extreme in Los Angeles. The development organization had great difficulty finding people to bid on the work and was constrained to take contractors with whom they were not entirely comfortable. The organization and quality of the work was a constant problem and resulted eventually in firing one of the contractors in mid-stream and arbitration proceedings. The Route 2 project was also privately financed. Most professionals in the field thought they would never get financing for the cooperatives and as discussed earlier it was exceptionally difficult.

The development process while in theory an empowering and community building activity can be just the opposite. The technical nature of the process can be disempowering and the disorder that can accompany the process can be disruptive to community formation. In

1987 I visited the Milton-Park project. The lead organizer told me that the development process, which included resident involvement in design and a degree of self-help in the rehabilitation, was the center of the formation of the cooperatives. Certainly the design and contracting process in the Weller Way cooperative was key to group formation even if they suffered from limited participation at points. In the Route 2 project the development period seemed in many ways a continuation of the political struggle with many enemies replacing one. There was a high level of participation, for example, in the relocation and rehabilitation committees. During this period about 70 meetings a quarter (three months) took place in the development corporation office. The chaos of the process, however, made much of this conflictual. It continued the process of bringing the people together in struggle, but as one might imagine it was not a positive community building process.

Stage Three: Operating the Cooperatives

Perhaps the most notable change when the development process is finished and the cooperative takes over full management of the property is that much of the technical assistance that was poured into the development process leaves. This was the case in the Route 2 project and was also true in New York City as found by Susan Saegert in her follow up study of a sample of the limited equity cooperatives developed in that city (Saegert 1989, p. 13)).[16] In Canada a continuing support structure has been developed to assist the cooperatives in their operations, but this is not yet true in New York City and is certainly not true in Los Angeles where only a handful of such cooperatives exist.[17]

Another important similarity between New York and Los Angeles is that many cooperatives were left in under-rehabilitated and under-funded condition at the end of the development process. As a result the cooperative leadership had to confront serious problems that materially affected the lives of the residents when the cooperatives were new and very vulnerable. Saegert finds the difficulty in meeting the challenges these problems present as contributing significantly to a great deal of internal conflict. Although the origins of the cooperatives in New York and Los Angeles are very different, these and other similarities make the New York experience useful in understanding the Los Angeles situation.

Saegert sets forth a broad list of problems that beset limited-equity cooperatives: communication; participation; factional conflict; management; finance; physical conditions; and isolation (pp. 8-9). All of these problems existed in forms similar to New York in the Route 2 project and have been discussed at length in various portions of the book. Saegert sees these problems as not only emerging from the shaky footing on which the cooperatives were placed, but from a misconception of the nature of the cooperative. She announces loudly that the cooperatives must be seen as "a process of social organization, not just the physical rehabilitation and legal sale of buildings" (p. 13). Saegert's point seems directed at the state and its abandonment of cooperatives when they are in need. She goes on to conclude that the state should provide continuing technical assistance not only to assist in the continuing physical and financial maintenance of the cooperative, but also to assist in the continuing development of the social organization.[18]

I could not agree with Saegert more. There is, however, a significant difference in the emphasis I give the various components of the needed assistance. In Saegert's study and her work with Jacqueline Leavitt (1990) the socio/ethnic characteristics of the coop residents are far more homogeneous than the residents of the Route 2 cooperatives. The cooperatives are also located in single buildings occupied by residents that tend to have established social relations. In contrast the Route 2 residents are a very heterogeneous mix and while many people have lived in their homes many years, the scattered site nature of the property reduces the likelihood of established social relations. Thus there is less likelihood of a socio/political consensus among the residents pre-existing the establishment of the cooperatives. Weaker consensus means there is less on which to base a common concept of the nature of the cooperative enterprise or a concept of how to proceed in carrying out cooperative affairs.

The outside assistance could be helpful in aiding the group toward a consensus on how the cooperative should proceed. This is not a single momentary need. Agreement on a process will likely need revision as experience presents additional challenges. Further, what appears to be a pre-existing consensus may or may not mean that the cooperative residents are equipped to meet the continuing challenges faced in the cooperative. In other words, the failure to accurately conceive the nature of the cooperative enterprise may not only be within the state. Few groups, even those with histories of survival in a hostile environment through reciprocity, have experience with the type and degree of collective responsibility potentially called for within a limited-equity cooperative. Winning, being in charge, changes the nature of many relationships. If the consensus breaks down internal social development will suffer.

Many of the problems the cooperatives face go to the very heart of debates about the nature of democracy. If a common concept of democracy is not broadly held or if the application of these accepted principles is not up to the challenge, problems will surely arise that will lead to a loss of legitimization and alienation from the cooperative. The cooperative will be perceived as yet another instrument of domination, oppression, and intolerance in the lives of people who are only too familiar with these experiences. The lack of positive resolution of these issues is expressed in Saegert's finding that in the cooperatives she examined "either the same people rule the building as 'benevolent dictators,' or a new faction gains power," and that even though it seemed people were empowered in the struggle to gain control of their building, disempowerment set in as participation dwindled from what she called "misunderstandings and personality conflicts" (Saegert 1989, p. 14).

In the larger society we learn a great deal about individual responsibility. We do not receive the same quality of lessons about collective responsibility and political obligation. Yet this goes to the center of the nature of a cooperative. What is our relationship to our neighbor? To what extent can the majority bind any of us to its will? What responsibility does the cooperative have to help a member who has become ill and cannot pay their carrying charges? Can the cooperative tax its members to support the ill members against the minority's will? Must the solution to such a problem be sensitive to, or even further, actively supportive of cultural and family difference?

What I have found is that over and over again such deeply political questions present themselves in cooperatives. The political standard of behavior among the people I've observed is that the solution to such problems must be "fair." The same was true in the Liverpool case (McDonald 1986, p. 152). If the process is not perceived as fair, alienation sets in. Alienation can lead to revolt either through the cooperative process if it is perceived as open, or more directly in interpersonal conflict if it is not, or it can lead to withdrawal. But what is fair? Is the even hand of fairness a flat surface or does it have textures that fit particular situations? None of these questions or the others presented in cooperatives are unique. What is unique is that a small collective of people must decided them.

In many cases, including those I've reviewed here, the people being asked to address these questions are among the more alienated and oppressed members of their respective societies. At a minimum they are the people who feel the pain of marginalized working-class existence, the racism of the racial state, and the sexism of long established patriarchy. Every act the cooperative takes is washed by this reality and subject to suspicion learned by years of experience. In society at large the failure of the state to be perceived as fair has contributed to a delegitimization of the state. Why should people expect the cooperative's governing board to be different? Is it not just another instrument of domination? If they do see the cooperative structure as different and are thereby empowered, how long will it take them to loose faith and return to an alienated condition? It seems an impossible task to be fair in such a context. As Saegert concludes, what is "miraculous" is that the cooperatives do function (Saegert 1989, p. 13).

What I have observed is that all but a few people, those so embittered by life that they can no longer hope, do not want to feel class-based marginalization, do not want to dwell in racism; do not want to endure patriarchy; and do not want to feel alienated. In the cooperatives I've studied I've seen people reach out to each other and withdraw, reach again and withdraw again. At the moments when people connect, when community is formed, you can see people fill up. In the moments of withdrawal you can see them shrink. Saegert states that in crisis people will participate, but that they will withdraw when the crisis abates.[19] There is a truth to this, many people will rally when a threat is presented, but I have also seen people participate because of the fullness they feel in the good times when community is achieved. Any scheme to assist cooperatives will need to explore how to organize in the good times as well as the bad.

The populist approach which I know best has only one real tool to achieve these moments of community. In the Route 2 project it is called keeping the process open. Benjamin Barber calls it public talk. Many others call it dialogue. The Route 2 project has one other element that has often made this approach work, the organic intellectuals who understand the process at its core. We will not always be so fortunate to have these individuals present. The alternative is to collectively learn more about how to sustain these moments of community, perhaps by collecting and collectively examining stories such as the ones told in this book. Gramsci saw this role as initially quite special, but he believed that we were all intellectuals and that it need not be such an exclusive role. We all have a lot to learn about democracy and the nature of dialogue particularly in our increasingly heterogeneous world. Community is possible. It is a struggle. There is every obstacle in its path, but it is possible.

Notes

1. See, for example, the reports of British housing cooperatives in Birchall (1987); Henry (1987); Campbell (1959).

2. I am referring to the work of the Housing Environment Research Group, Center for Human Environments at the Robert F. Wagner Institute of Urban Public Policy, The Graduate School and University Center, The City University of New York.

3.   This is interesting because one of the primary conclusions of the Leavitt and Saegert work is that buildings with pre-existing strong social relationships among the residents have a better chance of succeeding. In the case of the Route 2 Project they took whomever was there regardless of prior relations. The cooperatives were formed entirely by the happenstance of geography. The Milton-Park project is somewhere in between. The groupings were generally spatial but were modified by friendships.

4.   The Milton-Park protests started in the late 1960s when protest was in the air. Veterans of the 1960s were present in the Route 2 project and contributed heavily to the effort although the original action was not of their making. The residents of Milton-Park were greatly aided by an economic downturn in the mid-1970s (Helman 1968, pp. 101-102). The residents' plan was also aided by the electoral success of the Montreal Citizens Movement and Parti Quebecois in this same period (pp. 101-103). The situation in Liverpool was not as favorable. There was no equivalent political movement with progressive populist overtones. From McDonald's (1986) description, however, the resident leadership clearly felt alienated from all organized political groups. Even though the leaders of the Weller Way were strong union people they felt the Labor party's statist views were outdated. As one resident put it "the Labour Party . . . wanted this Mother Cow of municipal housing which should have gone out forty or fifty years ago" (p.54). They felt no warmth for the other parties either and became "'apolitical as far as parties were concerned, but very political as far as local politics is concerned'" (p. 53). Liverpool was certainly hit harder than Los Angeles and Montreal by the impact of restructuring. The degree of decline had to play a part in the generation of alternative ideas and breaking the hegemony of the Labour Party over the Weller Way leadership.

5.   The primary objection articulated by the Labour Party Councillors was that the coop amounted to "queue jumping."

6.   Homefront no longer exists. Some of the members of the organization later changed their position and supported the formation of limited-equity cooperatives.

7.   They did also receive political support (Helman 1987, pp. 101-102). Also many people connected with the university participated in the Milton-Park project. While in the case of the Route 2 project physical proximity and university connected residents were not present, my presence provided some of the same type of assistance. Some of the other people active in the Route 2 project have said I, through my contacts with the university, gave the project legitimacy in the eye's of those who would not usually respond to working-class people. Certainly I brought students to the project who did a great amount of work to make the project happen and made my network of contacts available to the effort. There were a number of times when my network produced key information that got the project past rough spots.

8.   In New York City there were many intellectuals within and outside the state that aided the process. Help came from churches, politicians, and tenants and neighborhood associations. It also came from organizations such as the Association for Neighborhood Housing and Development, the Pratt Center, and the Urban Homestead Assistance Board (Leavitt and Saegert 1990, pp. 109-125).

9.   There was an advocacy planning group active in the 1960s that did not follow this model, The East Oakland-Fruitvale Planning Council (EOFPC). This group had a small staff and spent much of its funding to pay community people for attending meetings. Most of the advocacy planning groups of the late 1960s and early 1970s worked heavily on issues of housing and transportation. EOFPC worked primarily on schools and law enforcement problems (Heskin 1975).

10.   A law suit also slowed the Milton-Park project.   During the protest period an internal fight with one side supported by the developer led to a law suit over the validity of an election (Helman 1987, pp. 73-74).

11.   An example of this problem occurred in one of the buildings studied by Leavitt and Saegert (1990).   The city required that rents be raised after the conversion to a cooperative in a building that had a long history of landlord-tenant struggles. The response of a dozen of the tenants out of 35 occupied units was to go on rent strike in protest. The protest ended with most of the rent strikers moving out (p. 46).

12.   The same is true in New York City.   Leavitt and Saegert's (1990) book is full of examples of problems with the execution of the city programs.

13.   See, for example, discussion of this problem in McDonald (1986, pp. 125-126).

14.   I am not sure whether the assisting housing association that worked in Liverpool was a non-profit.   I could not find clarification in McDonald's book. The group behaved as if it was, and I have assumed this characterization.

15.   He did an initial study of 99 organizations and a follow up in-depth study of 30 groups.   They were not necessarily organizations involved in developing cooperatives.

16.   The development corporation stayed on for a brief period in the Route 2 project and helped organize the management company. In the longer sense of what happened, this was the case.

17.   The only remaining technical help may come from a management company or managing agent if the cooperative is not self-managed. As indicated in the book this assistance may be problematic. Management companies may very well fight the cooperative's participatory structure preferring instead a more hierarchical structure which gives them a single individual with whom to interact. Also the management company has an economic interest in maintaining its contract with the cooperative which in any factional fight may cause the management company to take sides with the side favorable to maintaining its contract or worse exacerbate potential factional differences to maintain its contract. Improving the capacity and willingness of management companies to work with cooperatives must be part of any continuing technical assistance effort.

18.   This call for the social side of continued technical assistance is explained in detail, including examples of existing programs, in Saegert's book with Leavitt (1990, pp. 197-212).

19.   It should be noted that crisis can also cause withdrawal. If the conflict is internal to the cooperative, members can stop participating to avoid the conflict. As stated in one case in Leavitt and Saegert (1990): "A number of tenants who had participated in meetings told us they quit going because they disliked listening to the bickering" (p. 57).

Bibliography

Achelsberg, Martha A. 1988. "Communities, Resistance, and Women's Activism: Some Implications for a Democratic Polity." In: Ann Bookman and Sandra Morgen (eds.) *Women and the Politics of Empowerment*. Philadelphia: Temple University Press.

Adamson, Walter L. 1980. *Hegemony and Revolution: Antonio Gramsci's Political and Cultural Theory*. Berkeley: University of California Press.

Adler, Nancy J. 1983a. "Domestic Multiculturalism: Cross-cultural Management in the Public Sector." In: William B. Eddy (ed.) *Handbook of Organization Management*. New York: Marcel Dekker.

_____. 1983b. "Organizational Development in a Multicultural Environment." *Journal of Applied Behavioral Science*. 19(3): 349-363.

Alinsky, Saul D. 1971. *Rules for Radicals*. New York: Random House.

_____. 1969. *Reveille for Radicals*. New York: Vintage Books.

Althuser, Alan A. 1970. *Community Control: The Black Demand for Participation in Large American Cities*. New York: Pegasus.

Arnstein, Sherry R. 1969. "A Ladder of Citizen Participation." *Journal of the American Institute of Planners*, 35: 216-224, July.

Bachrack, Peter and Morton S. Baratz. 1970. *Power and Poverty*. New York: Oxford University Press.

Barber, Benjamin. 1984. *Strong Democracy*. Berkeley: University of California Press.

Barrera, Mario. 1979. *Race and Class in the Southwest: A Theory of Racial Inequality*. Notre Dame: University of Notre Dame Press.

Barton, Stephen. 1977. "The Urban Housing Problem: Marxist Theory and Community Organizing," *Review of Radical Political Economy*. Winter: 16-30.

Beauvoir, Simon de. 1961. *The Second Sex*. New York: Bantam.

Belenky, Mary Field, Blythe McVicker Clinchy, Nancy Rule Goldberg, Jill Mattuck Tarule. 1986. *Women's Ways of Knowing*. New York: Basic Books.

Bellah, Robert N., Richard Madsen, William M. Sullivan, Ann Swidler, and Steven M. Topton. 1985. *Habits of the Heart: Individualism and Commitment in American Life*. New York: Harper and Row.

Bernstein, Basil. 1973. *Class Codes and Control*. London: Routledge and Kegan Paul.

Birchall, Johnston. 1987. *Building Communities the Cooperative Way*. London: Routledge and Kegan Paul.

Bledstein, Burton J. 1976. *The Culture of Professionalism.* New York: W.W. Norton and Company, Inc.

Bluestone, Natalie Harris. 1987. *Women and the Ideal Society.* Amherst: University of Massachusetts Press.

Bocock, Robert. 1986. *Hegemony.* London: Tavistock.

Boggs, Carl. 1986. *Social Movements and Political Power.* Philadelphia: Temple University Press.

_____. 1984. *The Two Revolutions: Gramsci and the Dilemmas of Western Marxism.* Boston: South End Press.

_____. 1976. *Gramsci's Marxism.* London: Pluto Press.

Bookchin, Murray. 1987. *The Rise of Urbanization and the Decline of Citizenship.* San Francisco: Sierra Club Books.

Bookman, Ann and Sandra Morgen (eds.). 1988. *Women and the Politics of Empowerment.* Philadelphia: Temple University Press.

Bouchier, David. 1987. *Radical Citizenship: The New American Activism.* New York: Schocken.

Boyte, Harry. 1986. "Beyond Politics as Usual." In: Harry Boyte and Frank Reissman (eds.) *The New Populism: The Politics of Empowerment.* Philadelphia: Temple University Press.

_____. 1984. *Community is Possible.* New York: Harper and Row.

_____. 1980. *The Backyard Revolution.* Philadelphia: Temple University Press.

_____, and Frank Reissman (eds.). 1986. *The New Populism: The Politics of Empowerment.* Philadelphia: Temple University Press.

_____, Heather Booth, and Steve Max. 1986. *Citizen Action and the New American Populism.* Philadelphia: Temple University Press.

Brislin, Richard W. 1980. "Expanding the Role of the Interpreter to Include Multiple Facets of Intercultural Communications." In: Larry A. Samovar and Richard E. Porter (eds.) *Intercultural Communication: A Reader* (3rd. ed.) Belmont, California: Wadsworth Publishing.

Broadhead, Ronald and Ray C. Rist. 1978. "Why Social Science Discovered Morality." *Social Policy,* 9: 36-40.

Brooks, Michael P. and Michael A. Stegman. 1968. "Urban Social Policy, Race and Education of Planners." *Journal of the American Institute of Planners,* 35: 275-286.

Buber, Martin. 1970. *I and Thou.* New York: Scribner's.

_____. 1965. *The Knowledge of Man.* New York: Harper and Row.

_____. 1958. *Path in Utopia.* Boston: Beacon Press.

_____. 1955. *Between Man and Man.* Boston: Beacon Press.

Burgess, Rod. 1982. "Self-Help Housing Advocacy: A Curious Form of Radicalism. A Critique of the Work of John F. C. Turner." In: Peter M. Ward (ed.) *Self-Help Housing: A Critique.* London: Mansell Publishing Limited.

Campbell, Harold. 1959. *Housing: A Cooperative Approach.* Manchester: Cooperative Union Ltd.

Carnoy, Martin. 1984. *The State and Political Theory.* Princeton, New Jersey: Princeton University Press.

Chabal, Patrick. 1983. *Amilcar Cabral: Revolutionary Leadership and People's War.* Cambridge: Cambridge University Press.

Clavel, Pierre. 1986. *The Progressive City: Planning and Participation, 1969-1984.* New Brunswick, New Jersey: Rutgers University Press.

Cliff, Tony. 1970. *The Employers' Offensive.* London: Pluto Press.

Cloward, Richard A. and Llyod Ohlin. 1960. *Delinquency and Opportunity.* Glencoe, Ill.: Free Press.

Colfer, Carol J. Pierce. 1983. "Communication Among 'Unequals'." *International Journal of Intercultural Relations.* 7: 263-283.

Combahee River Collective. 1981. "A Black Feminist Statement." In: Cherrie Moraga and Gloria Anzaldua (eds.) *This Bridge Called My Back: Writings by Radical Women of Color.* New York: Kitchen Table.

Conklin, Nancy Faires and Margaret A. Lourie. 1983. *A Host of Tongues: Language Communities in the United States.* New York: The Free Press.

Cortes, Ernesto. 1986. "Education For Citizenship: A Profile." In: Harry Boyte and Frank Reissman (eds.) *The New Populism: The Politics of Empowerment.* Philadelphia: Temple University Press.

Coulter, Merton. 1983. *Issues in the Syndication of Limited Equity Housing Cooperatives.* State of California Department of Housing and Community Development.

Dalh, Robert A. 1961. *Who Governs? Democracy and Power in an American City.* New Haven: Yale University Press.

Davidoff, Paul. 1965. "Advocacy and Pluralism in Planning." *Journal of the American Institute of Planners,* 31: 331-338.

De Leeuw, Barbara. 1974. "Learning to Build Majority Organizations," *Just Economics.* 2(1): 2.

Dealy, Glen. 1982. "The Tradition of Monistic Democracy in Latin America." In: Howard J. Wiarda (ed.) *Politics and Social Change in Latin America: The Distinct Tradition.* Amherst, Mass.: University of Massachusetts Press.

Delgado, Gary. 1986. *Organizing the Movement: The Roots and Growth of Acorn.* Philadelphia: Temple University Press.

Derber, Charles. 1982. "The Proletarianization of the Professional: A Review Essay." In: Charles Derber (ed.) *Professionals as Workers: Mental Labor in Advanced Capitalism.* Boston: G. K. Hall.

Diamond, Irene and Nancy Hartsock. 1981. "Beyond Interests in Politics: A Comment on Virginia Sapiro's 'When Are Interests Interesting? The Problem of Political Representation of Women.'" *The American Political Science Review,* 75: 717-721.

Dietz, Mary G. 1987. "Context Is All: Feminism and Theories of Citizenship." In: Jill. K. Conway, Susan Carolyn Bourque and Joan Wallach Scott (eds.) *Learning About Women: Gender, Politics, and Power.* Ann Arbor: The University of Michigan Press.

Doeringer, Peter and Michael Piore. 1971. *Internal Labor Markets and Manpower Analysis.* Lexington, Mass.: D. C. Heath.

Donovan, Josephine. 1988. *Feminist Theory.* New York: Continuum.

Dutschke, Rudi. 1968. *Ecrits Politiques.* France: Christian Bourgois Edituer.

Edwards, Richard, Michael Reich, and David Gordon. 1975. *Labor Market Segmentation.* Lexington, Mass.: D. C. Heath.

Ehrenreich, Barbara and John Ehrenreich. 1979. "The Professional-Managerial Class." In: Pat Walker (ed.) *Between Labour and Capital*. New York: Monthly Review.

_____. 1979. "Rejoinder." In: Pat Walker (ed.) *Between Labour and Capital*. New York: Monthly Review.

Eisenstein, Zillah R. 1988. *The Female Body and the Law*. Berkeley: University of California Press.

Elkin, Stephen. 1987. *City and Regime in the American Republic*. Chicago: University of Chicago Press.

Ellis, Leroy. 1969. *White Ethnics and Black Power*. Chicago: Aldine Publishing Company.

Emerson, Robert. 1983. *Contemporary Field Research: A Collection of Readings*. Prospect Heights: Waverland Press.

Engels, Fredrick. 1954. *The Housing Question*. Moscow: Progress Publishers.

Epstein, Cynthia Fuchs. 1988. *Deceptive Distinctions: Sex, Gender, and the Social Order*. New Haven: Yale University Press.

Evans, Sara. 1980. *Personal Politics*. New York: Vintage Books.

_____and Harry C. Boyte. 1986. *Free Spaces: The Sources of Democratic Change in America*. New York: Harper and Row.

Feagin, Joe R. and Clairece Booher Feagin. 1986. *Discrimination American Style*. Malabar, Florida: Robert E. Krieger Publishing Company.

Fellman, Gordon. 1973. *The Deceived Majority: Politics and Protest in Middle America*. New York: Dutton.

Fields, Barbara. 1982. "Ideology and Race in American History." In: J. Morgan Kousser and James M. McPherson (eds.) *Region, Race, and Reconstruction*. Oxford: Oxford University Press.

Fraser, Graham. 1972. *Fighting Back: Urban Renewal in Trefann Court*. Toronto: A. M. Hakkert, Ltd.

Frederickson, Marilyn. 1982. "Four Decades of Change: Black Workers in Southern Textile, 1941-1981." *Radical America*, 16: 27-44.

French, Marilyn. 1985. *Beyond Power: On Women, Men and Morals*. New York: Ballantine Books.

Freire, Paulo. 1970. *Pedagogy of the Oppressed*. New York: Continuum.

Friedmann, John. 1988. *Life Space and Economic Space*. New Brunswick, New Jersey: Transaction Books.

_____. 1973. *Retracking America: A Theory of Transactive Planning*. Garden City, New York: Anchor Press.

Fuglesang, Andreas and Dale Chandler. *Participation as Process*. 1986. Oslo, Norway: Norad.

Gans, Herbert J. 1962. *The Urban Villagers*. New York: Free Press.

Gaventa, John. 1980. *Power and Powerlessness*. Urbana: University of Illinois Press.

Giles, Howard, Richard Y. Bourhis, and Donald M. Taylor. 1977. "Towards a Theory of Language in Ethnic Group Relations." In: Howard Giles (ed.) *Language, Ethnicity, and Intergroup Relations*. London: Academic Press.

Gilligan, Carol. 1982. *In a Different Voice: Psychological Theory and Women's Development*. Cambridge: Harvard University Press.

Gilman, Charlotte Perkins. 1911. *The Man-Made World, or Our Androcentric Culture.* New York: Johnson Reprint, 1971.

Gordon, David. 1972. *Theories of Poverty and Unemployment.* Lexington, Mass.: D. C. Heath.

Gorz, Andre. 1965. "Work and Consumption." In: Perry Anderson and Robin Blackburn (eds.) *Towards Socialism.* London: Fontana.

Gould, Carol C. 1988. *Rethinking Democracy: Freedom and Social Cooperation in Politics, Economy, and Society.* Cambridge: Cambridge University Press.

Grabow, Stephen and Alan David Heskin. 1973. "Foundations for a Radical Concept of Planning." *Journal of the American Institute of Planners,* 39: 106-114.

Graham, Robert. 1989. "The Role of Contract in Anarchist Ideology." In: David Goodway (ed.) *For Anarchism.* London: Routledge.

Gramsci, Antonio. 1971. *Selection from the Prison Notebooks.* New York: International Publishers.

_____. 1973. *Letters from Prison.* New York: Harper and Row.

Greer, Edward. 1977. "Racial Employment Discrimination in the Gary Works, 1906-1974." In: Gerald Erickson and Howard Schwartz (eds.) *Social Class in the Contemporary United States.* Minneapolis: Marxist Education Press.

Gumperz, John Joseph. 1982. *Discourse Strategies.* Cambridge, England: Cambridge University Press.

_____. 1976. Language, Communication, and Public Negotiation. In: Peggy Reeves Sanday (ed.) *Anthropology and the Public Interest.* New York: Academic Press.

Gyford, John. 1985. *The Politics of Local Socialism.* London: George Allen and Unwin.

Haas, Gilda. 1982. "Building People vs. Building Organizations: Two Approaches to Political Education." (unpublished).

_____ and Allan David Heskin. 1980. "Community Struggles in Los Angeles," *International Journal of Urban and Regional Research.* 5: 546-563.

Habermas, Jurgen. 1973. *Legitimation Crisis.* Boston: Beacon Press.

Hall, Peter. 1980. *Great Planning Disasters.* Berkeley: University of California Press.

Halle, David. 1984. *America's Working Man.* Chicago: University of Chicago Press.

Hampden-Turner, Charles. 1975. *From Poverty to Dignity.* Garden City, New York: Anchor Books.

Handell, Gerald and Lee Rainwater. 1964. "Persistence and Change in Working-class Lifestyle." In: Arthur Shostak and William Gomberg (eds.) *Blue Collar World.* Englewood Cliffs: Prentice Hall.

Harris, Philip R. and Robert T. Moran. 1979. *Managing Cultural Differences.* Houston: Gulf Publishing.

Hartman, Chester, Dennis Keating, Richard LeGates. 1982. *Displacement: How to Fight It.* Berkeley: National Housing Law Project.

Hartsock, Nancy C. M. 1983. *Money, Sex, and Power: Toward a Feminist Historical Materialism.* Boston: Northeastern University Press.

Hays, Allen. 1985. *The Federal Government and Urban Housing.* Albany: State University of New York, Albany.

Held, David. 1987. *Models of Democracy.* Stanford: Stanford University Press.

Helman, Claire. 1986. *The Milton Park Affair: Canada's Largest Citizen Development Organization.* Montreal: Vehicle Press.

Henig, Jeffrey R. 1986. "Collective Responses to the Urban Crisis: Ideology and Mobilization." In: M. Gottdfiemer (ed.) *Cities in Crisis*. Beverly Hills, California: Sage Publications.

Henry, Stuart. 1983. *Private Justice*. London: Routlege and Kegan Paul.

Heskin, Allan David. 1987. "From Theory to Practice: Professional Development at UCLA," *Journal of the American Institute of Planners*. October. pp. 436-451.

_____. 1983. *Tenants and the American Dream*. New York: Praeger.

_____. 1975. *The Lessons from Advocacy Planning*. Unpublished dissertation. Seattle: University of Washington.

_____and Mark Garret. 1987. "When Planning Fails: Protecting the Neighbor-hood in Vested Development Rights Disputes," *UCLA Journal of Environmental Law and Policy*. 6: 159-203.

_____and Robert A. Heffner. 1987. "Learning about Bilingual, Multicultural Organizing," *The Journal of Applied Behavioral Science*. 23(4): 525-541.

_____and Dewey Bandy. 1986a. "The Importance of Class," *Berkeley Planning Journal*. 3: 47-66.

_____and Dewey Bandy. 1986b. "The Dialectics of Community Planning." UCLA Graduate School of Architecture and Urban Planning Discussion Paper #8614.

_____and Dewey Bandy. 1985. "Peoples' Justice: Decision Making in a Federation of Limited Equity Housing Cooperatives," a paper presented to the Annual Conference of the American Planning Association, Montreal, Canada.

Hillery, George A. Jr. 1955. "Definitions of Community: Areas of Agreement." *Rural Sociology*. 20: 118.

Hinson, William. 1966. *Fanshen*. New York: Vintage Press.

Hochschild, Arthur. 1979. "Emotion, Work, Feeling, Rules, and Social Structure." *American Journal of Sociology*, 85: 551-575.

Hollingshead, A. B. and L. H. Rogler. 1963 "Attitude Towards Slums and Public Housing in Puerto Rico." In: Leonard Duhl (ed.) *The Urban Condition*. New York: Simon and Schuster.

Homefront. 1977. *Housing Abandonment in New York City*. New York: Homefront.

Hooks, Bell. 1984. *Feminist Theory: From Margin to Center*. Boston: South End Press.

Huber, Joan and William H. Form. 1973. *Income and Ideology*. New York: Free Press.

Hyman, Richard. 1977. *Strikes*. London: Fontana.

Jackman, Mary H. and Robert W. Jackman. 1983. *Class Awareness in the United States*. Berkeley: University of California Press.

Jennings, Thomas. 1972. "A Case Study of Tenant Union Legalism.," In: Stephen Burghardt (ed.) *Tenants and the Urban Housing Crisis*. Dexter, Michigan: The New Press.

Kahn, Si. 1982. *Organizing*. New York: McGraw-Hill.

Kallenberg, Arne L. and Larry J. Griffin. 1980. "Class, Occupation and Inequality in Job Rewards." *American Journal of Sociology*, 85: 731-766.

Kann, Mark E. 1986. *Middle Class Radicalism in Santa Monica*. Philadelphia: Temple University Press.

Kohn, Melvin. 1976. "Occupational Structure and Alienation." *American Journal of Sociology*, 82: 111-130.

_____. 1969. *Class and Conformity*. Homewood, Ill.: Dorsey Press.

Kollis, Karen. 1975. "Class Realities: Creates a New Power Base," *Quest*. Vol.I No.3 (Winter 1975), pp. 28-43.

Kolodny, Robert, assisted by Marjorie Gellerman. 1973. *Self Help in the Inner City: A Study of Lower Income Cooperative Housing Conversion in New York*. New York: United Neighborhood Houses in New York.

Komarovsky, Mirra. 1962. *Blue-Collar Marriage*. New York: Vintage Books.

Kornhauser, Arthur William. 1954. "Human Motivations Underlying Industrial Conflict." In: Arthur William Kornhauser, Robert Rubin, and Arthur M. Ross (eds.) *Industrial Conflict*. New York: McGraw-Hill.

Laclau, Ernesto and Chantal Mouffe. 1985. *Hegemony and Socialist Strategy: Towards a Radical Democratic Politics*. London: Verso Press.

Lane, Tony and Kenneth Roberts. 1971. *Strike at Pilkingtons*. London: Fontana.

Larson, Magali Sarfatti. 1977. *The Rise of Professionalism: A Sociological Analysis*. Berkeley: University of California Press.

Leavitt, Jacqueline and Susan Saegert. 1990. *From Abandonment to Hope*. New York: Columbia University Press.

Levison, Andrew. 1974. *The Working-Class Majority*. New York: Penguin Books.

Liebow, Elliot. 1967. *Tally's Corner*. Boston: Little, Brown and Company.

Lipsky, Michael. 1970. *Protest in City Politics*. Chicago: Rand McNally.

Loewenstein, Julius I. 1970. *Marx against Marxism*. London: Routledge and Kegan Paul.

Lowi, Theodore J. 1969. *The End of Liberalism: Ideology, Policy, and the Crisis of Public Authority*. New York: Norton and Company.

Luttrell, Wendy. 1984. "Beyond the Politics of Victimization." *Socialist Review*, 14: 42-47.

MacKinnon, Cathrine A. 1987. *Feminism Unmodified*. Cambridge, Massachusetts: Harvard University Press.

Mansbridge, Jane J. 1983. *Beyond Adversary Democracy*. Chicago: University of Chicago Press.

_____. 1990. "Feminism and Democracy," *The American Prospect*. 1: 126-139.

Maquire, Daniel C. 1980. *A New American Justice*. Garden City, New York: Doubleday and Company.

Mayer, Neil S. 1983. "How Neighborhood Development Organizations Succeed and Grow." In: P. Clay and R. Hollister (eds.) *Neighborhood Policy and Planning*. Lexington: Lexington Books.

McDonald, Alan. 1986. *The Weller Way*. London: Faber and Faber.

McKenney, Mary. 1981. "Class Attitudes and Professionalism." *Building Feminist Theory*. New York: Longman Inc.

Midgely, James. 1986. *Community Participation, Social Development, and the State*. Methuen: London.

Miles, Robert. 1982. *Racism and Migrant Labor*. London: Routledge and Kegan Paul.

Miller, David. 1989. *Market, State and Community: Theoretical Foundations of Market Socialism*. Oxford: Clarendon Press.

Miller, Joanne, Carmi Schooler, Melvin L. Kohn, and Karen A. Miller. 1979. "Women and Work: The Psychological Effects of Occupational Conditions." *American Journal of Sociology*, 85: 66-93.

Miller, Mike. 1974. *Putting People Power in Action: Reader in Mass Organization*. San Francisco: Organize.

Miller, Robert. 1982. *Racism and Migrant Labour*. London: Routledge and Kegan Paul.

Miller, S.M. and Frank Reissman. 1964. "The Working-Class Subculture: A New View." In: Arthur Shostak and William Gomberg (eds.) *Blue Collar World*. Englewood Cliffs: Prentice-Hall.

Minnich, Elizabeth Kamarck. 1986. "Toward a Feminist Populism." In: Harry Boyte and Frank Reissman (eds) *The New Populism: The Politics of Empowerment*. Philadelphia: Temple University Press.

Molina, Jose M. 1978. "Cultural Barriers and Interethnic Communications in a Multiethnic Neighborhood. In: E. Lamar Rodd (ed.) *Interethnic Communication*. Athens, Georgia: The University of Georgia Press.

Moraga, Cherrie and Gloria Anzaldua (eds.). 1981. *This Bridge Called My Back: Writings by Radical Women of Color*. New York: Kitchen Table.

Neeleman, Martin L. and Carolyn Emerson Needleman. 1974. *Guerrillas in the Bureaucracy*. New York: John Wiley and Sons.

Noddings, Nel. 1984. *Caring: A Feminine Approach to Ethics and Moral Education*. Berkeley: University of California Press.

Oakley, Ann. 1976. *Woman's Work: The Housewife, Past and Present*. New York: Vintage Books.

O'Brien, David. 1975. *Neighborhood Organizations and Interest-Group Processes*. Princeton: Princeton University Press.

Ollman, Bertell. 1971. *Alienation: Marx's Conception of Man in Capitalist Society*. Cambridge: Cambridge University Press.

Omi, Michael and Howard Winant. 1986. *Racial Formation in the United States: From the 1960's to the 1980's*. New York: Routledge and Kegan Paul.

Padilla, Felix M. 1985. *Latino Ethnic Consciousness: The Case of Mexican Americans and Puerto Ricans in Chicago*. Notre Dame, Indiana: University of Notre Dame Press.

Parker, Richard. 1972. *The Myth of the Middle Class*. New York: Liveright.

Pateman, Carole. 1970. *Participation and Democratic Theory*. Cambridge: Cambridge University Press.

_____. 1985. *The Problem of Political Obligation*. Berkeley: University of California Press.

Patterson, James M. 1964. "Marketing the Working-Class Family." In: Arthur Shostak and William Gomberg (eds.) *Blue Collar World*. Englewood Cliffs: Prentice Hall.

Parenti, Michael. 1978. *Power and the Powerless*, New York: Saint Martin's Press.

Peattie, Lisa R. 1968. "Reflections on Advocacy Planning," *Journal of the American Institute of Planners*. March: 80-88.

Peck, M. Scott, M.D. 1987. *The Different Drum*. New York: Simon and Schuster.

Peterson, Paul E. 1981. *City Limits*. Chicago: University of Chicago Press.

Plant, Raymond. 1978. "Community: Concept, Conception and Ideology." *Politics & Society* 8: 79-107.

Polsby, Nelson W. 1963. *Community Power and Political Theory*. New Haven: Yale University Press.

Powell, John Duncan. 1970. "Peasant Society and Clientelist Politics." *The American Political Science Review*, 64, 2: 411-425.

Pressman, Jeffery L. and Aaron B. Wildavsky. 1973. Berkeley: University of California Press.

Ramirez, Manuel, III. 1983. *Psychology of the Americas: Maestizo Perspective on Personality and Mental Health*. New York: Pergamon Press.

Red Apple Collective. 1978. "Socialist-Feminist Women's Unions, Past and Present." *Socialist Review*, 38: 33-57.

Reissman, Frank. 1986. "The New Populism and the Empowerment Ethos." In Harry Boyte and Frank Reissman (eds) *The New Populism: The Politics of Empowerment*. Philadelphia: Temple University Press.

Repo, Marjaleena. 1977. "Organizing The Poor Against the Working Class." In: John Cowley, Adah Kaye, Marjorie Mayo, and Mike Thompson. (eds.) *Community or Class Struggle*. London: Litho Ltd.

Research Group on the Los Angeles Economy. 1989. *The Widening Divide*. Los Angeles: UCLA Graduate School of Architecture and Urban Planning.

Rex, John and David Mason (eds.). 1986. *Theories of Race and Ethnic Relations*. Cambridge: Cambridge University Press.

Rousseau, Jean-Jacques. 1973. *The Social Contract and Discourses*, tran. G.D.H. Cole, new ed. London: Dent.

Rubin, Lillian Breslow. 1976. *Worlds of Pain: Life in the Working Class Family*. New York: Basic Books.

Sacks, Karen Brodkin. 1988. "Gender and Grass Roots Leadership." In: Ann Bookman and Sandra Morgen (eds) *Women and the Politics of Empowerment*. Philadelphia: Temple University Press.

Saegert, Susan. 1989. "Planning for Performance: An Evaluation of Sponsored Limited Equity Cooperative Housing in New York City," Working Paper No. 3. New York City: The Robert F. Wagner, Sr. Institute of Urban Public Policy, The Graduate School and University Center, The City University of New York.

St. Anthony, Neal. 1987. *Until All are Housed in Dignity.* Minneapolis: Project for Pride in Living Press, pp.77-94.

Sapiro, Virginia. 1981. "Research Frontier Essay: When are Interests Interesting? The Problem of Political Representation of Women." *The American Political Science Review*. 75: 701-716.

Sassen-Koob, Saskia. 1985. "Capital Mobility and Labor Migration." In: Steven E. Sanderson (ed.) *The Americas in the New International Division of Labor*. New York: Holmes and Meier.

Schon, Donald. 1983. *The Reflective Practitioner*. New York: Basic Books.

Schwadron, Terry (ed.). 1984. *California and American Tax Revolt: Proposition 13 Five Years Later*. Berkeley: University of California Press.

Scott, James C. 1985. *Weapons of the Weak*. New Haven: Yale University Press.

Sechrist, Lee, Todd L. Fay, and S. M. Zaidi. 1982. "Problems of Translation in Cross-Cultural Communications." In: Larry A. Sanovar and Richard E. Porter (eds.) *Intercultural Communications: A Reader*. Belmont, California: Wadsworth Publishing.

Seleskovitch, Dancia. 1976. "Interpretation: A Psychological Approach to Translation." In: Richard W. Brislin (ed.) *Translation: Applications and Research.* New York: Gardner Press.

Sennett, Richard. and Jonathan Cobb. 1973. *The Hidden Injuries of Class.* New York: Random House.

Shearer, Derek. 1982. "How the Progressives Won in Santa Monica," *Social Policy.* 12, no.3: 7-14.

Shostak, Arthur B. 1969. *Blue Collar Life.* New York: Random House.

Sidel, Ruth. 1978. *Urban Survival: The World of Working Class Women.* Boston: Beacon Press.

Siebel, Hans Dieter and Ukandi G. Damachi. 1982. *Self-Management in Yugoslavia and the Developing World.* St. Martin's Press.

Soja, Edward W. 1989. *Postmodern Geographies.* London: Verso.

_____, Allan D. Heskin, and Marco Cenzatti. 1985. *Los Angeles Through the Kaleidoscope of Urban Restructuring.* Los Angeles: UCLA, Graduate School of Architecture and Urban Planning.

Sontag, Susan. 1973. "Third World Women," *Partisan Review,* 60, p. 201.

Spencer, Charles. 1977. *Blue Collar: An Internal Examination of the Workplace.* Chicago: Lakeside Charter Books.

Stone, Clarence N. 1987. "The Study of the Politics of Urban Development." In: Clarence N. Stone and Heywood T. Sanders (eds.) *The Politics of Urban Development.* Lawrence, Kansas: University of Kansas.

Swanstrom, Todd. 1988. "Semisovereign Cities: The Politics of Urban Development," *Polity.* 21: 83-110.

_____. 1985. *The Crisis of Growth Politics: Cleaveland, Kucinich, and the Challenge of Urban Populism.* Philadelphia: Temple University Press.

Taft, Ronald. 1981. "The Role and Personality of the Mediator. In: Stephen Bochner (ed.) *The Mediating Person: Bridges Between Cultures.* Boston: Schenkman Publishing.

Taylor, D. M. and Simard, L. M. 1975. "Social Interaction in Bilingual Settings." *Canadian Psychological Review.* 16,4: 240-254.

Twelvetrees, Alan. 1982. *Community Work.* London: British Association of Social Workers.

United States Government Accounting Office. 1988. "Sales of Federal Assets," September. RCED-88-214FS.

Urban Homsteading Assistance Board. 1986. *Tenth Year Report and Retrospective.* New York: Urban Homestead Assistance Board.

Urban Planning Aids. 1973. *The Empty Promise.* Cambridge, Mass.: Urban Planning Aids.

Van Maanen, John. 1988. *Tales of the Field.* Chicago: University of Chicago Press.

Viguerie, Richard A. 1983. *The Establishment vs. The People: Is a New Populist Revolt on the Way?* Chicago: Regnery Gateway, Inc.

Walker, Pat (ed.). 1979. *Between Labor and Capital.* Boston: South End Press.

Ward, Peter and Sylvia Chant. 1987. "Community Leadership and Self-Help Housing," *Progress in Planning.* Vol. 27, Part 2.

Wekerle, Gerda R. 1988. "Women Building Communities." In: Karen Frank and Sherry Ahrentzen (eds.) *Alternatives to the Single Family House*. New York: Van Nostrand Reinhold.

Wiebe, Robert H. 1967. *The Search for Order*. New York: Hill and Wang.

Willmott, Peter. 1986. *Social Networks, Informal Care and Public Policy*. London: Policy Studies Institute.

Yack, Bernard. 1988. "Liberalism and Its Communitarian Critics: Does Liberal Practice 'Live Down' to Liberal Theory?" In: Charles H. Reynolds and Ralph V. Norman (eds.) *Community In America*. Berkeley: University of California Press.

Index

	DATE DUE		
MAY 1 3 1994			
MAY 0 9 1995			
OCT 1 7 2003			